Ellen Foster

Effigy of the Cloven Hoof

Ellen Foster

Effigy of the Cloven Hoof

By

Ellen Foster

Valparaiso Indiana
April, 2010

Lulu Press, Inc.

Copyright © 2010 Ellen Foster

First published in United States of America 2010

ISBN   978-0-557-39894-2

EFFIGY OF THE CLOVEN HOOF

By Ellen Foster

Table of Contents

Acknowledgments

I have many debts to acknowledge during the decades of preparation of this book. Throughout the years of our residence in Exeter, England I received a variety of ideas and concepts helpful to me in creating a living image of the year 1400 ad. through my association with the stewards and guides of the 14th century Cathedral of St. Peter in the city of Exeter.

Several members of the Departments of History and English at Valparaiso University have been especially helpful to me in opening the world of Geoffrey Chaucer and Julian of Norwich, as well as endorsing for me the benefits of personal research and study in the Kingdom of England of the 14th and 15th centuries

Further I have advantaged myself of a number of gracious friends willing to read the developing manuscript and am especially grateful to my family not only for their willingness to read but also their endurance, helpful comments, puns and on-going support.

My special thanks to Annette and Dennis Aust, Michele and Charlie Foster, and Ellen Corley. Your personal thoughts, reactions and suggestions helped me to better understand the readers' reaction to my story. Marilyn and Ted Foster consistently added their loving best wishes. But most of all I credit my best friend, technical advisor, grammar and punctuation consultant as well as patient, loving husband, Lou Foster, as the real enabler of my life and work.

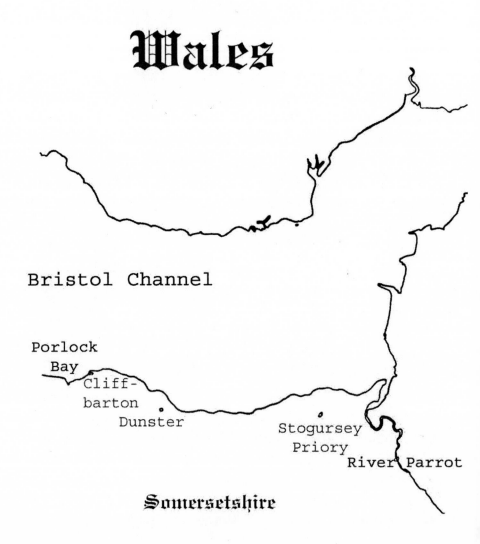

Wales

Bristol Channel

Porlock
Bay
Cliff-
barton
Dunster

Stogursey
Priory
River Parrot

Somersetshire

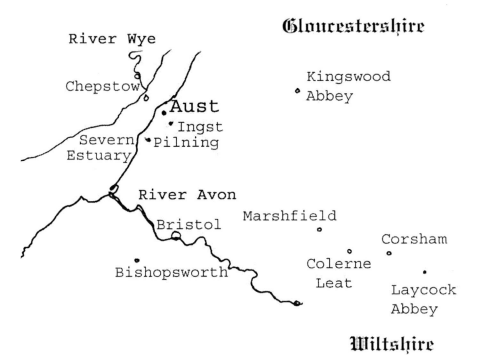

River Wye

Chepstow

Severn
Estuary

Aust

Ingst

Pilning

Gloucestershire

Kingswood
Abbey

River Avon

Bristol

Bishopsworth

Marshfield

Colerne
Leat

Corsham

Laycock
Abbey

Wiltshire

Axbridge

England

Somersetshire

EFFIGY OF THE CLOVEN HOOF

Introduction

Ravens' Menace

An aura of sullen air, heavy and thick with moisture, clung to her as she emerged into a sodden dawn from the chilly stone sanctuary of her family's ancient chapel. The fastness of its mould-patterned walls, heaving thatched roof and narrow lancet windows had barred from its interior all but the slenderest shafts of dawn breaking light. Lady Apollonia of Aust, blinded momentarily by the first brilliant beams of warmth and sunlight streaking from the east, drew herself up with a great sigh of relief finally able to straighten her prayer-wounded knees and welcome the hoped for gifts of a new dawn. Not one among her affinity noted her darting grey eyes and the constant succession of thoughts they betrayed. Finely sculpted lines round her eyes and mouth were rigidly set in her usual mask of calm only troubled by occasional tiny twitches of muscles taut and stressed beneath her ivory skin.

She had been torn from her bed mid night time, alarmed and forewarned to stormy malevolence within her own walls. During the darkest hours of the night wind-whipped rains had lashed the manor walls as lightening and thunder crashed reverberating fury through its corridors but the Lady had slept till roused to sudden consciousness by the screams of her terrified cook.

The panicked little Norman battering his Lady's chamber door, howling in fear as storm-savaged heavens seemed ready to shatter the earth, was unaware he had wet himself. A spreading dark stain grew from his crotch past the knees of his hose exaggerated in spurts by the effects of his thudding fist upon the massive oak door. Normally a coddled, effeminate man, fastidious with the placement of every curl of his locks and beard, Guise had been driven disheveled from his kitchen domain with hair on end and mustaches frayed.

"Holy Mother, protect us from the fiend!" he prayed in gasping sobs between shouts of alarm. "Madame, Madame, you must come to ze kitchen!"

Guise's eyes rolled frantically to every dark corner beyond the reach of the tiny flame of his trembling candle as his chest quaked with the stuttered breathing of a terrorized infant. A large crucifix bounced limply against undulating soft folds of his sagging chest and drooping abdomen, spilling from the constraints of hose and a hastily donned padded jupon. In the midst of his assault upon the door he crossed himself repeatedly with prayer beads tightly clasped in a fleshy hand. He squealed in shock as the Lady's maid, Nan, angrily flung open the chamber door. "What is this then?" she demanded of his impudence.

Nan's accusatory face equaled the lightening in flashing outrage at the cook's impertinence. Guise was reduced to a shattered fragment of a man sobbing aloud and screaming incoherently in his native French. Nan stared back at him in stunned incomprehension of his Gaelic torrent. At last, re-gathering the threads of his limited English, Guise spat his impatience at the petite but culpable barrier. "Summon my Laydee at once, you simple wench," he shouted, "We must flee to 'ze church. 'Ze deveels of Hell haf claimed 'zes house. We shall all be lost."

From the darkness of her bedchamber Lady Apollonia suddenly appeared beside Nan, stepped forcefully through the door and in towering silence walked calmly past the startled cook into the corridor. A furred train of her bedchamber robe flowed in her wake as she led the way for the trio's quick descent down the circling stone stairway leading into the hall and through its vaulted heights along to the cavernous darkness of the manor kitchen. Nan rushed ahead to lead their way, lighting her mistress' path with a wall torch held high above her shoulder creating jerking shadows amidst her spirited chiding of the hysterical cook.

"Cease this slobbering gibberish and tell us what ails ye, man!" she badgered Guise. "What has happened?"

None of the maid's reproaches could penetrate the fog of terror which ruled Guise so reduced in stature that he hid behind the ladies as they finally entered his dimly lit kitchen. Dumb with fear he pointed trembling hands towards the bodies of great ravens hanging over every portal round the service quarters. Their grisly corpses were iridescent in the violent illumination of lightening slashing down from high windows of the kitchen's vaults.

"Who could have done such a thing, my Lady? What does it mean?" Nan gasped in disbelief stunned by the macabre spectacle.

2

The birds were hanging by their feet; blue-black bodies and wings jerking in grotesque imitation of life. Their heads dangled loosely from narrow neck tendons twisted and slit allowing spurts of blood to fall and splash tiny crimson pools upon the flagstones below. Several servants of the house, aroused and frightened by the storm, peered curiously into the kitchen only to join Guise in a terrified communal howl as thunder crashed suddenly and roared quaking the very stones beneath their feet.

Deranged mad fear would have consumed them all had it not been for Lady Apollonia's presence. Silently she moved to position herself a caryatid in the center of the kitchen; her personal height and pillar-like body demanding the enforcement of calm as Nan strode among the staff, forcefully reminding each member of the household to attend instantly to his or her duties. Nan's small person spoke with the Lady's authority as she ordered trembling servants to light torches, stir the fires, fill huge basins of water and busy themselves with their early morning kitchen chores.

Lady Apollonia's searing gaze met Guise' watering eyes with an instant of conviction at his pathetic behaviour. Suddenly aware of having made an appalling display of himself, Guise wiped his nose with the back of one hand while smoothing his hair into a semblance of order with the other. He pulled his shoulders high in spite of jellied knees to don a massive apron reaching from his armpits to his ankles. Its fresh whiteness covered the humiliation of his lower body allowing the return of éclat while shreds of his personal dignity reassembled and girded him within the emblem of his position. Breathing deeply he called forth the normal tenor of his nasal voice and ordered the shaken kitchen boys seeing to the fires.

"Mon dieu! mon dieu! Look what you do, imbeceeles!" Guise shouted. "Dry wood! Bring dry wood not 'zis rain-soaked sponge! Sweet Jesu! A miracle would be to make 'zese burn."

Guise hovered over the lads stoking up the hearth fires and ovens until they filled the kitchen with triumphant light and warmth. Having driven away the last traces of predawn terror and humiliation, the irascible martinet of the kitchen marched, at last, to his massive tables fully restored to his appropriate sense of sovereignty.

Giles Digby, Lady Apollonia's household steward still in his night cap and robe, also summoned to the kitchen by its' pre-dawn chaos, walked to his Lady's side with his lips pressed to narrow consternation. Through the warming firelight reflected in moving

3

waves off the massive stone walls, he stared at the mutilated birds with more disgust than terror. Straightaway he chose several men of the household to assist him and he soon had the still warm feathered corpses carefully removed from their gallows, placed on a ledge for scrutiny by the Lady Apollonia. She had not altered her position but remained in the center of the now bustling kitchen.

"My Lady, you must retire to your chamber," Nan pleaded quietly whispering at her side. "The morning chill will bring sickness unless you dress and array yourself against it!"

But Apollonia refused with a gentle silent gesture to Nan, remaining in her sculpted posture until she was convinced a semblance of normal morning household routine had been restored and all traces of blood were washed away from the flagstones. Then the Lady of Aust moved quietly to the ledge and carefully examined each slaughtered bird.

It was an act of macabre intent recently done within this early morning. "But who could have done this thing and why?" she asked herself. "How am I to respond to such a lurid display obviously meant to frighten my household?" Once satisfied that she could learn little from their piteous earthly remains, Apollonia dispatched the carcasses to a speedy burial in the woods out of sight, out of mind.

"It is," she reminded herself, "as if the birds had been hung to bleed as the fowl of the kitchen were often left to hang bleeding after butchering. But what could such a threat portend?"

She knew black ravens could not be considered common kitchen fowl. What kind of nefarious threat would these known scavengers imply and what could their menacing positioning from the lintel of every door to the kitchen mean? If their blood was meant to spill into each entrance, surely it must imply a harbinger of evil intent against her household. "But then who intends such threats against us?" These questions stirred within the Lady's quick mind even as her calming presence in the kitchen seemed to those in her service to be quieting the slowly diminishing storm.

Chapel service had ended with the usual benediction of God's peace placed upon their heads by the gentle hands of Friar Francis, the household chaplain, but Lady Apollonia carried little sense of tranquility from her morning devotions. The world to which she returned outside the household chapel seemed as agitated and arrested in confusion as her own troubled spirit. In truth, glowing sunlight pierced the low leaden clouds oppressing the horizon replacing the violent gales of nighttime past. With a knowing gaze to the west, Apollonia reassured herself that the storms were truly ended but she knew in her heart that turbulence and disquiet was continuing to stalk the day. Dead ravens added only the most recent of threats to her peace of mind.

Lady Apollonia was not frightened by the prospect of Guise's nocturnal devils but she was forced to acknowledge that some source of human malice had invaded her home. Human hands had slit the birds' throats and carefully corded their legs to hang from pegs above her doors. Their morbid blackness added a strangely constructed personal threat to her while an already vitiating cloud of discord and distress haunted every lordship, manor and cottar in England's year of our Lord 1400.

Although she could maintain her stony calm in all outward appearance, Apollonia was as troubled in spirit as her poorest peasants by the continuing troubles of the kingdom; events far beyond her control yet capable of infecting the countryside of the far west with tension and violence. Greedy, lustful, over-mighty subjects found themselves more than willing to ignore the law of a weakened king and take what they wanted. She wished she were able to dispel the cloud of dread which gnawed at all of their hearts especially since the news had recently come telling of the deposed King Richard's death. She could think of no way to calm her own anxiety, no substantial deed which once done might alleviate the imps of disquiet nettling her usually tranquil nature. She and her household would pray daily but would God hear the prayers of a people guilty of the death of their anointed sovereign?

Autumn of 1400 had arrived in the west of England on the black wings of storm and unseasonable extremes of weather which many said were portents of far greater evil abroad in the land. In a series of howling gales villagers told of hearing the screams of a murdered king. When the harvest moon rose dark red, it was whispered, it betrayed royal blood shed by profane hands. King Richard II of England, deposed by Henry Bolingbroke, had suddenly died and yet the young monarch's corpse when displayed by his successor revealed no mark of violence against him. Still all knew he had died to suit the convenience of the Lancastrian usurper, now King Henry IV. Impious unholy regicide, the sin of a nation in its all encompassing judgement and guilt, ruled England. Where could one turn to escape from retribution being called down upon the heads of their unhappy, accursed generation? Even the church now in league with the usurper could offer no assurance of sanctuary or hope of grace, merely a dreadful silence.

Wary stillness ruled every tongue but guarded wondering escaped aloud when folk gathered in small groups to share their innermost fears. "God save us from the fiendish conspiracies of Satanas!" would be whispered in a private corner under cover of darkness. "God saved not the king," a voice would moan. "Yea, but verily it is said our righteous King Richard lives yet in Scotland," another would argue. "Then England's throne is the Devil's own?" a concluding whisper would trail away. Some folk wondered aloud if the end times had come. Was it not possible that the long-dreaded turning of the century had brought with it those latter days of creation foretold by the prophet of Revelation. Had the thousand years of the rule of the Fiend begun? Poor simple folk as well as their wealthier, better fed overlords seemed equally helpless to combat the corrupting fear of the times in which they lived.

To compound the chaos, Scotland and Wales were rising in rebellion along England's borders while storm and destruction battered its coasts. "Aye, its War, Famine, Plague, and Death, the Hellish horsemen of the Apocalypse," villagers said. "Verily, they were seen riding the lightening and hurling thunder during the demoniacal gales of the night." "In God's own truth," villagers swore to one another, "the devil was witnessed dancing in triumph on human graves."

Lady Apollonia crossed herself repeatedly but would suffer no foolish speculation in her presence and did all she could to halt the superstitious whispering within her household. It was her opinion that wagging chins and purposeless nattering only added to the confounding chaos and chaos was the ultimate design of the evil one. "The light of each new day," she was known to say, "provides God's opportunity for order and honest toil in His service." Having seen to the preparation of their souls in the chapel, all members of the Lady's household were expected to continue their work. That was her will and within her walls were none to gainsay her. Silence and order seemed to walk with the Lady of Aust and the respect of her household affinity guaranteed its maintenance. Lady Apollonia found good remedy in hard work and used its physic regularly to vindicate calm and purpose. Led by her personal example, her people too concentrated their minds and labors on the daily demands of the Manor of Aust: the care of its beasts and produce, the running of its mills, brewery and dairy, preparations for seasonal moves from pasture to pasture, the alternating resting and tilling of all demesne and villein fields.

Only those nearest to her in daily service heard the sound of Lady Apollonia's voice and even they sensed not the extent of her present unease. She was a woman who seemed to speak very little. Though her tall slender figure would appear regularly in kitchen or hall, barns or outbuildings, Lady Apollonia's presence would be marked only by the gentle whisper of her flowing black skirt. She never appeared alone; was always accompanied by Giles, her steward, or Nan, her personal maid. If orders were given, their voices pronounced the Lady's commands. Her chaplain and almoner distributed alms and good will liberally in her name. Their Lady's charitable concerns were common knowledge in the shire but always expressed through the voices of others.

At the advanced age of fifty-three years and thrice a widow, Lady Apollonia of Aust had achieved a tentative regard among her gentle neighbors who could only envy her obvious success in land management and her apparent accumulation of significant wealth. Having never adopted the inclination of the body assumed by those females who aped courtly ladies so as to protrude their stomachs and recline their tiny shoulders, Apollonia stood her full height, slim but large-boned and angular, straight and tall. Her garments were always black and unadorned except for a simple gold cross which lay upon her breast and the snowy white wimple which framed her oval face. Most folk who met her noticed at once her evenly spaced strong teeth. They were amazingly untouched by corruption for a Lady of her years. On those rare occasions when she was seen to smile her face was brilliant.

It was the Lady's custom to keep her grey eyes cast downward not in modesty, she loathed affectation, but in self-defense. She had seen enough of the violent realities of her world to prefer to distance herself from much that society valued. She regarded as priceless her hard won sovereignty and knew that she had the intelligence required to maintain it. But that acknowledgment she also kept jealously to herself, hidden behind her silent and nun-like withdrawal, poised to reveal nothing through casual conversation or by meeting the prying eyes of observers. Silence and withdrawal were her refuge providing the main lines of her defense by freezing out any who presumed to trespass upon her privacy.

In further support of her posture of retreat from the world, her personal religious discipline was as rigorous as that of any convent community and designed by her to complete the defenses about her person. She shared her intimate thoughts with no one. She distrusted the world of chivalry and gentle pretension to courtly manners, maintaining a deep inner loathing of the gentles' real worship of war, conflict and greed. She nourished through her own compulsion for order her real goals to protect all whom she knew to be in need, all whom she accepted as her dependents.

The Lady of Aust was suspected by her neighbors to have ears in every door, advance knowledge of surprising news and intuition which they considered quite extraordinary. Nearby ladies gathered in their solars would cluck and chatter across their needlework frames in critical wonder at her unseemly masculine control. In spite of the difficulties of travel, Apollonia of Aust was a frequent inspector of the operation of her farms and manors. She completed a round of visits to each site twice every year and might reappear at any time in the intervals. Constant and faithful to the church, she also supported retreats for herself in several monasteries located throughout the countryside. These, too, she was known to visit regularly in the midst of her routine travels. The Abbess of Lacock Abbey, it was said, had allowed Lady Apollonia the maintenance of her own cell within that convent for retreat and meditation whenever the Lady desired. Such retreats were temporary and only used when necessary. Lady Apollonia had chosen to live her life in the world but she determined to do so on her own unworldly terms.

Lady Apollonia's barns were well-built and as well-filled as those of any monastic grange. Her lands along the river were well-drained and delineated by regularly maintained canals. Her peasants and craftsmen seemed well fed, less prone to disease, unrest, or rebellion. Even the flocks of sheep seen feeding in her pastures were tended by careful shepherds fully aware that their mistress would personally inspect the lambing and shearing according to their season.

Amidst the workaday industry and diligence of the manors of Aust, however, a place was always set aside for wayfarers at the gates

8

and a table dormant stood ready in the Lady Apollonia's hall. Pilgrims or beggars, the dispossessed and masterless who roamed forests and country lanes, knew they would find food and sanctuary at her gates. They would also find themselves put to work and were ever required to wash before being allowed to enter her hall. In the mornings or at the end of a long day, however, plain meals and ale, warmth and refuge rewarded all those who labored under the Lady's protection.

Her almoner, Brother William, happily declared that he worked longer hours in Lady Apollonia's service than ever required of him by the church. And days were never so full that his Lady did not receive from him a detailed accounting of all those who sought her alms and sanctuary. She would pick carefully through each of his thoughts and collected opinions gathered from the vagabonds and pilgrims who paused on their journeys to beg hospitality of the Lady of Aust.

Her chaplain, Friar Francis, was constantly encouraged by his Lady to visit local villages, freely offering his good offices to those in need of pastoral care. Though his first love was preaching, he knew that his patroness expected regular reports from him of his cure of the souls of her manors and she wished to know everything. She made meticulous inquiries after the health, family, and living conditions of each of her tenants. She knew most of her people by family name; their children, gardens, and livestock were her concerns as well. Lady Apollonia's personal powers of observation were keen but she expected that her learnings would be regularly supplemented through the ministries of her clerics, her personal household, her steward and his reeves. She artfully created a network of discernment throughout her affinity, all those who's devoted service to the Lady of Aust was freely and wholeheartedly given but whose intelligence gathering was never allowed to lapse.

The innermost circle of servants surrounded the Lady of Aust with loyalty unknown beyond the closest ties of blood and kinship. Giles Digby, Nan Tanner, Brother William and Friar Frances, served her with the devotion of family. But loyalty to her person extended further; proudly given from her clerks and their assistants, the manor craftsmen, virgators and villeins, all were her people. They had been maintained, supported, educated, or elevated by her and their experiences were continually repeated in the lives of young people entrusted to her care. Her household received promising boys and girls from the immediate countryside, whose lives, marriages, and mysteries would be encouraged through her patronage. Many years of her life had been devoted to the careful selection and cultivation of her household affinity. Most gratifying to her of all her life's achievements was her awareness of the fidelity and devotion of all those who proudly wore the Lady's badge, an emblem of English ivy entwined about a pure red heart.

Chapter One

A Tide of Lepers

As she was leaving her chapel on that saturnine morning, Brother William, Friar Francis, and Giles, followed about the Lady on all sides. She walked briskly, quietly acknowledging the pinched faces and anchorless souls gathered in the brightening light of her courtyard awaiting alms. Each of her trusted servants was reporting in turn the clamor of rumor and accusation that had accompanied the morning's crowd of beggars at her gates. Giles described their terrified rush and push to enter as that of a frantic horde driven more by fear than hunger.

"The able-bodied were taken first to the trough to wash, then be fed, and put to work as usual, my Lady," her steward recalled. "But they moved dumbly, wild-eyed as beasts terrified by lightning", Giles said. "I've never seen such skittish clinging to one another. They fear the world has reached its end times, my Lady. Every man jack of them swore that the hellish horsemen were seen abroad in the storm again last night!"

"To confound our efforts of orderly preparations to break the morning fast for this unusually large assembly, my Lady," Brother William added hastily, "a group of lepers appeared at dawn, standing their required distance from the walls, crying for pity. Normally, they would be content to receive their food left for them down by the river. But after the ravages of the night they, too, were driven to your gates. Gentle Lady, their plight is most piteous and death has proved their unsought companion. They have come to us for succor in Christ's name and truly have no other hope of aid in their distress."

Lady Apollonia listened without interruption to the reports of her trusted minions as they walked with her through the courtyard and towards the hall where she customarily oversaw the assignment of the day's tasks. She soon became acutely aware that despite her desire for return to routine the manor's normal daily course must be put aside on this fateful morning. Giles, completing Brother William's tale informed her that the stormy violence of the night past had left in its wake a more deadly debris than anyone could have realized. To her surprise, even the serene Friar Francis was dishabille in his retelling of the tales brought to him. "It is as if the Lord God sent a great flood to punish this wicked world once again, my Lady and the beggars say that dead bodies are strewn along the Severn's banks."

Friar Francis' words were hurriedly followed by Brother William's addition of frightening detail. "We believe the great majority of the dead are lepers, my Lady, men and women, in varying stages of the dreadful disease. With their masks and robes washed away facial decay and putrefied limbs are all exposed to the horror of those who have seen them."

They entered the hall at its far end nearest the kitchen where pilgrims, beggars and members of the household were quietly gathering, standing in subdued queues waiting to receive the benediction and be offered their meal. Their mood was marked by none of the usual chatter and banter of the day's beginning. Each of Apollonia's hall servants was first required to whisper into her ear his or her collection of tales from the storm. Then each stepped back and awaited respectfully further instructions. With a simple gesture of smiling assent, the Lady nodded her thanks to each one of them and turned aside for a quiet conversation with her steward, Giles.

Her personal nagging concerns pushed to one side, Apollonia willingly allowed herself to be redirected by the urgent needs she was learning had been caused by the disaster of the night before. She had always harbored a suppressed terror of the dreadful disease of leprosy yet she was grateful to be able to offer some gesture of compassion to these poor souls she knew to be so valued by Christ and his saints. Here was something that she could do and she gladly threw herself into the mental tasks of arranging for the collection of the dead while making provisions for their Christian burial. But she also knew she must protect those of the leper band who had miraculously survived the river's treachery. Excommunicate from all of human society by law, lepers were forbidden to inherit, forced instead to exist in twilight of constant movement maintaining always a required distance between themselves and the rest of God's humanity. In normal times, they would be avoided by most country folk. In times of discontent and unrest, however, their disease marked them as easy targets of outrage and persecution at the hands of fearful, superstitious men. Apollonia was prepared to succor and protect them but she knew she must first engage the cooperation of her own people to perform the tasks necessary and then enlist an additional show of force to protect the working parties.

Giles assumed that his Lady would personally organize and supervise the morning's relief ministry, lending the weight of her presence as collateral to its ultimate success. To him alone, as was frequently her custom, she outlined the details of her project and entrusted their execution to his youthful but capable hands. He was only five and twenty, of medium height, ruddy complexion, and of meticulous disposition. His dress was of excellent cut and current fashion and he especially loved to wear the sinuously long pointed leather slippers, called Cracows, which startlingly elongated the line of his thin legs and narrow feet. His love of fashion could not be interpreted as likelihood of foolish conduct, however. He was no fop. Legitimately proud of his position in the Lady's household, he had earned Apollonia's complete confidence. He was thorough, practical, reliable, and intelligent. Giles' thoughts seemed to function as an extension of the Lady's mental processes. He was her agent of choice and her intellectual right arm.

Stopping first to converse with the Friar and Brother William, Giles asked them straightforwardly, "Will you both be willing to direct the lepers to gather their own dead? Lady Apollonia seeks your help but prays that you will answer her request with complete honesty."

Having gained their assured assent, Giles continued to describe to the clerics their Lady's plan of transport and proposed preparation of a burial site. Apollonia waited within earshot of Giles' conversation with her clerical servants as she wished to hear their responses and reactions. She knew them to be humble and sincere servants of their religious vocations as well as dedicated to her but, she insisted, they must be allowed to object to do her bidding. Leprosy was a truly fearful disease. She smiled to herself as she heard the good Friar and his brother in Christ assure Giles that the Lady's plan was excellent.

"Surely Giles," the Friar responded at once, "with the carts to help us, we shall have the job done this day before the sun is set."

"God bless her Ladyship," Brother William added, "and grant us strength to be worthy of her trust." Doing obeisance to the Lady, both clerics hurried out towards the kitchen to set her plan in motion.

Having abbreviated his own morning breaking of fast, Giles continued to issue orders to workmen of the household to gather necessary tools and set his foreman to select able-bodied beggars from the groups of men still standing about the courtyard waiting for work.

Lady Apollonia's servants were to supervise the conscripted laborers in digging a large pit some distance from the parish church of Aust but still within the bounds of sanctification. The recruits were quickly armed with shovels and led off towards the churchyard. It would be heavy labor after the soaking rains of recent days but they must have the pit ready when the grisly harvest had been completed and be prepared to shovel the earth over the lazar cemetery they were creating. The Lady's servants promised good coin to all willing hands and received an enthusiastic response from many who had been forced into beggary by hard times and dislocation. A large statue of the Virgin in her exquisite blue cloak was carried from Lady Apollonia's chapel to the worksite to add reassurance of the Holy Mother's protective blessing upon the work required of them that day.

Brother William and Friar Francis departed from the manor house kitchen with a small cart carrying baskets of food and drink to the surviving lepers cowering in the wood outside the gates. While distributing bread, cheese and ale, the clerics, too, recruited volunteers. Nearly all of the surviving men of the leper band and several of the able-bodied women as well were willing to return to Severn's banks to search out and retrieve the dead. To complete the Lady of Aust's provision, Friar Francis and Brother William explained to the leader of the leper band that he and his compatriots would gather the bodies, load them into the carts and transport them back to a freshly dug burial pit at the edge of the church yard for swift but prayerful internment they would all be allowed to witness.

Crossing himself repeatedly as he moved among the deferential, heavily shrouded and masked members of the leper band, Brother William calmed his inner fears by reciting to himself the admonitions of St. Francis to care for the leprous as they represent the suffering body of Christ himself. He tried to maintain his smile among them and greet each one with his blessing but he knew he couldn't possibly consider St. Francis enthusiastic willingness to pull them into his arms and kiss them.

Friar Francis, having served a leper hospital attached to a house of his order, was less apprehensive of the sights of human horror he knew they must see but he too, prayed silently. Francis wished no impiety but he found it so difficult to understand why the loving Lord of Heaven should will to heap tragedy upon these hopeless wretches who suffered constant mortification of the flesh. Lepers, he knew, endured greater suffering and humiliation than any of God's creatures

14

and yet he couldn't believe their sin to be greater than that of any other men. The gentle Friar sighed to himself and countered as always, troublesome questions with urgent prayers for instruction and obedience. So much to do and it must be done quickly, his nagging doubts dissipated in the urgency of the task before them.

Having ordered Lady Apollonia's horse and mounts for Nan and Owen, a young Welsh boy of the household who would ride to accompany the Lady and her maid, Giles sprang into his own saddle and galloped from the gates. He carried a hurriedly written note to his Lady's brother calling upon him to meet her at an appointed place near the River Severn and to bring with him a small company of his most reliable men, armed and ready to deal with any potential discord or strife. Hurrying his horse along the familiar path towards the manor house of Ferdinand of Marshfield, Giles, the only child of his parents, wondered to himself as he had on many occasions, how unlike a brother and sister could be. Lady Apollonia was a complicated enigma to him so unlike any other woman he had ever encountered. His Lady's brother, Ferdinand, was a gentleman so true to his class and the profession of arms that Giles always knew what to expect and how he must respond. Brusque, hale and hearty, brave and uncomplicated, Ferdinand had lived to ripe old age untouched by life's subtleties or shadings. The wonder of his peers for his candor and lack of ambition, he fought when and where his lord commanded and he hunted whenever his services were not in demand.

Chapter Two

Brotherly Service

The timing of Giles' arrival was perfect, though not regarded so by Lady Apollonia's brother. "Damn you Giles; give me your Lady's message and be off before the day is lost!" he bellowed. Giles, delivering the note directly into Lord Ferdinand's hands, quietly disregarded his preemptory dismissal and paused to allow the reading of it.

"In Christ's blood, what does my sister think armed men are for? A herd of drowned lepers needs no military escort." Giles knew to expect that his Lady's brother would shout protest and then proceed to act in accordance with his sister's wishes.

"The Lady Apollonia urgently requests your presence to avert any uprising or retaliation by the country folk against the lepers who survive, my Lord Ferdinand," Giles said in courteous explanation. "These troublous times excite the ignorant and can inflame their rage against the poor and outcast. My Lady acknowledges your strength and purpose in maintaining the King's peace in the shire. She will see to the details of the burial of the dead."

Muttering furious curses in all directions, Ferdinand called for his falconer. Lowering his massively gloved arm to allow the majestic bird to pass on to the arm of the trainer, he cooed lovingly to his treasured peregrine. Powerful and swift in flight, the slate-grey female with the buff breast commanded whatever luxury Ferdinand's household could provide for her. The Lord of Marshfield exulted in the mastery of the air which his precious hawk achieved so effortlessly and enjoyed displaying her prowess to his minions. "I shall miss you Guinevere, my beauty," he said as if addressing his lady love, "but it cannot be helped." Then addressing his Breton breeder, valued second only to the bird itself, Ferdinand exhorted him to lavish care upon his favorite. "Let her have her head when she flies this morning, Piers, exercise her well. Mind you, see to it that she awaits me in hall when I return."

Abruptly straightening in his saddle, Ferdinand's voice changed noticeably to his gruff utterances of command. "We shant hunt this morning, Devil take it!" he shouted. Singling out the most trustworthy men of his affinity, he ordered them to arm themselves and follow him. He offered no further details of the nature of their journey as, he reasoned, his men were to follow without question. Further, brave as he was, he truly did not know how they might react to an encounter with lepers. "Judas be damned, Polly, you find ways to make my life onerous," he swore under his breath.

Galloping at the forefront of his troop, Ferdinand's thoughts turned back to the strange events surrounding the day of his sister's birth. Ferdinand was eight years old at the time and regarded himself already a man. Although the passing years had robbed him of any memory of his mother's face, he could vividly remember her swelling body awkwardly moving about the private apartments of his father's moated manor house. Plagued continually by throbbing toothache through the whole of her pregnancy, his mother had been assured by her ladies that at the time of her birth travail the offending tooth could be extracted. Then, she was told, she would be so preoccupied with her labor that the pulsating pain of her jaw would sink from her consciousness and the babe in her womb would not be threatened by the drawing of a rotten tooth.

In honor of the protectress of this scheme, his mother had a special altar to St. Apollonia erected in the family chapel and she struggled to carry her swollen body into its incense filled vaults daily to offer her prayers for the safe delivery of her child and blessed relief from the ceaseless pain in her face. It seemed a perfectly reasonable safeguard as everyone knew St. Apollonia to be the patron of those who suffered toothache. With the Saint's blessing, the birthing chamber would become the place of entry of a new life dedicated to her and would also provide the long desired end to excruciating suffering which her martyrdom had memorialized.

Thus, when the early pangs of her approaching labor began, Ferdinand remembered that his frail mother seemed more than ready to get on with it. Leaving the women of the household in charge, Ferdinand and his father went off early in the morning. Returning late from the day's hunt, father and son learned of the birth of a girlchild. The saint had heard his mother's prayers, Ferdinand was told, and his healthy baby sister had been safely delivered. His mother, too, had achieved release from her agonizing pain.

He could remember visiting her bedside, repulsed by the hot fetid air of the chamber. To his boyish eye, the dreadful disarray of his mother's hair, damp and stringing limply across her grey drawn face, was most alarming. Still, she had seemed wonderfully happy, smiling ecstatically as she cried aloud to unseen spirits, "Blessed Apollonia, you are merciful. *Gratia, gratia plena.* My daughter shall bear your name and that of the Blessed Virgin." Frantic with delirium, his lady mother was unable to recognize Ferdinand when he bent to kiss her hot twitching hand. He had remained in his mother's chamber suppressing his urge to retch as his mother's ladies had insisted that his presence might aid her. Several hours passed and Ferdinand remembered his mother slipping into a lingering lethargy of shallow, gasping breaths. She never returned to conscious recognition of her son. Consumed by childbed fever, her body spent and exhausted, Ferdinand's mother died within three days.

Tiny Lady Mary Apollonia lay in her cradle cared for by her mother's maid. The Lord of Marshfield, looking down upon her from the heights of his obvious distaste and displeasure at the birth of a girlchild, would not bend to touch her. "Praise God, your lady wife was delivered of a healthy infant, my Lord. She is bonny and strong, may the saints protect her," the old woman had said hoping to console him.

"I shall see to it that you are properly rewarded for this day's service," Ferdinand's father had responded with a chill in his voice that some interpreted as gauge to his unbounded grief. But her father refused to approach the cradle because he could not countenance the tiny red body tightly wrapped in swaddling cloths, sleeping innocently in the unnatural warmth of the birth/death chamber. Heaven forced him to accept this daughter, he told himself, but he would not hide his irritation with its unfortunate sex. Already angry that his wife had dared to abandon her duty to him, he had withdrawn abruptly from the chamber declaring that all arrangements for the child's care could be made without his participation.

One wet-nurse was available in the household, a buxom dairy maid who had recently weaned her own sturdy son. Gwennie happily offered her bosom and her heart to the littlest lady of the manor. Overjoyed to have another sweet infant to suckle, she strapped her charge to her body and carried the infant throughout her work day. Singing and cooing to the baby between barn and kitchen, Gwennie cosseted the infant life with song and constant attention. By the time Apollonia was weaned, she was a well-loved toddler, cherished by the entire servant's quarter. Indeed, as a little child, she daily preferred to find herself in the company of the household servants who welcomed her with them into the hen houses, the barns and stables. In the face of her father's disdain, Apollonia reached out to and found good-natured affection from those of the household who seemed ready to acknowledge her estate but still encourage her to experience their views of life, planting, harvesting, and husbandry.

It was not a common name and yet, Ferdinand recalled, Apollonia suited his sister. She had always preferred it to being called by any other name. Polly was his personal selection and the only name by which he ever addressed her, within the realm of family only. It was his right as elder brother to use the diminutive and by this means re-emphasize his primacy in age as well as the superiority of his sex. In his most private thoughts and to his secret heart alone, Ferdinand acknowledged that he was intimidated by his sister. Her unwomanly acumen and unyielding determination seemed an affront to him. He often wished that he might know why she insisted upon being so different from other women but then, he told himself, if he knew he probably could not agree.

Ferdinand's reverie was interrupted by the sight of Apollonia's darkly robed figure seated as straight and commanding as any knight upon her palfrey, accompanied only by her maid and a boy. Calmly awaiting him at Aust Cliff, the lofty shelf of rock on the bank of the Severn a short distance northwest of the village, Lady Apollonia turned in welcome at the sound of Ferdinand's approach.

"Judas blood, Polly, why will you prance about the countryside with no one to accompany you," he shouted as he guided his mount beside hers. "There are footpads and thieves aplenty in these forests as I have warned you; you risk too many liberties for a woman of your station." He seemed to warm to his subject. "Why must you allow any beggar, now indeed whole bands of lepers, access to your lands? You tempt the fates, gentle sister, and one day your kindness may well be repaid by ingrates' foul play."

Quietly waiting for her brother to finish speaking, Apollonia knew it would serve no purpose to argue the facts of the lepers' innocent choice of her lands below Aust for their campsite. In the hope of finding themselves admitted to the Benedictine leper hospital at Shrewsbury, the band had traveled away from human habitation and avoided the byways of common travelers keeping as close to the banks of the River Severn as a guide to their route as they dared. Stopping to rest for several days near Aust, they were caught unaware when the flash tide of the night before roared up through the Severn's perilous estuary. A gigantic tidal bore had driven a wall of water crashing over the river's banks and inundating their sleeping bodies huddled together against the rain. Credulously unaware of the river's lethal treachery, only the strong and the fortunate had been able to cling to some trees or brush to protect themselves from the pounding surge. The weak were sucked into a swirling fury of the water like struggling ants washed away by a carelessly toppled bucket.

Without lifting her eyes, Apollonia leaned across to kiss Ferdinand's cheek and pressing her hand over his, she whispered into his ear, "Brother, grant me the favor of your protection whilst I direct the gathering of these poor souls for burial." Ferdinand made no reply but turned to his men ordering them to arrange themselves around the periphery of the wooded banks of the river. He charged them to see to it that no strangers be allowed to pass without reporting their presence to him. Then looking over the cliff, he saw the daunting task his sister had taken upon herself. The tide was out and had left in its sinister retreat a litter of human refuse scattered among the skeletal roots and stripped vegetation lining its muddy venue of death.

The leper workers had returned to the site well before Ferdinand's arrival and were struggling into the mire to retrieve their dead comrades' bodies upon carriers improvised of rough poles and stout hemp. Lady Apollonia's carts, which had carried the outcast living to the flood site, were now slowly being filled with remains of bodies rotted in life and liberated by death. Covering hideous disfigurement whenever possible, carefully placing bodies in attitudes of arm-crossed devotion, the leper workers seemed eager to bestow small displays of respect and dignity to their dead. Immune to hope in this life, many wept and moaned quietly as they prayed for solace in the world to come. Death and mourning were frequent visitors to their community, too fearful to be welcomed but tolerated as daily existence trudged on.

Brother William and Friar Francis moved encouragingly among the heavily masked and enshrouded leper workers. Lending their gloved hands where hands were missing and assisting in the location of bodies overlooked by diseased eyes, Lady Apollonia's chaplain and almoner gently lifted the dispirited and consoled the bereaved by their willing presence among the gentle pariahs. An ascending sun sliced through fading banks of heavy cloud, heating the grey steamy stagnant air. The lepers' ragged robes dragged with perspiration, their garment hems quickly coated with thick mud, yet no one among them requested a respite. To find such compassion with their plight and the promise of burial in consecrated ground for their companions was a very great blessing. The surviving lepers worked in earnest as if their toil were an offering of appreciation to the Lady whose gift to those dead meant that their dispossessed souls might await the judgement in holy ground.

Ferdinand, with admiration for the compassion and courage of his sister and her servants, was reduced to uncharacteristic silence as he surveyed the remains of human disaster lying along the bank below them. Then somewhere, bursting the stillness of the moment, the air rang suddenly with shouts from an unknown trouble spot upstream. It was impossible to determine the nature of the commotion from the height of Aust Cliff. Ferdinand accompanied his sister as she urged her horse down the path towards the alarm. Nan and Owen followed at a respectful distance. Forced into single file along the rain-soaked river path and carefully picking her way past the mired slough which the elements and traffic had combined to create in the wood along the bank, the Lady suddenly looked up to find herself surrounded by several of the larger and stronger of her leper workers. Ferdinand, reacting with first instincts of self-protection, put his hand upon the hilt of his broad sword and urged his horse to his sister's side. Not daring to approach too near the Lady, the lepers fell upon their knees in the thick mud where they stood and their muffled voices cried out from behind heavy masks, "Have mercy Lady and do not withdraw your protection. It was not we who did this thing!"

Friar Francis struggling through the mire, hurried to his mistress' side. "This way, my Lady, forgive me but you must come this way." Taking hold of the bridle, Francis led Apollonia's palfrey along the upstream bank to a place where normally well-maintained drains from her fields were clogged with oozing mud, matted vegetation and fractured tree limbs. As he walked the friar was trembling and distraught. He seemed to feel compelled to offer an explanation but could not order his thoughts. "My Lady, you and my Lord Ferdinand must understand. We found it as it is. The lepers fear that they will be blamed for this horrible thing. Be gracious and help us to know what we must do with it?"

"God's Death, foolish friar, speak not in circles," commanded Ferdinand. But Lady Apollonia, knowing explanations would be forthcoming, allowed her faithful Francis to turn her horse away from the river bank and continue along the sharply cut drainage canal. A short distance inland, a pool had been formed by a dam of vegetation left in the canal as flood waters retreated. There, lying in the midst of the murky pool of water was another corpse. Dressed in homespun peasant tunic and hose, the body had once been a large man with huge hands and unusually large feet.

"Holy Mother of God," the Lady thought to herself, "'tis no wonder your poor lepers were terrified of this discovery." Furiously decapitated, the corpse seemed to have had its head torn out from the gaping hole between its shoulders now pouring forth points of slivered spine and shreds of ripped tissue.

"Stop where you are, Polly", Ferdinand growled, "Don't look upon this horror." Dismounting, he sent Friar Francis to fetch two of his trusted companions; then he plunged into the waist deep pool and doggedly dragged its occupant to the grassy bank. Ferdinand had seen too much of death in his warrior's lifetime to be squeamish at the sight or touch of corpses. Rolling the corpulent torso onto that which had once been its back, Ferdinand's eyes grew narrow with understanding. "This is no leper, Apollonia," he barked, "this was a gentleman."

To the casual observer, Lady Apollonia would not have been seen to lift her eyes. But beneath the hooded lids, her eyes darted in a flurry of activity, swiftly noting many additional curiosities evident to her. As her brother had said, the corpse was of gentle birth in spite of his homespun garments. Its ankles and huge feet were swollen with big toes inflamed from gout. The grotesquely fat, putty soft hands had never known hard labor and deep indentations in its chunky fingers suggested digits swelled to fat around huge rings now missing.

"Decapitation must have occurred before the body fell or was pushed into the water," she thought to herself. "There is no head for this creature anywhere near. And, the flesh of the neck shows no sign of sword or spear. In God's name how could this have happened?" Then, with an involuntary shudder of sinister familiarity, she noticed a crusty, blood red, crab-shaped growth covering the back of the right hand now thrown limply across the bulging belly.

"Mother of God, after all these years!" she thought frantically longing to interrogate the dead. "Was it you who wished to terrorize my household?" Grown corpulent and flabby since the days of their last encounter thirty-six years before, the insolent corpse hurled hateful repressed memories into her consciousness. Against her will Apollonia remembered this creature; there could be only one man of such gross extremities marked by Cancer's hideous sign.

Lady Apollonia quietly signaled her brother to her side as he climbed up from the bank. Leaning down from her horse, her head nearly touching his, she whispered quickly. "Brother, kindly throw your cloak over the wretched creature."

"What, my cloak upon that?" Ferdinand retorted. But Apollonia interrupted his flow of speech immediately.

"Let no others see this thing which has happened. Accompany your men in the delivery of these tragic remains to the Abbot at Kingswood. Tell the reverend Abbot that I shall request his presence later this day." Speaking quickly so that she could not be interrupted, Apollonia stopped her brother's growing objections before they could be uttered.

"I believe I can assist him in identifying the body of this wealthy gentleman but," she emphasized with her eyes fixed upon her brother's, "impress upon his grace the need that great caution must be employed in any release of the news of this tragedy. He must do nothing until I have told him all."

Ferdinand grunted his assent not wishing to inquire after any further details of his sister's plan. Apollonia added only, "God speed you, dear brother, haste and secrecy are our best weapons at this moment against which I know not what."

Always grateful for any quick solution to irritating problems, Ferdinand pulled off his dark brown riding cloak, spread it quickly upon the bank, and rolled the body into it. Using its cord to tie the cloak in place, he tested its surety with a hearty yank. Remounting his horse, he had resumed an attitude of nonchalant command when Friar Francis was seen returning along the river's edge with the summoned knight of Ferdinand's affinity and his young squire. Before these men could dismount, Ferdinand began barking orders to each of them to hoist the shrouded body lying upon the river bank onto the backside of the squire's horse. Then the knight was sent to collect the disbursed contingent still keeping watch around the perimeter of the area.

"Have them all return to me at once!" Ferdinand shouted after the disappearing rider. "We ride for Kingswood and the sun is already lowering to mid day!"

As if anxious to be done with these unwonted tasks, Ferdinand grabbed his sister's hand passing his lips roughly over its proffered back. In unstoppable movement, he turned to chide the young squire who struggled to secure the fleshy corpse to the hindquarters of his skittish horse.

"You cannot wake him. Matthew," he growled. "Stop mincing about with the delicacy of a maid! Put a bit of muscle into the lashing, lad. Sit atop him if you must and let us be done with it!" he shouted in irritation.

Ferdinand's company slowly gathered and as the last man galloped into the clearing, the Lord of Marshfield turned his horse abruptly and rode away leaving his sister without another word. Lady Apollonia seemed not to notice his departure as she had resumed her normal face to the world, eyes cast downward and her hands folded in her lap. But her mind was searching through the events of the morning in a frantic attempt to select her best course of action.

Giles rode up to join the Lady as Ferdinand and his men departed. He could see that she was unusually distracted as she offered him no greeting and remained silent as he moved his mount to her side. Feeling that he must speak, Giles cleared his throat and quietly addressed her. "There were not so many bodies as we thought, my Lady. The lepers say they have found all of their missing fellows. Eight adults and several children have been removed to the pit for burial." The Lady nodded but made no comment.

To elicit her concern for that which he felt were new developments, Giles continued, "My Lady, Brother William and the Friar have done all they can to console the lepers in their mourning but with the discovery of this gentleman's body, the leaders of the leper band fear reprisals. They do not wish to remain in this area. With good reason, my Lady, they are anxious to move on towards Shrewsbury where they believe they will find permanent sanctuary within the monks' lazar hospital."

Apollonia nodded her agreement but continued in silence.

"If you will allow an opinion, I believe they should be encouraged to continue on their journey, my Lady," Giles said with conviction. "It is highly unlikely that stricken and unarmed lepers would have attempted such a crime."

As if her mind had finally focused upon his words, Lady Apollonia shook her head in assertive agreement. Thus shaking off her distraction, she sat forward in her saddle and took a deep breath.

"Sickness of the body frequently breeds patience and endurance, Giles. Indeed, you are quite correct. We have nothing to fear from the lepers but I do fear there may still be others about who seek to do us ill."

She looked at the sun and hurried on. "We must act very quickly. It is possible that we may all be in jeopardy from a very ancient grudge against me. I believe it best that we prepare our defenses."

Providing a brief explanation and a series of messages, Apollonia waited as Giles conveyed her instructions to Nan, Owen and her clerics. On Lady Apollonia's orders, Nan was to accompany Friar Francis and Brother William back to the manor. They were instructed to see that the surviving lepers were well provisioned and safely removed to an unused barn in an empty north pasture near to the Gloucester Road where they might rest and regain their strength. Nan was to provide adequate supplies for the final portion of their journey to Shrewsbury then she was to follow her Lady to Kingswood.

Once Friar Francis and Brother William were convinced that the leper band was safely out of harm's way, Apollonia was adamant that they must return to the manor and bathe thoroughly after which they were to be given four leaves of columbine to chew several times each day for a week against the appearance of any scrofulous corruption of their skin. The household was to be told that the Lady was about to retreat to Kingswood Abbey for some period of time. During her absence, the work of the manor must continue as if nothing unforeseen had occurred.

And finally, young Owen was given a special mission, one much to his liking. He was directed to find Alwan whose forester's hut he knew well in a secluded copse downriver from Aust and speak this message to him: "My Lady Apollonia greets you well and requests your service. Beginning near the place where the leper band has camped, search the woods along the Severn for any sign of knights' destrier or armed parties involved in ambush or struggle. Most especially look among the tree limbs overhead. Bring word of your findings to the manor."

Once Owen, Nan, and the clerics were underway, Lady Apollonia and Giles turned their horses east, leaving the rutted paths and cutting cross country towards Kingswood Abbey. Giles had never learned to ride more than adequately. He had no interest in horses other than their being the means of traveling from one point to another. Lady Apollonia, he noted admiringly, was a true horsewoman. She had been in the saddle most of the day and yet she rode now as if inexhaustible and fresh. Her long body seemed to move in concert with the forward thrusting of her palfrey's neck and her face revealed the joy she found in riding full tilt, unrestrained and fluidly leaning into the pounding motion. Giles could see that his Lady was not only enjoying the ride but also she had taken up a challenge. A gauntlet from an unknown hand had been hurled at her feet and she clasped it to her like a grail quest. Puzzles and mysteries always pricked her quick intelligence, Giles smiled to himself. He knew she would not release this strange sequence of events from her scrutiny until the truth of the violence in the night past had been completely revealed to her satisfaction.

Chapter Three

Abbatial Meddling

Ferdinand would waste no time. Having delivered his charge to the care of the monks he would gladly depart with his company, leaving behind some assurance that his sister would follow shortly and explain all to the satisfaction of the Abbot of Kingswood. Apollonia knew that she could depend on her brother to do as he had agreed and would not allow himself to be pressed into the slightest additional comment. She was also confident of the ambitions of the aggressive Abbot Harold of Kingswood. She knew he could be trusted to receive this mysterious body and hold it secretly until it could be proven worth his while. Still, she sensed an urgent need to meet with the Abbot promptly and establish a connection between herself and the pursuance of the public identity of the body. In part, Apollonia's well-honed instincts of self-preservation also urged her to position herself at the center of the inquiries. But added to her self defense, her curiosity was aflame and continued to ignite her thinking as she considered every unexplained peculiarity of the presence of the body found upon her lands and its singular mode of execution. Beyond that, moreover, she was fearful that the death of the headless corpse might signify a struggle between people of rank and privilege, a far more dangerous prospect than one death at the hands of vagabonds. If some aristocratic vendetta was being unleashed in her region, she wished to expose it, protect against it but keep from revealing her interests until she deemed it safe to do so. For the moment she would initially seek an appropriate and acceptable cover for her activities and rational for her involvement through her gentle manipulation of the Abbot Harold. Riding slightly ahead of Giles, Apollonia organized the simplest and most convincing explanation of events that could be offered to the perpetually inquisitive Abbot of Kingswood. She was certain he could be motivated to act in her behalf but it was better, she told herself, that he act assuming to pursue his own interests while she shielded her larger suspicions tightly concealed within her own counsel.

Reform-minded Abbot Harold Somerton was an aristocrat who presumed high position within the cloistered life to be his by right of rank and birth. No caricature of the cavalier hunting monk, Harold was driven to protect the landed interests of the church through rigid discipline and despotic control. He was singularly proud of the severity of his rule in the Cistercian Abbey of Kingswood. Founded in 1139 by William de Berkeley, the Abbey had been supported through the centuries by ongoing patronage of aristocratic families and Abbot Harold was determined that their benevolent foundation would remain unsullied by accidie or indolence. He wished to leave Kingswood, as monument to his abbacy, increased in lands, wealth, and influence upon the surrounding countryside. Kingswood Abbey's diligent white monks and conversi had already extended, through careful husbandry, the number of flocks of sheep upon which the wealth of their monastery grew yearly. Monastic lands and tithes had more than adequately supported the extension of the glorious Abbey church and the recently completed gabled gatehouse. But having suffered severe depopulation through reoccurring years of plague, the ambitious Harold was being frustrated by a simple conundrum of numbers. He needed many more assiduous tonsured brethren to keep the flocks and maintain the farms that could multiply the Abby's wealth.

Abbot Harold steadfastly refused to resort to leasing the monastery's patrimony. He preferred, instead, to devote his efforts towards the increase of the community, its monetary endowments and gifts in order to bring about the completion of his grander dreams, an Abbey in Kingswood to rival the power and glory of Glastonbury Abbey in Somerset. Solutions to the lack of manpower and temporary inadequacy of funds, he was convinced, could be achieved through the direct straightforward means of pressuring local landowners and wealthy merchants to do more for Kingswood. At every opportunity, the zealous abbot would remind local heads of families of the transitory nature of life. Heaven's gates would swing more swiftly open to welcome that lord or knight who encouraged some sturdy young man of his family or affinity into the severe apostolic life of the Cistercian order. Generous financial endowments were also encouraged to accompany the postulant, substantial enough to support in perpetuity the prayers for the giver's soul and the holy work of the Abbey.

When Lord Ferdinand of Marshfield and his men were announced by the gatekeeper as having arrived in the outer courtyard and awaiting the Abbot's presence, Harold's agile mind immediately began forming requests for novices or, at the very least, endowments from Ferdinand's sizeable holdings and flourishing household. Accompanied by his clerk's flapping sandals marking the rhythm of their hurried pace along the flagstones, the Abbot rushed into the courtyard to welcome his guest's visit and ply him with visions of the blessed benefits of Abbey patronage.

Before Harold could utter his opening words of welcome and greeting, he was stunned to see that the Lord of Marshfield had arrived with a body slung across the hind quarters of one of his horses. Ferdinand had already dismounted and assumed command, ordering several of the monks to assist his henchmen in carrying their burden into the Abbot's chapel. With his martial foot-pounding stride, Ferdinand strode quickly towards Harold and seized his arm. Abruptly halted in mid-step, the startled Abbot was hastily reversed and pulled along by Ferdinand into the slype towards the chapel with him. Pressing his finger to his lips to indicate a secret shared by them alone, Ferdinand hurried the Abbot through the chapel entrance preemptively ordering everyone else to leave them. As the heavy clank of the iron strap lock fell into place on the chapel door echoing from the ribbed ceiling vaults, he noted with satisfaction that they were enclosed alone with the recumbent body lying upon the chapel altar. Before the Abbot could speak, Ferdinand walked to the altar table and ripped away his cloak covering to expose the full horror of his delivery.

"My Lord Abbot," Ferdinand spoke quickly, "My sister, the Lady Apollonia of Aust will soon arrive to beg your counsel. This wretched soul, whom she believes she knew in his mortal life, was discovered upon the banks of the Severn River along her lands, apparently the victim of some evil executed during the night just past. She begs your indulgence and gracious pardon for this inconvenience but, confident in your extreme care for the souls of the living and dead, she trusts that you will reveal nothing of the horrible nature of the death of this unfortunate until she has been able to parley with you."

Dumbstruck, Abbot Harold's arms dropped limply to their sides, his face fallen in a wide-eyed, open-mouthed gasp of revulsion. Ferdinand's voice droned on in its unhurried recitation whilst he continued walking. Inconspicuously wrapping the cloak around one arm he proceeded slowly but steadily towards the main entrance of the chapel. Before Abbot Harold could regain his composure or marshal the slightest objection, Ferdinand opened the door and walked through the exit. "By your leave, Your Grace," he announced loudly and backing out, slammed the chapel doors behind him. His feet pounded their rapid march upon the stones of the passage as he walked back into the Abbey courtyard. Within moments it seemed, Ferdinand's loud rasping voice was heard issuing orders to mount up immediately. The thunder of hooves marked his noisy departure.

Struggling to overcome nausea at the sight of the headless horror impetuously abandoned upon his altar, Abbot Harold's calmer instincts began to reassert themselves. Holding his ringed gloved hand across his nose, he forced himself to examine the body more closely in the hope of identifying it. In spite of its curious peasant garb he could see, at once, that this had been the body of a man of consequence. "Oh indeed," he thought excitedly to himself, "compassion and consolation to the bereaved family of this gentleman, once his identity was secure might earn substantial benefit to him." Abbot Harold was painfully aware of the extraordinary opportunity squandered by his predecessor of seventy-five years earlier. The body of King Edward II had been brought to Kingswood Abbey for burial after the King had been murdered at Berkeley Castle. The earlier Abbot, terrorized by the prospect of aristocratic reprisals, refused to accept the dead king's corpse and it was taken, instead, to be interred in Gloucester. Throughout the seventy-five years since King Edward's death the Benedictines of Gloucester had received the benefit of royal attention as Edward III caused a magnificent alabaster canopy to be carved to mark his father's memorial tomb and royal effigy in their great church. "Worse still," Abbot Harold muttered to himself, "the Benedictines of Gloucester continued every year to receive the largesse of hundreds of pilgrims who traveled to Gloucester to pray at the tomb of the martyred king." In his own mind, Abbot Harold was certain he would never allow such an unworthy and short-sighted mistake to be repeated within the tenure of his abbacy. "But," he thought with growing excitement, "if aristocratic martyrdom could be established in this instance, pilgrimage could surely bring large gifts to the Abbey's treasury."

Harold's eyes sparked with anticipation as his thoughts continued to indulge in a flurry of speculation. Walking silently around the recumbent corpse, the Abbot was, at first, unaware of quiet knocking on the side chapel door. A hesitant little crack appeared between its massive panels and a timid voice ventured into the silence.

"Father Abbot, the Lady Apollonia of Aust has arrived and awaits you in your lodgings."

Abbot Harold turned angrily towards the offending voice. "Anyone who dares to enter this, my personal chapel, without my permission will be severely punished, Brother Lionel," he responded with icy command. "See that the Lady is informed that I shall meet with her after I have completed my prayers for the dead."

Born the third son of a fecund but impoverished noble family, Abbot Harold customarily spoke to members of his community with a tone of imperious distance, expressing that which he believed existed between his social position and theirs. His irritated angry response on this occasion however, was more truly directed at the unexpected happening so recently thrust upon him. He wanted no questions yet; he needed time to deliberate.

If there were ways to turn this event to his service, Abbot Harold wished to take time to think through every avenue of opportunity. And he thoroughly disliked dealing with the Lady of Aust as he never felt he could control an interview with her. He preferred to direct conversations, to be in charge but attempts to pilot discourse with the Lady Apollonia had always proved most illusive. He wanted time in peace on his own to collect his thoughts before encountering the inscrutable Lady quietly waiting in his parlour. Her life and reputation for good works spoke of a meek and acquiescent woman, obedient to the rule of the church in all things. But Abbot Harold sensed an unspoken wall of will in her silence which frustrated him completely. He assumed the Lady to be under the restraints of some holy vow for, whenever he met with her, her servant gave voice to the Lady's conversation. It was most disconcerting to deal with a woman who not only refused to speak but who also insisted upon keeping her eyes downcast and unreadable. "Still," the Abbot thought, "I must not allow myself to overestimate her." Lady Apollonia had wealth and local influence, all of which she dispensed according to an agenda of her own devising. But as he searched for an Achilles' heel in her armor of distance, silence and self-composure, the Abbot reminded himself that the Lady was getting on. All older women, he knew, were eventually amenable to his pastoral counsel that they direct their thoughts from this life to the next. Patronage of his monastery always received Abbot Harold's highest recommendation as a sound commitment to future blessedness.

Then, he happily remembered in a moment's afterthought, the Lady had come to him for his assistance her brother had said. 'Whatever it is that she requires," the Abbot thought to himself, "it is likely that I shall be able to bore my own purposes into the cracks of her temporary dependence." Further, Lady Apollonia promised to be the key to identification of the ghastly deceased lying in his chapel. "The Lady of Aust unknown to her," Abbot Harold thought smugly, "may very well be offering me yet another beneficial avenue of increased patronage." Thus encouraged and impatient to learn the full meaning of this curious visitation, the Abbot hurried off to his parlor, stopped before its door to compose his features and entered the room as if preceded by a fanfare of the heavenly hosts.

"Ah my gracious Lady, we live in the latter days of trouble and wickedness. Will there be time enough on this earth for us to prepare our souls for the certain judgement which awaits?" he expounded as he burst into the room where she was sitting. "How did this horrible crime occur and how shall we ever know the identity of the tragic victim?" Pausing for a moment to observe his effect upon the visitors, the Abbot was intercepted before his next outburst by Giles' profusion of thanks in the name of Lady Apollonia.

"Cognizant of your reputation for militant fidelity to the true faith and encouraged by your earnest concern for souls committed to the care of Kingswood Abbey my Lord Abbot," Giles spoke in his best courtly manner, "My Lady of Aust humbly seeks your counsel in a most delicate dilemma." Seeing that he had captured the Abbot's complete attention, Giles continued to explain, "We of the Lady Apollonia's household of Aust have no insight as to the nature of the gentleman's death. His body was discovered by one of her clerics after the evil gales of the night past. However, the identity of the gentleman whom we have delivered into your care is probably known to my Lady and she urgently requests your assistance in contacting the surviving heirs as she fears they would not welcome any message from her hands." Dropping his voice to a level suitable for the confessional, Giles adopted a player's stage whisper. "My Lord Abbot, my Lady believes that the deceased, discovered in the state of horror which you have undoubtedly witnessed, in a drain from the Lady's fields north of Aust, is none other than Sir Wilfrid de Guelf, the lord of Cliffbarton."

Pausing long enough to allow the Abbot's calculating mind to understand the significance of his revelation, Giles went on. "Being liege man to my Lady's first husband, Sir Wilfrid was well-known to her and she calls your attention to an unusual growth, shaped like a crab, upon the back of the deceased's right hand." The Abbot's eyes maintained a glassy calm but his mind whipped these seeds of information into a mental file for potential future growth. "Sir Wilfrid and his affinity may have regarded my Lady with enmity these many years since she refused the gentleman's hand in marriage upon the death of her lord, Geoffrey Montecute of Colerne Leat."

The Abbot was well acquainted with the bare facts of the Lady's first marital alliance. It had been regarded a triumphant match for her family, allying them to the fortunes of a famous lord, comrade in arms to the Black Prince, hero of Poitiers, and a Garter Knight. Geoffrey Montecute had joined the company of the Earl of Salisbury and sailed to France as a nineteen year old knight in midsummer of 1355. Serving with Prince Edward through miles of plundering, raiding *chevauchees* from Bordeaux to Narbonne and back, the young knight's baggage train bulged with booty plundered from the prosperous lands of the Armagnac. Carts full of carpets, draperies, jewels, gold and silver plate, any object worth carrying away, Geoffrey had continued to send home to await his return to England. He remained in France, reveling in the harrying and wasting of the French countryside, the Black Prince's punitive expeditions meant to heap suffering upon his French subjects.

Finally challenged by a host of French Chivalry in September of 1356 in their camp below Poitiers, the English armies were confronted by a vastly superior force led by the King of France himself. Geoffrey Montecute was with the Earl of Salisbury, commander of one of two front divisions of the English defensive lines. By a miracle of circumstance and monumental bungling on the part of the French, the Oriflamme standard of St. Denis and the French King John, fell to the English that day in the midst of unbelievable carnage. Young Geoffrey lost one eye during the battle but returned to his native land wholly enabled to afford the lifestyle of a nobleman. His fortunes actually increased back in England as he grew richer with each passing month through the ransoms and payments in gold guaranteed by his stable of French hostages captured from the battlefield of Poitiers.

Royally feted as a hero upon his return to England and invested with the Garter by Edward III, Sir Geoffrey remained with the royal court, cultivating his tastes for its debaucheries and continuing the habits of careless cruelty he had acquired in the service of the flower of chivalry. By 1361, it was made singularly clear to him that his honor and fortune were without an heir. Therefore, he begged leave of the court to return to his estates. It would be a brief absence, he assured his gaggle of lovely paramours, only long enough to marry, beget sons, and correct the one outstanding inadequacy of his honor.

Lady Apollonia was not yet fourteen when her father announced to her that she would be married to Geoffrey Montecute within the month. Having maintained her through her thirteenth year and arranged a brilliant match which would guarantee the lifestyle of a great lady for her, her father considered his duty fulfilled. Whatever his daughter's feelings were in the matter he saw no need to inquire after them. At thirteen, she was of marriageable age approved by canon law. Tall and large boned, Apollonia gave the impression of being older. Silent and efficient, she impressed others with her maturity but her prodigal intelligence was as bookish and naive as one born and bred in the convent. For guidance, Apollonia was told to address her prayers to Saint Nicholas, the patron of maidens.

Lady Apollonia refused to recall the years of her first marriage unless compelled by circumstances to do so. Sir Wilfrid's body, lying in the flooded drainage canal had forced her mind to delve into the dreaded past. She was prepared to deal with bad memories she told herself as she sat silently in the Abbot's parlour but now they must wait for other moments of consideration. Her immediate concern was safety and self-defense and Apollonia reckoned that Kingswood Abbey, being nearest at hand, would be perfect sanctuary for her now while Abbot Harold served as her agent of cautious inquiry. To this end, while Giles was completing his prepared message to the Abbot, the Lady sat in motionless silence, her purpose securely veiled behind her posture of meditative withdrawal. "In the interests of peace and justice, my Lord Abbot," Giles concluded, "Lady Apollonia begs that you graciously consent to send word to the family of de Guelf asking them to identify and claim these remains of their kinsman. She further requests your care to avoid revealing the name of Aust or the place of the body's discovery, thereby protecting her from the evil possibility of any undeserved reprisal or acrimonious charges." Giles turned to Lady Apollonia as if to assure that his message had been delivered to her satisfaction.

As his attention also shifted to the silent woman, Abbot Harold was shocked to see the Lady slump forward in her chair. Giles rushed to support her. "My Lord Abbot, could you have your servants show my Lady to a guest chamber. The events of the day have brought her near to faint and I fear she must retire to bed."

"God save us from female corruption!" Abbot Harold swore to himself irritably, "how similar they all are; notorious troublemakers, gossips, venal daughters of Eve." Still, he had achieved a good deal of information and could begin to act without further need of the Lady. Therefore, feigning smiling concern, he summoned his servant and allowed Giles to assist the Lady to the guest apartments maintained by the monastery for important persons who might require accommodations through the night. Once the Lady was installed in her own room, seated comfortably in a chair with the fire in the hearth roused and glowing warmth into the prepared space of the guest lodge, Giles sent the Abbey servant away. He knew that his Lady and he must have a few moments to speak privately before his own hurried departure. Apollonia began by insisting that he return with all possible speed to Aust.

After the Abbot's chamber door closed behind the departing figures of Giles Digby and his fainting Lady, Abbot Harold retreated to his own fireside chair in pensive mood, the fingers of both hands unconsciously weaving themselves together then releasing as his unseeing eyes focused on a distant void. Turning over in his mind the facts of the situation, he could see at once why Lady Apollonia wished his intervention in this matter and he was certain that she would be generous. His heart warmed slightly as he considered her handsome payment for the Abbey guest apartment and anticipated additional gifts for his services. But if the body in his chapel was truly the Lord de Guelf of Cliffbarton, Abbot Harold would need to employ extreme caution in notifying that notorious family of a death in their midst.

The de Guelfs were rightly feared throughout the West of England. Though they had produced warrior knights in succeeding generations, the men of the family had a reputation for cruelty and wanton destruction impervious to correction by the king or modification through the good offices of the church. The sons of the family, it was said, were conceived, born and bred with the pursuit of evil as their only celebration and purpose in life. Prone to uninhibited and bizarre outbursts of violence, the progeny of that dreaded family earned their unfortunate neighbors' undying gratitude only when marching off to war--any war, anywhere.

One infamous story, often told of the brothers of the family de Guelf generations earlier, was of their relentless pursuit of their own sister who had run off with a monk. Finding her in bed with him, the brothers cut away the private organs of the monk's manhood and while her lover lay screaming in agony, forced their sister to eat those parts which they said had made her a whore. Brazenly stripping the castrated monk and exposing his gaping wounds to the eyes of the gawking town, the brothers nailed him to a tree, taunting him with his own crucifix as their model. Then the Brothers de Guelf carried their screaming sister home to Cliffbarton where, it was whispered, they buried her alive.

Rumors of the depravity of Sir Wilfrid de Guelf had generated gossip enough to penetrate even monastic walls. Tales of Sir Wilfrid's favorite village pastime, the famous cat fights of Cliffbarton, were common knowledge. Groups of young villeins, hands bound behind their backs, were forced to compete against each other. They were each ordered to kill a cat with its tail nailed to a post using only their heads and mouths. While the terrified animal struggled to avoid being butted and bitten, the boyish gladiators rewarded their master with an entertainment of cheeks clawed and torn or eyes scratched and bloody.

Then, too, Harold thought, there was that matter of the de Guelf effigy in the parish church of Cliffbarton. No doubt it was superstitious nonsense but stories had been prevalent for generations that members of the family de Guelf celebrated the Black Mass. Their wealth and success in eluding justice was made possible, rumor implied, by their worship of the Lord of the Underworld. The Devil's mark was said to be upon each of their bodies. "Of course it must be he," Abbot Harold suddenly recalled, "the Lady Apollonia recognised a large crab-shaped growth on the back of the deceased's hand."

Still, Harold thought, the wife of such a man as Sir Wilfrid might well feel a very great need to endow a chantry in her husband's memory, supporting a number of monks to pray for the soul of her lord and master. She would be intimately aware of the hundreds of prayers needed to assist his blackened spirit through millennia of purgatory earned in a lifetime of evil. Abbot Harold decided he would send a sympathetic message to the Lady de Guelf, urging her to respond to his inquiry as soon as possible if her Lord had been unexplainably absent from his home. After all, bodies did not keep well; speed was necessary especially if the remains were to be disposed of in a manner expected by those of rank and privilege.

Calling his servant, the Abbot ordered his clerk and the most trustworthy of the monastic lay brothers to be sent to him straightaway. When timid Lionel arrived with quill and paper which he always carried to such a summons, the Abbot began to dictate a note of pastoral concern to the Lady de Guelf. Should her Lord Wilfrid have been missing within recent weeks, the Abbot requested the Lady to come personally to Kingswood as she was urgently needed to assist in a most unpleasant task. Until he received her response, Abbot Harold assured her of his fervent prayers in behalf of her family.

When the scribe had completed the letter, the Abbot added his grand signature with a flourish. He watched the little clerk respectfully roll up the document, now transfigured into significance by the abbot's seal, and then put it into the hands of the burly lay conversus who regularly served his master in matters of questionable but confidential activity. Abbot Harold was brief in his instructions to his messenger. "See that this is delivered directly into the hands of the Lady of Cliffbarton and none other. Wait until an answer can return with you," the Abbot commanded with crisp pronunciation of each word. Turning to the humble clerk, his voice became dark with intimidation. "Now Lionel, you shall forget everything you have seen today as well as this message you have penned." The Abbot's eyes bored into his pale twitching face, "and if there is any discussion within these walls of the events of this day, you will report the names of the offenders to me immediately."

Chapter Four

Wifely Duty

Lady Apollonia was a survivor. Like the waxy green ivy leaves of her heraldic cognizance, she had endured through all seasons of her long life. During her fifty-three years she had known brutal unrestrained power; she had witnessed other women of her class wantonly abused by the men who controlled their lives. Wife beating and humiliating subjugation were not only expected; they were recommended to husbands as proper measures for the maintenance of spiritual discipline and lordly authority. If ever free from the constraints of marriage, a single woman's independence could only be maintained through the exercise of quick intelligence, substantial monies carefully invested and the display of an impenetrable mask of vulnerability and insignificance. Above all, Apollonia had learned to live in a state of wary watchfulness, never allowing herself to become entrapped in unknown corners of others' devising.

She knew great families often took the law into their own hands; in the shires they were the law. Vengeful grudges were violently pursued, especially when one family member assumed some offense had been committed against his honor. Years earlier Wilfrid de Guelf had felt himself insulted and injured by Lady Apollonia's escape to avoid marrying him. Young as she was, Apollonia had been fully aware of the bestial character of her husband's liege man. Fleeing into the sanctuary of Lacock Abbey at the time of Geoffrey's death, Apollonia had remained under the protection of its Abbess until her brother Ferdinand had arrived with sufficient escort to take her to his home. She had escaped but she knew Wilfrid de Guelf may well have felt himself publicly humiliated. Rumors had circulated that Sir Wilfrid may have married several times in the intervening years. But what remained of his immediate family? Did he have brothers or sons who would pursue the malice against her, especially now that his body had been discovered in mysterious humiliating circumstances on her land? A rich and juicy plumb for any strongman's taking, Apollonia recognized her susceptibility to attack by vengeful clan members who could easily assume themselves justified to kidnap her for ransom, pillage her farms, steal her sheep or simply enjoy wreaking havoc and destruction against her and her affinity.

The Abbey's guest apartments were quite comfortable and a lay servant was provided for her needs until Nan Tanner could be fetched to her mistress' side. Apollonia settled herself, fully prepared to remain within Kingswood's cloistered security until the time came when she would be assured of safe return to Aust. Giles had been sent home to maintain a state of vigil among the men of Aust manor. Nan, meanwhile, made haste to reach the Abbey within two days of her Lady's arrival bringing fresh linen and personal items required. Once Nan had joined her, Apollonia felt in her heart, everything had been done to protect her person and her household. They were all vigilant and on guard, as well as readied to seek out the identity of those who might wish to do them harm.

While patiently awaiting word to return from Cliffbarton to Kingswood, Apollonia and Nan left their guest apartments only to attend the *opus dei*, services sung at each of the canonical hours of the day by the monks of Kingswood's beautiful church. After services when they returned to the privacy of the Abbey guest apartments, they mended, enjoyed stitching their embroideries and continued to examine and discuss between them the sequence of events passed since the night of the great storm. Nan was obsessed to search out the meaning of the mysterious dead ravens. She returned to that subject many times as she truly feared the episode exposed a traitor in their midst. She had also heard frightening rumors that a knight's destrier had been found near the village of Ingst. "My Lady," Nan's voice was fraught with worry, "why would the horse of a knight, a gentleman, be found in such a humble place?" Apollonia suggested that after they returned to Aust, Nan might float several innocent questions with obvious rewards implied within the kitchen and servants' quarter, testing the waters to see who might be drawn out by the bait.

At week's end, a small party arrived at the gatehouse of Kingswood Abbey, announcing the arrival of Lady Anne de Guelf of Cliffbarton and asking to be received by the Abbot. Lady Apollonia and Nan stationed themselves inconspicuously beside the stone mullions of their tiny chamber windows overlooking the outer courtyard. They noticed that the lay brother who had served as messenger and guide left the party upon its entry to the courtyard. He scuttled into the corridor leading to the Abbot's lodge, no doubt under orders to report first to the Abbot in private. It was a sad little entourage awaiting the Abbot's pleasure in the courtyard below. Two surly men accompanied several women, none of whom seemed the least bit comfortable or at ease being inside monastic walls. Lady Apollonia, as she searched among the feminine faces, sought to determine which one was the wife of Sir Wilfrid. It was not difficult to identify her. There was only one lady among the group and that was an elegantly dressed young girl who was struggling to carry herself with dignity. "She's hardly more than a child," Apollonia thought as she watched her servant assist her dismount. Cowed and unsure of her position, Lady de Guelf walked in the shadow of her serving woman as she was directed to proceed to the Abbot's parlour.

Several hours passed before Nan and Apollonia noticed the traveling party was gathering once again in the courtyard. They were obviously preparing to take their leave but a noticeable change had occurred in the assumption of rank and authority among them. Now, the Lady de Guelf moved with an assumed assurance, giving orders to her company as if she was, at last, the mistress of it. The male servants uncovered their heads when she addressed them and the serving women ceased to smirk in her presence. "She has broken free of his chains of control," Apollonia said happily to Nan. "What a marvelous transformation in her. Look Nan, see how she moves. Knowing Wilfred is dead, she as mistress of his household knows how to assert her class!" Then in her personal thoughts, Apollonia's mind returned to other ancient memories pressed deeply into her own awareness. "Seeing Wilfrid's body has granted this young widow the liberation I first knew after Geoffrey died? Dear Lord, let it be so." The thought was encouraging.

Lady de Guelf's company departed in haste, apparently grateful to be leaving the solemn grey walls of Kingswood Abbey behind them. It was not long before Brother Lionel called upon the Lady of Aust to deliver a message: "Abbot Harold requests your Ladyship to meet with him after Vespers." At the evening service's end, Nan followed her silent and withdrawn mistress into the Abbot's parlor. Appearing the perfect penitent, Apollonia entered the chamber with clasped hands hidden beneath her dark mantle and her eyes lowered. She genuflected to the Abbot and moved quickly to take the chair indicated for her by his Grace while Nan took her position standing behind the chair of her mistress.

"My Lady, you have done a great kindness indeed, by assisting in the identification of the deceased Lord Wilfrid de Guelf," Abbot Harold began. "His young wife, Lady Anne, has definitely confirmed the identity of her husband and has made arrangements for his internment here, within our Abbey Church. She has also agreed to endow a chantry chapel in his memory and to provide adequate income in support of prayers for his soul in perpetuity. I have encouraged her," the Abbot continued, "to return often and she has indicated that she will also be a faithful visitor to our Lady Chapel each year bringing her infant son, Sir Wilfrid's only family and heir, to observe the *placebo et dirige* in his father's memory." Abbot Harold's eyes searched the Lady's meditative posture for any sign of reaction. Nan thanked him graciously for his reassurances to them but Apollonia's dark figure remained silent. At least Abbot Harold could see the Lady's head bow slightly in acknowledgement of his news yet her lidded eyes continued to cap any escape of emotion or expression.

"The Lady Anne preferred to know none of the details of her husband's death and I could see no reason to add to her burden of grief," the Abbot said pointedly for Lady Apollonia's benefit. "Lady de Guelf rejoices in the knowledge that the soul of her revered Lord will be assisted through the fires of purgatory by the regular recitation of prayers in his behalf by pious and holy men." Having finished all that he intended to say, the Abbot paused meaningfully.

Rising from her chair, Lady Apollonia put her hand on Nan's arm. "My Lady wishes me to express her heartfelt thanks for your good offices, my Lord Abbot. She would like to return to the church to offer her own prayers for the soul of Sir Wilfrid." The Abbot nodded his approval. "Then, by your leave, we shall prepare to return to Aust in the morning after Prime." Depositing a bulging money pouch upon the Abbot's table, Nan continued, "My Lady of Aust begs your blessing, your Grace and asks that you accept this small token of her gratitude for your hospitality and sanctuary."

The Abbot rose rapidly to bestow the requested blessing upon both women but his eyes looked through the kneeling women as he prayed and signed over them. The words of his mouth droned the familiar blessing but the Abbot's heart sang a different song of triumph. "Kingswood has known a glorious increase, this day! My prudence and insight have been rewarded indeed!" His thoughts had taken flight, already beginning to count the variety of potential blessed rewards he could foresee pouring into the Abbey's coffers and thinking to himself that he may wish to summon his master mason. He had always wished to add a porch to the south entrance of the Abbey church. It would be the Harold Porch, dedicated to his abbacy and filled with the carvings of his name saints and the Herald Angels!

Chapter Five

Lady's Grace

Nan Tanner had entered her Lady's service as a child of the household of Sir Geoffrey Montecute in Colerne Leat. An unacknowledged orphan of the village, Nan was thought to be the offspring of a barber, as tanners were sometimes called, wandering from Bristol towards the hope of work in Coventry. Receiving bread from the kitchen door, he had also advantaged himself of the favors of one of the kitchen wenches who abandoned their eventual progeny in the manor barn. Whether such origins were true or not, Nan's infancy was careless at best. Her entire life's memory was bounded in the walls of the scullery and Colerne Leat manor house kitchen. Small for her age and pitifully malnourished, the child was often fatigued and clumsy with the heavy trenchers and kettles delivered to her for scrubbing. Her name, forgotten in irritation, became expressed instead through curses and blows against her perceived laziness. "Devyl take thee, worthless imp!" The cook would laugh as kitchen wenches raged against her helpless errors and sought to impose corrective discipline by a sharp thump against the side of her easily accessible head.

Nan stayed, whenever possible, within the kitchen with its large fireplace and massive ovens glowing warmth against the raw cold and damp. But the noisy strife and clashing tempers of older house wenches found ready outlet in teasing and tormenting a lazy bastard girlchild always on the brink of tears. Even the unruly dogs, so highly valued by their master that they enjoyed sovereignty over the household servants, sensed her childish defenselessness against their arrogant snapping. At the very bottom of the household pecking order, Nan learned to retreat whenever possible to hide away from taunts and blows liberally given in vented frustration upon any lower creature near at hand. Largely unaware of her Lord's marriage or the meaning of the servants' whispered speculation regarding their new mistress, Nan's world of terror changed little until the new Lady of Colerne Leat personally entered her life.

Apollonia's husband had allowed her to bring no one from her father's affinity with her as maid servant, clerk, or chaplain. Sir Geoffrey informed his young bride that he would allow her to choose from any of the females of his household. He would see that she was well-served, he sneered lewdly looking past her to the smirking eyes of his henchmen. Having begun to scrutinize Geoffrey's people soon after her arrival, Apollonia decided that she could accept none of the badly used wenches who fawned upon her husband with slavish fear and jittery attention to his ever-changing mood. Her isolation and barren loneliness at Colerne Leat drove the young Mistress to daily supplications that God would help her find one sympathetic person whose allegiance she could trust to serve her alone. Surely God would listen as Apollonia prayed desperately. There was no other hope of assistance open to her.

One bright summer morning, as Apollonia walked through the service corridors leading out to the garden, she thought she could hear the soft whimpering of a child hidden somewhere inside the darkness of the arched undercroft. Waiting for her eyes to adjust to the gloom, the Lady moved quietly towards the sound, finally discovering its source in a trembling, ill-fed, dirty little girl hiding in the depths of a dark bay used for storage of wood. The gaunt childish face was smudged and wet with tears which continued to pour out of eyes reddened from long weeping. When Apollonia attempted to touch the little one, the child's body recoiled from her outstretched hand as a mongrel would instinctively retreat from an anticipated kick.

"Little one, I mean you no harm," Apollonia said gently to Nan. "Come with me into the garden for a few moments in the sunshine." Never allowed in the garden, Nan was overwhelmed by the prospect. Looking down, she said nothing and simply curled more tightly into her corner. "You may follow me," Apollonia said quietly, "and I shall show you a pond full of fish." Then the new Lady of the household slowly began to walk away. Intrigued by her invitation and encouraged by the warmth and aura of protection which this grand Lady seemed to offer, Nan silently crept from her corner and cautiously followed Apollonia into the sunshine like a tiny darting shadow several paces behind.

Lady Apollonia did not stop until she arrived at a small bench placed in the shade of overhanging willows moved by a gentle breeze to caress the bank of the manor pond full of fat, well-fed fish. She seated herself then quietly waited for the little girl who hastily withdrew to the shadow of a nearby tree. Apollonia noted her strange halting gait, as if the child were walking in pain. Having carried from the house a basket of bread scraps leftover from the trenchers of the weeks' meals, Apollonia threw several pieces into the middle of the pond and watched as the bread floated along the surface of the water. Suddenly the surface was a bubbling whirlpool of fish thrashing about in feeding frenzy. Nan cautiously peered from behind her tree in wonder at the motion and sounds bubbling out from the stirred waters of the pond. Her curiosity overwhelmed her apprehension and she emerged from the tree's shadow approaching the Lady to see what was being thrown into the water. Gently, Apollonia took several large scraps of bread from her basket and laid them on the bench next to her, indicating to the child that she might toss them to the fish. Timidly taking the pieces of stale bread soaked in meat juices into her hands, Nan quickly turned her back upon the Lady and stuffed the largest chunk into her own mouth, then rushed to the water's edge and hurled the rest at the surface of the pond. The splash of entry was greeted by a rush of fish mouths seizing bread pieces and churning the pond into a brief, boiling swirl. The child squealed with delight and turning back to the Lady saw that she, too, was smiling and holding out additional food for the fish. Nan ran up to Apollonia to take the bread then ran back to the pond bank to repeat the toss, sometimes with a single piece, keeping the rest for her own consumption, sometimes with several as her own hunger began to diminish. Her face flushed and excited, Nan giggled aloud then clapped her little hands over her mouth as she turned to confirm the Lady's response. Apollonia smiled and offering the bread basket to Nan bade her new friend to continue the game.

They stayed together in the garden for several hours. During that time, Apollonia learned her companion's name. She also learned that young Nan Tanner had no father or mother; that she lived, worked, and slept in Sir Geoffrey's kitchen. A very appealing idea formed quickly in Apollonia's mind. It would be unusual but seemed so perfect a solution to her needs that she knew she would act upon it immediately. By the time the bread was gone and Nan realized that they must leave the lovely fish pond, Lady Apollonia announced to Nan Tanner that she no longer lived and worked in the kitchen. Apollonia would teach Nan to serve as her Lady's maid and she would live within the Lady's chambers!

Keeping well within the benevolent shadow of the Lady of the household, Nan re-entered the kitchen with her mistress. There the cook was told that Nan would have to be replaced in the scullery as she was being taken for training as her Lady's servant. The kitchen staff, standing about with their sneering mouths agape, watched in disbelief as their mistress departed the kitchen through the great doors leading towards the manor hall accompanied by a very dirty but shining little girl.

Before Lady Apollonia could bring herself to tell Geoffrey of her choice from among his servants she knew that she must make some changes in the child's appearance. Nan was taken to the Lady's chamber and put to soak and scrub herself in a large tub. She was an extraordinarily plain child with white complexion and transparent blonde hair. She appeared to have no eyebrows at all, small pallid lips hiding tiny teeth while her pale blue eyes seemed a startling flash of color from an otherwise blank little face. Watching the child dry her thin body after the bath, Apollonia noticed how cautiously Nan touched herself between the legs. Obviously bruised and sensitive, Apollonia wondered for a brief moment if the child had been kicked in the groin for some perceived error.

But Apollonia's thoughts first concentrated on the problem of finding something appropriate for the child to wear. Throwing Nan's filthy rags into the fire, Apollonia selected from her wardrobe a shift and linen chemise, cutting away their excess length. She pulled from her garment chest the smallest of her tunics to serve as overdress and tried its size against Nan's body. Standing naked but yet in awe and wonder, Nan carefully took into her hands and put on the newly abbreviated shift. She didn't know what to do with its cords so the Lady Apollonia tied its silk cords at the neck then dropped the chemise over her head, rolling its long sleeves up and tacking them into place. On top of that she dropped the shorter tunic, pulled and tacked its abbreviated sleeves above Nan's elbows. Finally Apollonia knelt to tuck and gather in the too-large waist. While Nan held the gathers in place with two hands, Apollonia found a sweet blue girdle from her own childhood lying in the bottom of her chest and wound it twice around Nan's little waist. A pair of Apollonia's short hose was gartered in place on each leg about the child's thighs and a white linen kerchief was tied over Nan's smooth, clean hair to provide a crisp headdress. At last a small white barmclooth furnished the newly appointed maid with an apron. Stepping back to admire the hastily assembled costume, Apollonia thought they had done very well

46

indeed. She would inform Geoffrey of her selection at the first opportunity when she felt it safe to risk speaking with her husband.

Well-fed and nurtured through her Lady's gentle encouragement; Nan was transformed in the weeks that followed. She grew visibly in body and in spirit. Her face and figure filled out nicely and soon she was able to walk at her full height past other members of the household without cringing or wincing. She was taught to move silently next to her Lady Mistress and to curtsy politely with hands touching her skirts in acknowledgement of any person of status whom they may encounter. Apollonia also noticed an absence of the halting discomfort which had arrested Nan's walking on their first days together.

Several months would pass in the Lady's service before Nan could bring herself to reveal the cause of her limping and the name of her molester. To the Lady's horror, she learned that her husband's favorite companion and closest comrade, Wilfrid de Guelf, had raped Nan shortly before Apollonia found her weeping in the undercroft. Apollonia's dislike of Wilfrid grew into icy loathing but she was forced to acknowledge that many men of her Lord's affinity were capable of abusing a child. Sir Wilfrid was not constrained to suppress his depraved sport with children--male or female. He entertained the table in hall with his perverted tales of pederasty and hunts for little virgins. Geoffrey refused to listen to his wife's pleas to curtail Wilfrid's wantonness as unholy reflections upon the entire household. He found his friend's preferences common enough and always the possible butt of a good laugh between them.

As to his wife's choice of maidservant, Geoffrey expressed studied indifference. "Keep the brat out of my way," he had warned. If truth were told, Geoffrey did not wish for any creature to provide solace or companionship to his young wife. He preferred that she remain isolated, insecure, and malleable. But a little scum to do her bidding would not threaten his control, he reasoned, did not even deserve his attention. Therefore, he dismissed the choice as a womanish whim now satisfied.

Apollonia betrayed no emotion as she heard his decision. Her eyes cast downward; she curtseyed to her Lord and left him. But her heart leapt for joy as she hurried to her solar where Nan was hard at work sorting Apollonia's silks for embroidery. She knew she would find a special delight in sharing her Lord's approval with Nan and Apollonia also knew she need not bother to repeat Geoffrey's warning that Nan stay out of his sight as the little maid in waiting lived in terror of the Lord of Colerne Leat. Constantly at her Lady's side, shiny, clean and always busy, Nan would disappear at the instant her Lord's footsteps were heard approaching their chamber. Like a wary cat, the child instinctively felt his approach, would scurry away and remain hidden until Geoffrey departed. But in the welcome silence of his absence, Nan would rush to Apollonia's chamber and reassume her cherished position at her Lady's side.

Apollonia taught Nan to read and to do basic sums. She recognized immediately the child's complete ignorance of common forms of worship and stories of piety. Therefore, each day after Nan had accompanied her mistress to chapel, Apollonia and she remained in the sanctuary to study the Bible stories in the stained glass windows and speak of the lives of the saints represented in niches of the altar screen. Apollonia also arranged for an old sewing woman of the household to instruct the maid in expert use of a needle. As often as weather would permit, Apollonia and Nan spent their most treasured and pleasant hours alone in the garden near the fishpond. The Lady, in Nan's eyes, could only be compared with the haloed feminine figures in the candlelit chapel. While still a child, she recognized that Lady Apollonia had rescued her from an existence of animal terror. In her mature years, Nan would freely testify that her mistress had not only clothed and fed her, Lady Apollonia, she would say, had granted her a soul.

Chapter Six

Devyl's Henchmen

Nan Tanner, in return, provided Apollonia the one tiny flame of hope in a black wilderness of marriage into which she had been unwillingly contracted. On the day she had left her father's house and accompanied her new husband to the place that would become her home, Apollonia prayed in silent desperation to suppress her inner terror of the arrangement. Silent through the entire journey, she could find no humor in the bawdy exchanges between her new lord and his companions. Painfully ignorant of the behaviour of men, Apollonia's innocence thwarted her understanding of their ribaldry while her intense shyness hobbled any attempt to speak. Geoffrey seemed to enjoy exposing her child-like naiveté. Her feverish blushing and humiliated retreat into silence only encouraged her husband's vulgar japes at her expense.

Geoffrey's extraordinary rudeness towards her only magnified Apollonia's instinctive fear of him. She had observed his conduct closely throughout their brief betrothal and wedding celebrations in the vain hope of discovering some small element of compassion in his chivalrous character which she could clutch as a reassuring possibility of any warmth and gentleness in his person. Though her husband played the game of courtly love with the skill of an experienced courtier, Apollonia recognized his feigned affections as a gauzy counterfeit. He preferred to use his considerable gifts to shock and to inspire fear.

Geoffrey's face was scarred and sunken round the purplish socket of that which had been his right eye. In spite of the disfigurement, he was still considered handsome. The ladies admired his fine complexion, exquisitely chiseled cheek bones and classically sculpted head crowned by shining black hair which fell to his proud shoulders. He was the perfect figure of a paladin, tall, long-muscled, and fluidly graceful. But cruelty lined and distorted his thin curling lips; swaggering arrogance emanated from his presence like a searing aureole. Geoffrey Montecute acknowledged no restraint, allowed no question of his capricious will, and was only content when other creatures cowered in his presence.

Apollonia dreaded her wedding night. How could she share a bed with this man? What was she to do? She had never been allowed to remain alone in the company of gentlemen and could not imagine sharing a sleeping chamber with one. Her father had guarded her maiden innocence like a dragon, forbidding anyone in his service to speak of carnal relations in her presence. When taking leave of his daughter for the last time, her father's words were spoken in his usual tone of command. "You will be amiable and obedient, Apollonia, seek to please your husband in all things and obey him as you were taught to obey me."

On the night of her arrival at Colerne Leat, Apollonia excused herself early from the boisterous company at table, leaving the raucous hall and escaping to the Lord's private apartments in the hope that she might calm her throbbing fear before her husband came to her. Being shown the bedchamber, she rushed to the prie-dieux and dropped to her knees as her body shook with hysterical weeping. Her ritual of prayers seemed empty and sterile; she knew not what to ask for. Calling upon Saint Nicholas, the Holy Virgin, every holy martyr she could think of, Apollonia begged the saints to come to her aid and assist her through the night ahead. Visibly trembling as she rose from her prayers, she began to remove her clothes. When she was completely naked she hurried into the bed and modestly pulled its fur coverings to her chin to await her husband. The noise from the hall below continued unrestrained and unabated.

Hours passed, the candles in the bedchamber burned slowly down, and Apollonia began to feel calmer in the hope that Sir Geoffrey might not come at all. Eventually, her body succumbed to exhausted sleep. Suddenly, as if in a frightening dream, she felt herself struggling to determine where she was, as a man's angry voice growled above her, "Is this the way you await your Lord, Madame?" Geoffrey was drunk and staggering from side to side. Fully clothed, he had entered the bedchamber with his dagger and sword still dangling in their scabbards from his belt. "Out of bed, woman," he shouted. "I want to see what I have bought."

"Please, My Lord," Apollonia began to object sleepily, shyly holding the coverlet to her shoulders. Roaring at behaviour he deemed blatant disobedience, Geoffrey ripped the bedclothes from her body and drew his sword.

"You will never disobey me, woman," Geoffrey snarled. "I own you body and soul and will have you as I wish. Now stand!"

Slipping her long white legs over the side of the bed, Apollonia struggled to suppress her wildly beating heart and stem the flood of fear pounding through her veins. Numbly obedient she stood next to the bed, keeping her head bowed and eyes lowered. She started with an involuntary gasp as Geoffrey's hand roughly seized the back of her neck and steered her into motion like a haltered beast. Pushing his wife towards the hearth where the firelight danced upon her exposed white flesh, Geoffrey steadied himself by leaning heavily upon his sword with its point now stabbed into the wooden floor. Slowly his left hand moved from her neck across to her shoulders forcing her to turn as he began what seemed an interminable examination of her naked body. Running his open hand, thumb and fingers L-shaped, down the full length of her torso, he bent slightly as he reached the tops of her legs to focus his single eye upon the taught skin and long muscles stretching from her hips through the length of her thighs. He forced her to continue to turn as he squeezed and manipulated muscle, joints and tendon in the manner of scrutinizing an unknown horse.

"I shan't ever take you to court. What a laughable clod you should be, big and clumsy as a Flanders mare." Geoffrey's flaccid mouth seeped spittle from the corners of its lips. His body lunged from side to side, staggering then regaining a tentative balance. "A good breeder," he shouted, "that's what I want and that is what you are for, woman. Are you a virgin?" he shouted, "I don't fancy any man's leavings."

Apollonia kept her eyes closed unable to take in the extent of her humiliation. She nodded her head as she could not bring herself to speak. "Ah, shy tender maid art thou? We shall see," Sir Geoffrey snorted. He pushed her to the bed and thrust her backward across it. "Now spread your legs." He spat at the floor and pulled himself erect. Still holding his sword in his right hand he lifted it over her trembling body. Placing the full length of its steel blade flatly upon her torso, he pressed its point at her throat with its blade passed between her breasts and its hilt pushed painfully into her groin.

Quaking with fear Apollonia clenched her eyelids tightly closed to blacken and shut away the images of unbelievable degradation being done to her. Her facial grimaces excited Geoffrey.

The creases in his cheeks twitched and his open mouth drooled as he savored her helpless terror. "You're young and strong," his breathing grew heavy, "and broad in the hips, sign of good breeding stock, by my faith! You are to give me sons, do you understand?" As if his insistent command could cause male conception, he repeated his words, "I will have sons."

Belching in sudden drunken rage against her, Geoffrey pressed his full weight against the hilt of his sword between her legs. "Mark me well, woman, if I ever catch you swiving another man, I' shall push this sword from your crotch to your chin and carve you in twain. One whoring half will be sent to your father and the other nailed to my gate. Do you understand me?" Apollonia had put one arm across her eyes but nodded ascent as Geoffrey finally pulled the sword off her and threw it to the floor. Ripping away his sword belt and tearing open his own clothes, he lunged onto the bed, too drunk to undress.

It was not long till dawn but Apollonia truly wondered if she would survive to see another day. Geoffrey had mounted her twice, flushed and excited by the generous flow of blood released by his battering of the hymeneal tissue. He laughed out loud as he smeared the hot sticky fluid along her legs. "Such a pity, virgins never seem to last," he roared at his own sickly humor. When he finally rolled from her body Geoffrey collapsed into a deep drunken sleep, his limp semi-nakedness carelessly flaunting its finish with her.

Geoffrey snored loudly through slack gaping jaws while Apollonia, rigidly awake, counted his long steady breaths inhale and snorting exhale. She waited like a caged animal watching for the earliest opportunity to flee from him and from the accursed chamber where he lay. Pain throbbed in her lower abdomen, back, and hips when she attempted to steal from the bed. The silence of her escape was shattered as she fell helplessly to the floor. Geoffrey's snoring continued undisturbed and she tried once again to pick herself up but her battered hips and trembling legs seemed unable to carry her weight. "I must get away," Apollonia hissed to herself, "I will get out of this room." Cursing her weakness, she forced her legs to support her, willed them to move. Leaning against the stone wall, she was able to pull herself away from the bed along the wall and towards the chamber door. A wardrobe chest stood near and from it she snatched a robe, wrapped it round her shivering, naked body, and limped from the room. Stealing silently down the hall towards the garderobe, she slipped into its cold blackness and pulled the heavy door closed behind her.

As she seated herself onto the icy stone opening, she felt an anguished scream rising from the depths of her soul. "Holy Mother" she cried in silence, "is this the holy sacrament of marriage?" Huge soundless sobs racked her body as visions of the brutal, degrading humiliation swept over her again and again. She felt nauseous at the thought of her odious husband. And she began to grow angry; a fierce anger born of helplessness began to overcome her shame and revulsion. Unaware of her fists pounding against her knees, she swore to herself that she would find a way to resist him. Geoffrey Montecute owned her, controlled her but she would thwart him. She could not fathom the depths of his bestiality but she would not participate in it; she would withhold her person from his bestial violence.

Urinating into the pit below and feeling Geoffrey's disgusting seed dripping from her, she pulled the furred robe more tightly to her torso and neck against the cold draughts whistling through cracks in the plastered stone garderobe walls. The frigid air seemed to clear her mind and numb her tortured body. With fierce determination, she thought, "Damn you to Hell, Geoffrey! I shall resist you!" But in the blank darkness of the tiny cubicle, her logic could only provide the inescapable truth that she possessed no option to refuse him; she could not openly rebel against her husband and survive. She could turn to no one in his household for protection. "So be it," she decided desperately. She would find a course of silent passive resistance.

She remained sitting in the gelid garderobe until every drop of Geoffrey's lust dripped from her body. Then she reached into the basin of water left by the servants and washed her body, her privy self, again and again with the icy water, until her skin felt sleek and clean of his slime. One important truth of life was known to her from her childhood exploration of the barns in breeding seasons on her father's estate. When male animals were roused to copulate, they climbed upon the female pushing into them again and again until their seed had been planted, she had been told. She had seen in the barnyard the same animal lust she had just endured. "I shant have it remain in me," she declared into the darkness. "I will expel any seed of Geoffrey Montecute. His hoped for heirs will never germinate in me."

Retreating to her dressing room, Apollonia prepared to go about her morning household tasks as the Lady of the manor would be expected to do. No one would ever know, she vowed to herself, the degradation she was subjected to by the loathsome man forced upon her as husband. That was her secret shame. Sir Geoffrey wanted sons but, she swore to herself, he would never get them off her. If she could successfully drain his fluids from her and pray God that she might never conceive, that may be her avenue of escape and it would remain her constant prayer.

Society assumed that every goodly woman turned to the church as her consolation in this life and hope for the next. Therefore, Sir Geoffrey saw nothing unusual in his young wife's request for masses to be said daily in the manor chapel. Nor did he find it surprising that she would wear a hair shirt next to her skin beneath her shift. That she often visited the Abbess of Lacock Abbey and established a lay relationship with the Augustinian nuns of the Abbey there did not concern him either. Such were acceptable applications of the female mind. As he kept his Lady confined in the country where her duties to him and the care of his large household were manifest, he thought nothing out of the ordinary in her growing interest in the church.

As the early months of marriage passed, Geoffrey was delighted to discover Apollonia's obvious skill in management. He readily extended her authority within his affinity to encourage her maintenance and supervision of his estates. She was an unexpectedly well-educated woman, able to read French, English, and Latin and skillful in computations which eluded Geoffrey. She had the polish of a diplomat in dealing with the church and a clerk's ability to ferret out important points of law which served his interests and profit. Pursuit of adventure under the guidance of Mars and Venus was the only business worthy of the knight in Sir Geoffrey's estimation. Leaving administrative clap-trap in Apollonia's competent hands encouraged his attendance at Court and his favorite pursuits of blood sports and bawdy women.

Largely due to her father's lack of interest in her, Apollonia had been well-schooled throughout her childhood years. When her brother, Ferdinand, was sent off at age twelve to serve in the household of a great lord and continue his education in arms and manners of the gentles, his tutors were retained by Apollonia's father. It was his opinion that clerics were adequate to occupy the time of his motherless daughter until she reached marriageable age. Before her fifth year, Apollonia surprised everyone with her prodigy's ability to learn. Ferdinand's tutors were soon scurrying to find new lessons and manuscripts to serve her quick mind and voracious curiosity. Once a married woman however, she thought it wiser to conceal many of her intellectual interests from Geoffrey, content to be allowed the freedom of movement which the management of his estates guaranteed her.

Three years passed and the Lady of Colerne Leat betrayed no sign of pregnancy. She was young and he had time Geoffrey assured himself smugly but it was an obvious source of frustration to him and he did not like the idea that he might appear impotent in the eyes of his companions. Not achieving the desired heir only stimulated him to greater demands upon Apollonia in their bedchamber and his sexual performance grew ever more aggressive. His body attacked hers as if assaulting her closed womb with the battering ram of his lust. His open mouth heaving blasts of foul breath, Geoffrey thrust his body hard upon hers determined to penetrate her silent will and destroy her inability to conceive by his superior weight and physical strength. Apollonia allowed herself to display no response to his sexual demands and she swore he would never see her fear and loathing. As patient as Griselda, her eyes remained closed and her emotions held in strict check throughout his pounding ravishment of their nights together. During the day, she would always appear composed and submissive, obediently and competently serving her Lord. That is how she was determined she would be seen.

After each sexual tryst while Geoffrey slept, Apollonia slipped away to the garderobe. There she could weep, repent, and mourn in silence as the slime of his passion dripped from her. The fury of her defiance seemed to translate into vigorous washing of her entire body as she strove to wipe away the slightest remnant of his touch. But as months went by her anger against Geoffrey dissipated into numb animal submission, her willful disobedience grew in her mind as mortal sin, sin which she could not confess, sin which remained unforgiven. But Apollonia endured her willful sinful acts as she would endure all: silently. There was hope, she knew, in being a barren wife. Geoffrey would denounce her, their marriage would be annulled and she would be free.

Geoffrey Montecute's favorite sport was hunting boar. He kept packs of dogs, teased, restrained, and ravenous at the ready for his summons to a day's hunt. On such a day, his companions and he would be mounted and keen to be off as the dog handlers brought out their chaotic packs of snarling charges. Unleashed upon the scent of the forest beast renowned for its strength, cunning, and viciousness, the hounds could apply their superior numbers and hungry desperation against the brawny savagery of the boar.

A huge male had been sighted in Geoffrey's forest, biggest of the boars ever taken in the shire, it was said. Killing such a beast would assure a hunter's fame and prowess and its tale would become the song of his glory. Geoffrey could barely contain his excitement as he boasted freely that the swine's head would soon decorate his hall. Swaggering among his men, he swore that his sword alone would pierce the beast's proud heart.

The day of the boar hunt began early and with great enthusiasm for the kill shared by men and dogs. The company charged off amidst a din of thundering hooves, horns and baying hounds. Following the scent for miles, the dogs approached and snarling encircled a copse of trees, rushed into its midst then seemed to grow confused, disbursed, then rushed off in a clamorous pack again. The riders rode on and on in the wake of the yowling hounds as they circled and soon began to retrace familiar ground. At last, it became appallingly clear that dogs and huntsmen were being confounded by the wily swine. After several fruitless hours had passed, Sir Geoffrey grew bored with the chase and called it off.

Returning to the manor, he arrived in an unusually black humor. "By God's death," Geoffrey swore at everyone within earshot, "I shall waste no time in finishing this matter." He summoned all of his foresters, ordered them to trap the boar alive and send word to him as soon as it was taken. Determined to wreak vengeance upon the cunning devil, Geoffrey's frustration mounted as days passed and the boar remained at liberty. By his name and his honor, as if his personal renown were at stake, Geoffrey swore that he would have his triumph but on his terms and at his pleasure.

Harried by their Lord to produce the boar with haste, the foresters gathered an army of men and organized the digging of a deep pit in the heart of the boar's territory. Skillfully brushing away their own scent and concealing its entrapping net with boughs and branches, Geoffrey's men baited the entire trench with garbage. For two weeks, the boar avoided his destiny but scavenging early one morning, his appetite overcame his caution. Sir Geoffrey's men sent word to the manor the instant it had been confirmed that the boar was captured.

Securely trussed to a mighty spar, the beast was brought around for Geoffrey's inspection. He was enthralled by the size of the brute; the sturdy pole upon which it was strung, was bent to a crescent by its great weight and lunging ferocity. The boar's curled tusks were enormous and Geoffrey charged his handlers, upon pain of their own deaths, not to damage them in any way when they removed the hempen rope which clenched the muzzle shut.

All of the dogs in the pens near at hand set up a great howling, as the scent of the wild animal whipped them into salivating fury. Sir Geoffrey and his men, flushed at the capture of such a mighty beast, congratulated each other in anticipation of the great show which they felt they had in store for themselves. Geoffrey, boasting of his triumph, announced his plan to chain the captured boar to a stake in his bear pit. There being no need to pursue the quarry till exhaustion, fresh dogs could be loosed to attack the captured boar within the confined area of the pit while every man of them could enjoy the spectacle in comfort. Wagers could be made on how long the boar would last, which combination of the hounds might prove strong enough to survive and how many of the dogs would finally be needed to kill the boar. "Am I not providing a spectacle worthy of ancient emperors for your enjoyment, my Lords? Put up your wagers; add spice to the meat as I have already provided for you the game." Geoffrey felt lordly indeed as he taunted and roused the bloodlust of his henchmen.

Sir Geoffrey was captivated by the struggling boar, drawn to the hairy mass of power and fury as if by some unseen force. He walked beside the group of men carrying the boar to the pit, feeling sexually aroused and trying to imagine how the sport might be prolonged. "Why rush the game?" he thought to himself. "Why not let in two or three dogs to harry the beast and tire him more slowly?" he smiled at his ingenuity. While his foresters struggled to chain the raging creature to a stake in the pit, Sir Geoffrey went to the dog pens to select the most vicious of his hounds, those most persistent in pursuit. Singling out several groups of aggressive dogs to the handlers, he ordered that they be released three at a time into the pit with the boar.

"So, gentlemen," Sir Geoffrey shouted when all was ready, "Shall we attend to the play?" His companions were delighted; every one of them eager to place himself as close as possible to the spectator wall of the pit. Servants walked amidst the shouting, wagering, and swearing party, offering wine cooled in the nearby spring. Geoffrey's herald called for order and then, with trumpets sounding, the contest was announced. Anticipation was keen as the first trio of dogs was unleashed into the pit.

Slyly, the hounds crouched and circled, attempting to separate themselves and attack the boar two at a time whilst he was occupied by the third. But the wily beast refused to be distracted. With his haunches pressed to the stake, he kept his head lowered until all three dogs ventured within his range. In one mighty back and forth slashing motion of his great head, he dispatched all three amidst howls of pain and the gush of blood and spilled canine intestines.

Three more of Sir Geoffrey's best dogs proved unable to wound, much less trouble, the boar. They were all gored with dispatch as the bear pit began to reek of hot blood and mortally wounded dogs. Still the huge animal remained in his attack position, wary and undistracted by the noise and offal lying about him. Irritated by the boar's apparent ease in slaughtering his dogs, Sir Geoffrey ordered that a small pack be unleashed to try the stubborn mettle of the great beast. In the crowded pit, there was only room to charge en masse; dogs howling, snarling, and snapping at the boar. Although the brawny beast threw several dogs over his head ripped and torn in screeching agony, two other hounds managed to clamp their jaws upon the exposed throat of the struggling boar. Others tore at his legs and others went for his soft underbelly until at last the great beast dropped. The bear pit had become a frenzied, foul-smelling, steaming cauldron of death.

58

Confident that the boar was dead, Sir Geoffrey called to have the frenzied dogs removed before they could damage the boar's head, his excellent trophy with its noble tusks. Then he climbed into the pit to look more closely at his wild and worthy adversary, its massive body and powerful legs, and especially the terrifying head. He bent over the fallen beast so that he might gain a better view with his single left eye. Unaware of twitching in the beast's powerful neck muscles, Geoffrey stooped to measure the tremendous tusks against the size of his hand as the boar's body began to recoil. The Lord of Colerne Leat did not see what happened next from his blind side. The tusks which he had admired so extravagantly, ripped upward through his abdomen, pouring forth his own entrails into the blood and stinking viscous of the pit floor. Geoffrey's scream pierced the stone walls and reverberated across the vaulted ceiling as the boar collapsed in a great mortally wounded heap.

Sir Geoffrey's death was agonizingly slow. Howling with the passion of the disemboweled, he was beyond comfort. His body had to be lashed onto the bed. Lady Apollonia could see at once that her husband's injury was passed any known physic or cure. She pleaded with his leech to soothe his pain, to administer any opiate potions which might quiet him. But Sir Geoffrey could not be made to drink; amidst maniacal screaming, he choked horribly and spewed the well-intended liquids out from his gasping mouth.

"He is, as ever, his own worst enemy," Apollonia repeated to herself. Geoffrey Montecute had purposely been her nemesis, her announced possessor but she could not help but feel pity at the extent of his suffering. Forcing herself to remain at his bedside, Apollonia tried to keep cool compresses laid upon his feverishly thrashing head. All her efforts were futile and cast off in his torment.

Priests were summoned to attend Geoffrey's chamber but were helpless to do aught but maintain a murmur of prayer beneath the hoarse wailing cries of the victim. Apollonia remained upon her knees at the bedside begging God to bring an end to Geoffrey's suffering. Hours grew into a day and half of nerve-piercing horror until death released her husband's tortured spirit from his powerfully strong body. When at last he grew silent, she burst out from the chamber and rushed to her solar dazed, trembling and chilled to the bone. Collapsing into

Nan's arms, Apollonia's hysterical screeching drove her senses to the brink of madness as her own grasp upon life wavered and surrendered.

Refusing to leave her mistress' side, Nan nursed her Lady day and night; warming her, begging her to take nourishment and supporting her through the funeral mass and the graveside internment of her Lord in the parish church yard. Not yet ten, plain little Nan had grown in her Lady's confidence; evolved into a slender but unyielding pillar of her strength.

When Sir Geoffrey's will was read, Lady Apollonia discovered that she had become an heiress through her sizeable widow's portion of the honor of Montecute at Colerne Leat. But as there were no other claims to inherit, the Manor of Colerne Leat was hers.

Chapter Seven

Divine Revelation

The realization of her personally acquired wealth as the widow of Geoffrey Montecute terrorized Apollonia. Though weak and tremulously unstable after endless hours of nursing her mortally wounded husband, she recognized her personal danger. The services of the men of the affinity of Colerne Leat could be available to the highest bidder; they felt no loyalty or constraint to defend their lord's widow. Apollonia's person had now become a prize waiting to be seized. If she and Nan stayed in the manor of Colerne Leat they remained friendless and defenseless. Apollonia knew they must escape; they must seek sanctuary and do it quickly. Carefully calculating their first opportunity to leave unnoticed, Lady Apollonia bribed a young stable lad to lead out two horses, saddled and ready on the designated night, to a dark and deserted corner of the village church yard. Arriving at the appointed place after the rest of the household was fast asleep she and Nan were surprised to find three horses waiting for them. Gareth, the stable lad stood with their mounts hat in hand, prepared to flee with his Lady.

"M'Lady, I cawn't stay 'ere awfter 'elpin thee," the young man pleaded. "Of course, Gareth, you must come with us." Apollonia said with conviction. She could not understand why she had not realized the jeopardy into which she had cast the village lad. In serving her now especially, he too, would require her protection but they could not waste precious time in deliberation. Laying her hand upon Gareth's shoulder, she spoke sincerely, directly to his hearing, "We will be grateful for your protection and I shall never forget this risk you have taken in my behalf." Mounting their horses quietly but quickly the little party carefully picked their way into the night, following familiar paths to Lacock Abbey.

Unknown to them at the time, their haste proved a prudent precaution as Wilfrid de Guelf had already summoned his henchmen from Somerset, clumsily scheming to kidnap the young widow of his dead lord. Wilfrid's crashing fury when Apollonia's escape was discovered the following morning was vented upon the entire service quarter of Colerne Leat all of whom were only too ready to point out they had done nothing but the missing Gareth was the obvious culprit most deserving of the lord's wrath.

Apollonia's friend and confidant of recent years, the Abbess Clothilde, ordered the gates of Lacock Abbey opened for her pitiful little party as it arrived at dawn. The Abbess volunteered to Apollonia that she was fully prepared to guarantee their safety through the protection of her convent and did not hesitate to offer them sanctuary. Gareth was sent to the Abbey stables where he might rest and remain hidden until a plan could be devised for his transferal to Apollonia's brother Ferdinand's protection at Marshfield. Abbess Clothilde assumed that Apollonia and Nan would be housed in the guest chambers until she noticed to her alarm the frightening condition of the usually composed and controlled Lady of the Manor of Colerne Leat.

Within the safety of the Abbey walls, Apollonia's conviction of sin and guilt overcame her. Visibly trembling and consumed by fear that her secret rebellion had contributed to the agonizingly bestial death screams of her husband, Apollonia fell prostrate before the Abbess begging that she be placed in a punishment cell. The recent memories of Geoffrey's hideous torment had grown into Apollonia's personal inner Hell; the advent of damnation, she reasoned, for her years of secret disobedience against her husband. Her voice trembling and rising in hysteria, Apollonia offered to give away every possession as she begged to be accepted into the convent.

"Accept me as a postulant, Reverend Mother, I beg you to receive me into your community," she wept. "I must speak with a confessor. I will become a pilgrim," she murmured on disjointedly. Her burden of guilt so agitated her mind that Apollonia refused nourishment and began to ramble madly of her urgent need to make a pilgrimage to the shrine of Our Lady at Walsingham as a barefoot penitent. Confused and dazed, Apollonia could not order her thoughts; could not consider anything except her guilt and monumental sin.

Abbess Clothilde had always welcomed Apollonia's visits in the past. She was a quiet but pleasant companion who was well-read and able to discuss the Confessions of St. Augustine, writings of the Church Fathers or even Boethius' Consolation of Philosophy with an older woman who hungered for a renewal of the intellectual pursuits of her early years as a German nun. The aged Abbess had guessed that this self-contained young woman carried a heavy, secret burden in her heart. She knew that Apollonia was married to a man celebrated for his chivalry but her marriage had never been a topic of their discussions. Obvious enough to the Abbess, the Lady Apollonia had always seemed happiest when away from her lord and full of dread when she was forced to prepare to return to his side.

Shocked by Apollonia's shattered condition, Abbess Clothilde immediately summoned the Abbey Infirmaress, Sister Mary Redemptia. Recognizing symptoms of grave illness, Clothielde turned sharply to her young friend. "Apollonia, I command you to cease this meaningless chatter. I further require you to take to your bed immediately and remain there until released by the Abbey Infirmaress." To calm her agitation, the Abbess added that Nan would remain at her side and she, Clothielde, would personally see that the Abbey chaplain should visit her in the infirmary. "Father Peter will come to you in the morning, my child, and hear your confession," the Abbess promised. "But now you must go with Nan and Sister Redemptia." Allowing no further discussion, the Abbess watched as the wretched Lady submitted to the pleading of her faithful little maid and with faltering steps walked off towards the infirmary.

Redemptia, was a creature of startling jerking movements and squeaking sounds, small and nervous as a chipmunk. She was tone deaf and discouraged from ever singing in service because of the disharmony she always created. Faithful to her order she seldom spoke but since her teen years had acquired a habit of making little sniffling noises which hissed unconsciously from her nose and lips unaware of their destruction of the rules of silence. Many of her sisters in the convent found such persistent little gasps and exhalations most distracting. But Abbess Clothilde valued the skinny erratic little nun and never missed an opportunity to express the convent's good fortune in having such a highly skilled leech as Sister Mary Redemptia among their community. She was even known throughout Wiltshire as an excellent herbal healer.

In short but jerkily rushing steps, Redemptia hurried her charges along the corridor towards her domain in the Abbey Infirmary and made Nan put Apollonia straight to bed, warmly wrapped in flannel with warm stones placed at her feet, then completely covered in wool. Sniffing with high-pitched squeaks as she ground her herbs, little gasps continued to escape her mouth whilst she stirred her resulting potions. Hovering over the recumbent figure of Apollonia, examining her hands, her skin, her mouth and eyes, Redemptia began to breathe audibly but more regularly once her diagnosis was complete and course of treatment decided. She began by administering a large goblet of barley water made from her own recipe of barley, liquorices, figs and sugar. Apollonia attempted to refuse to drink after half the sweet contents of the cup but Redemptia snorted indignantly at the offense causing the Lady to drink to the dregs in silent obedience. Next the nun approached with a liquor of selected herbs and simples especially prepared to calm Apollonia's spirit and make her sleep. Quickly succumbing to the sedatives, Apollonia drifted in and out of slumber for several days. Whenever the Lady's eyes opened, Nan was sitting next to her bed, offering soft foods and warm broth which she ate without question. Given quenched wine to begin and end every day, Apollonia's mind seemed to float in a warm and comfortable state of utter relaxation and peace. Her fever subsided and her spirit calmed and slowly her strength also returned. At this point in her recovery Sister Redemptia allowed her to sit up in bed.

Father Peter had come to the Lady's bedside regularly to pray with her and hear her confession. But Apollonia's anxiety seemed to return with her restored health and she began to press her confessor to be allowed to set out on her pilgrimage. He refused to listen to her plea for penance, gently admonishing her to remember that she was now subject to the rule of the Abbess. "Daughter, give thanks to God that your body is healing," he responded. "Now you must allow your soul the same opportunity. Speak with the Reverend Mother and let her be your guide."

During Apollonia's earliest days of recovery, the Abbess Clothilde called Nan into her presence. "Nan, child, I know you are nearest to our dear Apollonia as any living person," she said quietly, "but I must have you tell me what has occurred to drive your Lady to such an extreme state of disturbance?" In response, frightened little Nan, still traumatized by her own childhood hell and the possibilities of being left alone in the world, fell to her knees in tearful trembling and begged the Abbess to continue to protect them. "Please my Lady Abbess, help her, grant her some peace. You cawn't imagine how my Lady Apollonia has suffered, how she remained at the bedside of our Lord of Monticute through hours upon hours of screaming torment." Nan went on to describe in detail the dreadful manner of Geoffrey

Montecute's death and Apollonia's subsequent terror of being forced into yet another marriage simply because of her large inheritance as his widow.

When the Abbess finally came to her bed in the Infirmary, Apollonia welcomed the opportunity to speak with her as she felt convinced that her plans for pilgrimage and the offering of her own life to the convent would receive the Abbess' firm endorsement. To her great surprise she was gently told that she was being exceedingly silly preparing to leave a world before she had discovered what her contributions to it might be. "You are not yet twenty, my child," the Abbess said quietly. "Ravaged by a brutal experience of death in one near to you, your troubled spirit must be allowed to heal before you make decisions of such consequence."

"But holy mother, I have sinned. I am the cause of my husband's suffering. I must suffer as he suffered." Apollonia fell to her knees and began to weep. "I loathed my husband, recoiled at his touch and refused all possible spousal obedience to his will," she sobbed.

Without changing her countenance the Abbess took a small manuscript from her sleeve and gave it to Apollonia. "These are the Revelations of Divine Love, as experienced by a great woman whom I have met." Abbess Clothilde continued, "Mother Julian of Norwich is a simple woman, Apollonia, but one who truly experienced divine insight. Before you leave this place, I require you to read this. Only then, will I agree to discuss your future plans."

Dismissed from the infirmary by the Abbess, Apollonia took the manuscript to the room she now shared with Nan in the Abbey guest apartments. The writing of Mother Julian was surprisingly brief and written in common English. While Nan slept soundly on the pallet prepared for her, Apollonia read it straight through in the candlelight of that evening; nourishing her wounded spirit with the consolation of another who had longed to punish herself. The words of Mother Julian's showings seemed to speak directly to her, to understand the suffocating pain of her shattered spirit.

"Christ told me not to accuse myself so much, nor think that my distress and grief is my fault. He showed me that he does not wish me to be unreasonably depressed or sorrowful," Mother Julian had written.

Apollonia was struck by the wonder of it. "How can she say that? How could a mystical hermit of Norwich alone in her cell write as if she had a window to the world's need," she wondered, "even more a glass peering directly into the secrets of my soul?"

"We may well recognize our lives as prison and penance but Christ has not willed it," Mother Julian continued. "He has suffered enough for us and wants no more suffering; he wants us to rejoice for the Lord is supremely friendly and all courtesy. To be perfectly like our Lord is our true salvation." Apollonia read the sweet words again and again.

Unaware of tears beginning to well up again in her aching eyes, Apollonia said the words aloud, "To be like our Lord is salvation." Her tears grew into sobs, "Mother Julian I would do as you say." The pent up sorrow of the past three years gushed from her wounded heart. "I have been trying to do good in spite of my sin, in spite of the evil all around me." Overcome by tears and suddenly limp in her chair she sobbed in silence as the guilt seemed to drain from her spirit and wash away through her eyes dissolved and released. When at last her weeping ceased, Apollonia felt empty and ravenously hungry but she also felt strong. She stood up and spoke out loud into the darkness of the room. Without opening her eyes or betraying any change in her slumber, Nan awoke to hear her Lady's confession.

"Hear me Lord God. I did not choose my husband nor could I love or respect him. But Blessed Lord, I did not cease to love you." Walking about the narrow cell, Apollonia grew assertive and defiant. "Lord Jesus, I humbly acknowledge my sins but beg you to see they were committed to oppose evil and cruelty," she said to the walls.

Pacing back and forth, Apollonia began to accept her decision to thwart Geoffrey as she had no other path of escape from him and she knew in her innermost heart that she had never wished for his suffering and death. She had tried to counter his evil by refusing to take part in it. "And I would do it again, if forced to," she whispered into the darkness.

Returning to the candlelit table, Apollonia read on. Mother Julian's words seemed to urge her to continue such opposition. "Everything opposed to love and peace comes from the Fiend and his set," she read to herself. "God is not angry, He is our loving Mother," Apollonia stopped abruptly at these words. Julian of Norwich knew God in a shocking way which Apollonia had never encountered in all of her reading of church sermons and saints' lives.

She rushed on, anxious to grasp Mother Julian's meaning. "God is our patient Mother who does not want us to run away from him. He wishes that we do as a child would do when in trouble or frightened. The child runs to mother for help as fast as it can."

Miraculously, Apollonia's mind was consumed by an awareness of the presence of her own long dead mother reaching across the chasm between this life and the next, down from heaven to her through Mother Julian's showings. Julian of Norwich had experienced God as mother and the willing Giver of all good gifts of hope and peace. If Apollonia's mother had lived, Apollonia thought to herself she would surely have welcomed her home now. Her mother would have renewed her spirit after the soul-scaring misery of a hateful marriage.

An exquisite feeling of liberation grew in Apollonia's spirit and yet, for the first time in her life, she did not feel alone. She moved to the prie-dieux, kneeling, crossing herself and speaking from her heart: "Father in Heaven, have I denied your grace and goodness to wallow in self-righteous guilt? Help Thou my unbelief," she asked prayerfully. Saying over and over to herself the prayer Christ taught she was filled with peace as shattered portions of her being seemed able to reassemble. With receptive spirit she sensed herself becoming whole again, not as a lady of consequence, not as a wealthy widow but as a child of God.

The following early dawn, as she and Nan walked the cloister to the Abbey Church, Apollonia saw with great pleasure that the night had passed as she could see the first timid pink streaks of light appearing in the East. "What a miracle morning is!" she said joyfully to Nan. "Out of the darkness light dares to return to shine upon the just and the unjust alike. Who are we to refuse such gifts?" "Yes, my Lady," Nan nodded her agreement quietly but felt thrilled to hear Apollonia's voice so full of hope.

In her own mind, Apollonia felt truly embarrassed by her unworthy attempt to use the dear Abbess and her convent as an escape from personal guilt. She felt humiliated thinking back to her demands that she be allowed to retreat from the world; smiled at her childish simplemindedness. Until this moment, she had given no thought to the safety and protection of her dear little Nan or the responsibility she had taken upon herself for the protection of Gareth. "Abbess Clothilde was correct," she thought, "I was being very silly."

After morning prayers, Apollonia requested another interview with the Abbess. Their meeting was a brief one but from it both parties withdrew smiling. Nan was waiting expectantly outside the Abbess' door as Apollonia emerged from her apartments. Apollonia said nothing but Nan knew from her posture and her long purposeful stride that she had decided to leave Lacock Abbey. They walked away together quickly from the Abbess' lodgings, hurrying towards the scriptorium to find paper and quill. Apollonia could hardly wait to send a message to her sturdy, dependable brother.

Ferdinand, greatly relieved with the news of his sister's whereabouts, arrived at Lacock Abbey the following day, visibly agitated by rumors rampant in the countryside of Apollonia's abduction and forced marriage to Wilfrid de Guelf. Accompanied by armed men sufficient to deliver his sister safely home to Marshfield, the party took their leave of the Abbess Clothilde and her ministress of healing, Sister Mary Redemptia. With her whole heart Apollonia thanked the twitching, sniffing little nun whose eyes remained downcast while her cheeks inflamed to vibrant rose amidst the Lady's praise and thanks for her gifts of healing. Then Apollonia knelt to receive her spiritual Mother's parting blessing. Pressing a manuscript copy into her arms, Abbess Clothilde blessed her in the name of Father, Son and Holy Spirit, then added, "Go in joy, my child, and take Mother Julian with you. 'All shall be well!'"

Chapter Eight

Marriage Again

Ferdinand had indulged no attempt at conversation on the journey to Marshfield from Lacock Abbey. Apollonia rode at his side in the midst of his men at arms, grateful for her brother's company but distressed with the role of one requiring armored defense. Nan and Gareth too, rode behind the lord and lady within the ring of Ferdinand's protection, his soldiers' eyes and ears alert against any possibility of ambush, their sword arms prepared to draw and fight at their lord's command. When finally the party reached the safety of Ferdinand's lands within the Manor of Marshfield, he turned in his saddle to face his silent sister and made a brusque declaration: "You know you must marry again, Polly, immediately."

Apollonia could feel her body recoil as if Ferdinand had struck her. The chilling shock of his words brought forth a silent palisade of instinctive denial and objection. "No! No! Not yet! Mother of God, it is too soon, I must have more time," she pleaded in her thoughts. Her right hand moved quickly to cover her face and suppress welling tears. But tightly closed eyes could not enable her to escape seeing the urgent truth of her brother's concerns. Her widowhood now declared her eligible, her dower proclaimed her valuable and her sex ensured her vulnerability. Someone in the hierarchy of power would take matters into his own hands if she did not act first. Her husband's overlord could assume his right to arrange a marriage for her, granting her lands and fortune as reward to a favored retainer. Any unscrupulous bachelor, covetous of her wealth and scornful of the requirements of church and custom, might be tempted to ply his suit by force. Wilfrid de Guelf was not the only single male in the kingdom willing to resort to kidnap and rape with the blessing of a priest bought to provide a coerced but legally binding marriage. Apollonia knew the extent of her choices. If she did not take the veil she must marry.

Observing the pain in his sister's expression as she pondered his abrupt demand made Ferdinand regret he could not wait a bit longer to speak of it. He was grateful that she did not weep and humiliate him with the hysterics of female humors. She could be trusted to act with discretion and dignity, he observed to himself. Still, he was aware that Apollonia refused to look at him. She kept her head discretely bowed and silence provided her only response. Ferdinand decided he would say little more but pursued his logic far enough to suggest a candidate, "Edward Aust is a mere franklin, Polly but he has proven his friendship and honor to me as a solid and loyal justice of the peace, up Aust way." Ferdinand paused briefly but not wishing to elicit any response at this juncture bolted on with his oblique proposal. "His holdings include some of the best lands in Gloucestershire and I should not be surprised if he is sent to Parliament to sit with the commons at the next summons." Apollonia remained silent. No longer looking at his sister, Ferdinand said more gently, "I shall arrange a meeting."

Apollonia was picking raspberries in the Marshfield garden on the day Edward Aust arrived. Ferdinand and his wife, Cicely received their guest warmly, extending the customary expressions of county hospitality. They escorted him into the hall offering him a refreshing drink which he politely refused. At last they sat together near the fire to share a neighborly chat discussing the weather, the rumored outbreak of sheep murrain in Devon and the status of the war with France. When the conversation began to lag, Ferdinand suddenly stood up causing his young guest to leap anxiously to his feet also. Walking out of the hall, Ferdinand led Edward through the courtyard and into the garden where Apollonia had chosen to remain. The sun was shining brightly and sweet scents of the survivors of summer blossoms as well as mature piquant herbs perfumed the restrained air of the walled garden which lay in the sheltered warmth of the south side of the manor house.

Ferdinand was obviously uncomfortable in his role as matchmaker but since his father's death two years earlier; it was required of him as *pater familias*. Arranging a good marriage for his sister was as important to family stability as any other sensible strategy to extend and safe-guard family lands and influence. He was prepared to do his duty in this contractual agreement and he expected Apollonia to be fully cooperative in every aspect of her portion of the understanding as well. His curt introduction of his younger sister to Edward merely emphasized the intended purpose of the meeting which both parties already knew. "Edward Aust, this is my sister, the Lady Mary Apollonia. I think you two would do," he said and promptly left them.

Apollonia was keenly aware that her brother and Cicely would be grateful to have her marital status decided and her person removed to a new husband's home. It wasn't that they disliked her but Apollonia could sense she made them uneasy. Her sister-in-law, Cicely, was a good woman of excellent family and genuinely fond of Ferdinand. She sang pleasantly, plied a very fine needle and delighted in creating the most recent of fashionable court headdresses. In honor of this day she had worn her newest creation, a two-horned frame covered in yellow brocade, which was reputed to be the rage in the elegant Court of Burgundy. But, Cicely was prone to say at times, "Polly is too solemn," when discussing her brother's sister. "I can find nothing to chat about with her." Ferdinand agreed wholeheartedly with his wife. He felt a real affection for his sister but she annoyed him with her obstinate questioning of acceptable social behaviour. Ferdinand had come to the conclusion that Apollonia purposefully refused to take part in the social norms expected of gentle ladies. When lighthearted banter and flirting were employed by the gentles at table in the hall or contests of courtly love were devised to brighten and entertain long dark evenings, Apollonia withdrew into her reserved shell inserting an empty space in the courtly language and tinkling laughter which struggled to continue round about her. Ferdinand feared that any suitor would find her silence formidable and he heartily wished stout courage and persistence to the young squire now attempting to breach the stone walls of his sister's solemn aspect.

"Your brother, my Lord of Marshfield, is very direct, my Lady," Edward Aust said as he approached the silent figure in the garden. His soft hat failed to contain a full head of ginger colored hair curling about his neck and ears, the perfect compliment to his widely spaced toothful smiling face full of large freckles falling over his nose and onto both cheeks. He walked towards Apollonia hoping to continue in conversation but there was no response to his smile or his words as the Lady did not lift her eyes. Apollonia could not bring herself to look at him. Instead, she silently continued to pick berries and add them to her basket. Trying again, Edward moved to the bramble across from where she was picking and began to help himself to the plump ripe fruit. Eating some and adding handfuls to her basket, he continued speaking in a soft but encouraging manner, "By your leave, Lady, I can't resist raspberries and these are at their prime." They picked for awhile, till all the ripest and sweetest had been claimed then Edward suggested that they might sit together for a few moments.

Moving to a shaded area among the fruit trees, Edward laid his cloak upon the ground and Apollonia quickly sat upon one corner of it. He knew he was inadequate with any semblance of courtly behaviour so Edward sought instead to present himself as honestly but as kindly and well-intentioned as he could. Settling himself next to her, he cleared his throat and began to speak slowly trying to select his words with great care as he feared this proud Lady might well be scornful of his intentions, "I am a man of lower estate and can understand your reluctance to. . ."

Apollonia looked up suddenly and interrupted his prepared speech, "I haven't the slightest objection to your estate, Squire Aust, but I should be very grateful if you could promise me your patience whilst I learn to be your wife." She had lifted her face quickly and the grey eyes which suddenly met Edward's startled gaze were swimming with tears ready to fall. Her request was so very forthright and her sad face so completely earnest that Edward was momentarily stunned. This abrupt announcement of her acceptance after a total absence of conversation caught him completely off guard. He could remember nothing of the sweet phrases he had created to win her affection.

"Gracious Lady," he responded without thinking, "what breed of monster do you think me? I shall happily be patient with you if you will grant me similar favor."

Holding her eyes towards Edward and looking directly into his face for the first time since their introduction, Apollonia's heart was seized by the realization that he was blushing. His large hands with their red raspberry stained fingers searched awkwardly for proper placement in his lap. Beads of perspiration formed on his forehead and clean-shaven upper lip. He was at a total loss for words, madly searching his memory for any words to break the humiliating silence which hung like a curtain of fog between them, Edward could only feel the pain of utter failure fill his chest and paralyze his tongue. "He is shy!" Apollonia suddenly looked up and realized to herself. "He is intimidated and he is as ill at ease as I." Her sympathy slowly blossomed into a brilliant smile and the rigidity of her body relaxed.

She liked his face as she studied it; Edward's was a ruddy, sober and honest face with deep blue eyes now searching the heavens as if prayerfully begging direction. "Please forgive my outburst, Edward." Apollonia noticed that he drew breath sharply and turned to face her as she spoke his Christian name. His heart nearly burst as he looked upon her beautiful smile. "I have not been well of late but your presence cheers me.

Emboldened by her soft voice and glorious smile, he took her white hand in his freckled paw. His heart, he feared, made audible thumping as he sensed her long fingers press her palm against his. He lifted them to his lips and allowed his eyes to search her face now looking inquiringly into his own. "By all the saints, she is lovely!" Edward exulted to himself. "Plain spoken honesty radiates from her, not the disdain of which I had been warned." Her grey eyes reminded him of his favorite Madonna but it was her smile, so open and candid yet tentative and vulnerable, which won his heart.

"My lord, your brother has helped me to understand the terrifying injury and death of your husband, Lord Montecute, my Lady," Edward spoke quietly. "I truly wish by all the saints that I may be able to bring healing to the suffering you have endured. But as you are able to recover from your loss, please allow me to add assurances of my love and admiration for you, not only as your husband but as your truest friend."

Apollonia had never heard any man of her acquaintance speak in this manner. Edward Aust was being truly gentle with her not only seeking to understand her ordeal he was adding his willingness to express his love for her in terms of utmost friendship. "Perhaps we can learn patience together", she said gently. "Two heads are always better than one."

"We may as well join Ferdinand and Cicely," Apollonia said with a twinkle in her eye. "They will be standing on either side of the garden door awaiting our announcement." Chuckling to himself, Edward felt the tension which had griped his back, neck and shoulders since his arrival at Marshfield was slipping away. Happily, he stood to offer his hand in assistance as she rose from his cloak lying upon the grass. Apollonia discovered when they stood upright that she was as tall as her intended but Edward seemed undisturbed by her unfeminine height. His heart was filled with the joy of her acceptance and the wondrous ease with which their quiet natures seemed to intertwine. Apollonia shyly took his arm and his stature grew visibly in joyous pride as they walked together back into the house.

They were betrothed that day, the bans were published and within a matter of weeks, Edward and Apollonia were married in the grey stone porch of the hilltop parish church of Aust. Surrounded by large oak trees and protected from the winds off the Severn by their deeply bowed branches, the old church had no other name and was strangely bereft of a patron saint to claim it. Local stories suggested that Christian saints rejected the hilltop sanctuary as it was built on a fearful pagan site dedicated to the Celtic god of the River Severn. Apollonia would never accept that explanation as she grew to love the small village and especially the church of their marriage and baptisms of their growing family. "Aust church is Christ's church and beloved by him," she would always defend. "What greater patronage could one wish?" Aust Manor, the village, and its beautiful setting along the banks of the River Severn, became and remained Apollonia's home and her preferred title. She would choose to be called the Lady Apollonia of Aust until the end of her long life.

Squire Edward and his Lady were married for twenty-seven blessed years. They often jokingly reminded each other of their vows of being patient with each other made that day in Ferdinand's garden, especially after their family grew to include a boisterous quiver of five sons: Hugh, Chad, Thomas, Alban and David, each named for a saint native to the British Isles. Edward liked to tease his wife in her choice of names. "Lonia, my love," he would say, "do we continue to bear sons dedicated to the saints or are we compensating Aust for its lack of holy patronage?" She would only smile mysteriously and suggest that he construct his own answer.

Her years as Edward's wife had passed too quickly. Being spouse and mother completed her, fleshed out her living portrait in an aura of happiness and joy. Her greatest delight was the exultant wonder which the birth of each of their sons brought to Edward. His stocky frame would swell with pride as his huge arms cradled each new infant while the older siblings pulled at his legs and clung to his back. As the boys grew, her daily prayer was simply that they be allowed to become men like their father, a righteous man, unquestionably noble in her eyes who received her undying love and ever-growing respect.

It was probably her motherly instincts that first drew her to the plight of a young creature she found sitting in the village stocks one autumn morning ten years after her arrival in Aust. Apollonia

74

assumed he was young from the size of his body but his face had been so disfigured that it was nearly impossible to guess his age. His left ear, as she looked at him, was missing altogether and the skin of his cheeks badly scarred as if torn and twisted, pulling one eye into a permanent squint. Boys of the village were throwing garbage at him and to increase the sting of their game began to fill the rotten bits with pebbles and rocks. Slops rained upon the victim while the concealed missiles pounded away at his arms, legs and body. The lad in the stocks maneuvered helplessly, ducking his head beneath his arms while pulling his chin against his chest in a futile effort to make himself less a target.

Lady Apollonia walked straight to the stocks as she sent spirited Nan on vigorous counter attack. Even at her adult height, Nan was little taller than the imps she chased. To compensate for her delicate size and birdlike build, she swooped at them like a jay transforming her colorless face into bright red, her light blue eyes into a glaring vengeful icon. Shooing the village boys away with the real threat that her Lady, whom they knew, would personally speak to their parents should they do such a thing again, Nan sent the young rogues off in a cloud of dust. Apollonia approached the figure in the stocks to ask after the nature of his crime. Hearing in his accent a Welsh pronunciation of shire English, he told her simply that he was a beggar who had crossed the ferry at Aust hoping to find work on this side of the Severn. The village did not want beggars and meant to make an example of him.

Sending Nan to find the village warden and bring him to her, Lady Apollonia continued her questions of the young beggar, using her presence to provide the awkwardly restrained boy a protective shadow from the rays of the sun. It wasn't long before Nan, with the puffing warden in tow, hurried up the hill path towards the church where the stocks stood next to its entry porch. In his own mind, this village worthy was conjuring justification of his actions, should his judgement be called to question. Instead he found himself warmly greeted upon his arrival. "Master Worthing, how good of you to come." Apollonia addressed him warmly and assured him of her respect for the difficulties of his office.

"I am so fully aware of the village difficulties with beggars," Lady Apollonia told the Warden. "However, I am presently in need of youthful assistance. Would you release this young man to me to be considered for service?" If he allowed her to take the boy, Apollonia added that she could find work and would assume full responsibility for him.

Godfrey Worthing expelled a great sigh of relief and wiped his brow. "My Lady, your goodness is legendary. Let me assist you," he said heartily. His worst fears allayed, he refrained from risking any objections to the will of the lady wife of the local justice of the peace. He swiftly unlocked the stocks as she waited and lifted the splattered youngster to his numb feet all the while extolling the Lady's good graces. The boy, thrilled to be released from the stocks, stretched his body enthusiastically and rubbed his ankles with obvious pleasure and great relief.

As they walked together back towards the manor house, Lady Apollonia was shaken to learn the young man was no more than ten years old. Raised by his grandparents until they died, his name was Alwan and he had been caught near his native village in Wales earlier that summer trapping hares and squirrels on his lordship's land. The punishments for poaching were serious but the lord had been considerate of his youth. After ten strokes of the lash, Alwan was sentenced to have his ear nailed to a cart wheel. This punishment was meant to serve as warning as well as entertainment for the rustics. Many villagers gathered to witness the spectacle of the boy's desperate attempts to grasp the turning wheel, powerless to keep his ear from being twisted and ripped from the side of his head. Alwan's face had been permanently disfigured on the wheel of a dung cart.

Apollonia found it difficult to believe the simple goodness and sweet nature of this Welsh beggar boy. His twisted visage and purple scars marred the depth of his facial skin but touched no part of his unspoilt, willing spirit. Taught survival skills from infancy by a grandfather who refused to recognize any crime in taking from an English usurper's forests that which he needed; Alwan was an excellent fisherman, tracker, and trapper. Completely at home in the forest for days on end, he seemed to prefer to be in the woods and along the streams which fed the mighty Severn.

That evening by the fire Apollonia discussed Alwan's obvious natural gifts with Edward, knowing full well that her husband would agree to her assignment of a permanent place for him within their household. But she would not make a decision until she was convinced that the most suitable position for the boy's abilities had been selected. "Surely you have noticed that our Alwan is far more content in the forest than serving in hall," Apollonia told her husband. "With such ready skills in trapping and fishing why not encourage him to use them?"

Edward enjoyed teasing his wife especially about her serious "schemes" which he said were part of her design to finish off the loose ends of creation. "No one knows the wiles of young chaps better than you, Lonia," he smiled, "especially when you have calculated long and hard over the best means to design good character and occupation. God surely meant Alwan to be a forester. Amen to that!" Apollonia tossed a soft cushion at his impious face in retribution for an ironic hectoring of her careful decision already made. She knew he trusted her instincts and he readily agreed with her proposal to put Alwan in charge of providing hares, birds, and fish for the kitchen from their woods while he learned to become keeper of their game and forests. Through the succeeding years, Apollonia's confidence in Alwan's natural gifts was more than repaid by his excellent grasp of hunting and husbandry matured and developed through his experience in service. Alwan earned his way into a permanent home and plentiful supply of all his needs as the Squire's valued forester. But the village folk knew him by one name only and used it as a title of admiration and respect. Anyone in Aust could tell you where to find Alwan the Poacher.

Chapter Nine

Alwan's Recount

Alwan's hut in the woods was as familiar as his own home to the young page Owen, happily carrying his Lady's message along the banks of the river on that glorious early autumn day following the end of the great gales and the Lady's departure for Kingswood. Son of a wandering Welsh poet, Owen's father managed a poor but satisfying existence by living on the road and entertaining the halls of the great with his bardic songs and tales of heroic princes. Owen admired his father but saw him infrequently these days. His cherished mother had died young from a simple cut on her foot which festered, corrupted and swiftly destroyed her frail body like wild fire consuming dry grasses. Advised of the Lady of Aust's interest in the nurturing of promising young people, the poet-minstrel had appeared with his motherless son one morning two years earlier, begging the Lady to examine the boy and his considerable gifts. Since that time Owen had served as a page and personal servant to the Lady as she superintended the years of his education and preparation. Apollonia would have confessed to being unsure as yet, of the eventual career best suited to Owen but, of one thing she was absolutely certain, he was intelligent and bright; learned very quickly and truly enjoyed his studies. The lad must go to university and towards that goal she was directing his preparatory studies. A talented singer and storyteller from early childhood, Owen was drawn as if by nature's dictates to the company of his older countryman in the Lady's service. Innocent of any social difference between them, Owen regarded Alwan as his greatest friend and thought of the forester's mature face as wrinkled into a permanent lop-sided grin. Alwan's scars had become so tanned and darkened by his years in wind, weather and sun that the boy was unaware of them.

During leisure hours spent together, Alwan and Owen would share every Welsh tale they could scrape from their memories and add embellishments and enlargements as suited their mood. Alwan had grown into manhood, probably twenty-three or so years old he believed himself to be, retaining his boyish wonder and pure joy of life. Having never thought of marriage and family, he loved Owen like a cherished younger brother nature had denied him. Together they completed family for each other in many ways, sharing not only their

Welsh language and its wealth of folk legend but also each expanding for the other the realities of the world. Alwan, as the wizard of the Lady's forests, transmitted to Owen his knowledge and love of the natural world. Owen, being filled with the accumulated knowledge and philosophy of the academics, brought to his friend's woodland hut images of lands and peoples far beyond Alwan's ability to imagine.

     Not finding Alwan at home when he arrived, Owen instinctively knew the most likely whereabouts of his friend. Carefully guiding his horse towards the river, he found Alwan knee deep in the flowing water, replacing mended eel nets and minding a series of fish traps. Shouting out his Welsh greeting, Alwan responded with a hearty welcome and they sat together on the bank while Owen delivered his Lady's message. Delighted to be the first to tell his friend of the huge decapitated body which had been discovered in the drains north of Aust Cliff, Owen repeated Apollonia's message verbatim, beginning with her own words, "My Lady Apollonia greets you well and requests your help. She asks that you search out from the leper camp for any sign of bloodshed or struggle always being certain to look regularly to the tree limbs overhead."

     Alwan listened intently then wondered out loud. "Do m'Lady think the birds done it, then?" he asked laughingly to Owen.

     Owen's bright eyes grew wider as he launched into a lusty description of the gaping hole in the shoulders and torn flesh of the horrible corpse he had seen before the Lord Ferdinand covered it. "How do you think it could have been done, Alwan? Do you reckon someone caught his head in a noose and then pulled it away like criminals are hung, drawn or quartered?"

     "T'ere be many ways 'ter chop 'awf an 'ead, Owen, but 'oi nefer reckoned on 'ow to pull 'er awf." Alwan could only think of butchering when carcasses were trussed then gutted and he could not conceive of one man pulling another to pieces. He did not like his young friend to be thinking on such unholy things but Alwan knew his Lady would have reasons for being so specific in her instructions to him. So he wrapped a parcel of eels for Owen to take back to the manor kitchen and then shared a mug of ale with his young friend whilst they skipped rocks across the surface of the water. Finally, walking with Owen remounted upon his horse, Alwan saw him off where the wooded trail began leading back to Aust Village. Quickly returning to the river, Alwan tied off his nets, picked up his game sack and began his trek towards the washed out mud banks which had been the leper camp.

More than a week passed before his long loping stride brought him into the manor courtyard asking to speak to her Ladyship. He carried a full game sack with him but said he had nothing to deliver to the kitchen this time. He was told that the Lady had not yet returned from Kingswood Abbey but he would happily await her, spending time with Owen when freedom from his lessons allowed. Preferring to sleep in the Lady's great stone barn, Alwan kept his game sack in one of its deep, cool storage pits. On the day when the Lady returned to Aust, she asked that Alwan report to her straightaway.

Seated with Lady Apollonia in the main kitchen, Alwan was given a tankard of ale and allowed to slake his thirst fully before he spoke. Then Giles, standing by his Lady's side, began by asking, "Were you able to discover any clue which might help us, Alwan?"

The twisted face shone triumphantly, his grin stretching to both sides of his face and his eyes sparkling. "Aye, Mawster Giles, Oi believe that is so." At first, however, Alwan explained that his search had taken so long because of the distance he had to cover and the amount of destruction left in the wake of the flood. "Oi began at river's edge," he said, "an' for leagues, 'long the bank all seemed to 'ave been stripped awoay and warshed clear."

Daily expanding the perimeter of his search, Alwan persisted looking farther into the woods away from the Severn and yet within an area radiating out from that which had been the lepers' camp. "Twere not fur from the Pilnin' road where Oi foun' it, Mawster Giles." Turning to Lady Apollonia, Alwan's face glowed with admiration. "Twere in 'te tree, just as ye' said, m'Lady."

Alwan described the ground below the tree for his listeners so that they would recognize how it had been very fortunately left undisturbed and thus retained good tracks from the horse's shoes unique in their markings. He told them that he found the tracks of one horse only but he would recognize them again if ever he saw marks left by those horse-shoes. They were quite clearly the tracks of a destrier, a war horse which could only have belonged to a man of knightly rank.

"E must 'ave been riding 'ell bent fur fear, m' Lady. 'Is 'ead jammed into the crotch o' the branch zo 'ard, it were pulled awf." Then Alwan took the Lady and Giles to the barn and showed them the contents of his game sack. Eyes already eaten away by carrion birds and dangling neck flesh and skin decaying from exposure of the weeks past, Wilfrid de Guelf's graying head was unmistakably familiar to the Lady of Aust. "My ancient enemy," Apollonia said quietly, "I do grieve to find you come to such an unworthy end." As she looked away, Alwan returned the head to his bag and lowered it back into the pit.

Walking back to the manor, Apollonia recognized at once the extraordinary triumph delivered to her in Alwan's grisly trophy. From an endless expanse of forest along the river, he had discovered for her the place and instrument of Wilfrid's death. "Alwan," she said to her forester with honest enthusiasm, "your skills have shed great light on this troubling mysterious death! Whilst I was merely guessing you have discovered the truth of where and how the deed occurred and we are all in your debt." She did not hesitate to lavish praise upon him as she felt it Alwan's due having expertly extracted a significant nettle from a haystack of obscurity. Alwan beamed with pride, seeing no great accomplishment in his task but thrilled by his Lady's approval. He was encouraged to remain one more night at the Manor, to join them at table and possibly favor the company in hall with songs which he and Owen could sing so beautifully. Apollonia felt so completely relieved, in her grateful thoughts a celebration was in order.

"When you return to the forest," Giles asked Alwan directly but quietly and with a serious darkness in his tone, "please remain watchful for any other unusual tracks or unexplained marks which might suggest strangers still lurking about." Alwan looked quite puzzled by Giles' request. "It may be an unnecessary precaution, good friend," Giles said to reassure him, "but your forester's eyes and quick senses serve as our first line of defense should there ever be cause for alarm."

"And I am certain we shall need you to help us further in finding a solution to the mysterious death of that unfortunate gentleman who's head now lies in the barn," Lady Apollonia added with emphasis. "Whether or not we are in jeopardy, Alwan, may well be explained when we learn at last why he died here upon our lands."

Though sobered by the thought of responsibilities newly entrusted to him, Alwan still felt magnificent. Never before had he experienced such a surge of feelings of importance in his Lady's service. "Oi shall do moi best." he said proudly.

Retiring to her solar for quiet reflection before their evening meal, Giles could see that the Lady was agitated by Alwan's findings and the macabre trophy he had brought them. He was certain that she was not unnerved by the dreadful state of the head; she seemed to have expected that. Rather Giles felt, she was more disturbed by the collection of unanswered questions which continued to grow around the demise of Wilfrid de Guelf. Lady Apollonia finally looked up from her mental rummaging and asked her steward to tell her what he thought had happened in that stormy night.

Pausing for a moment's reflection, Giles began to list those parts of the riddle which he felt they already knew. "First," he said, "I think that Sir Wilfrid probably died during that night of the fearful storm, my Lady. The body, when found, appeared fresh and uncorrupted. Secondly, he may well have ridden in storm driven panic into the fork of the tree branch and decapitated himself. Therefore, his head remained in the tree whilst his horse rode on to pitch its headless rider into the river." Giles thought again, as if to justify his bizarre conclusions. "Perhaps it was terror of the storm that panicked his horse into a mad dash in the middle of the night, my Lady," Giles summarized. "I doubt we shall ever know precisely what happened but from Alwan's description of the hoof prints of one horse only beneath the tree, it seems quite plausible that Sir Wilfrid's death was a fearful accident." Pausing to complete the gathering of his thoughts Giles put both hands behind his back and leaned slightly forward. "But I still see no explanation for the ravens, my Lady. Why or how would this gentleman or his followers wish to intimidate you and frighten your household in such a bizarre manner?"

Lady Apollonia nodded slowly, "You are as orderly as ever, Giles, and have outlined the facts carefully. I believe you may be quite correct in the assumption that Sir Wilfrid's death was an accident of the storm." Then, she began to gently question Giles' summary. "But what would have been his purpose in riding out during such a storm and what brought him to Gloucestershire?" she asked. "I know Sir Wilfrid to be capable of unholy practices but I can think of nothing to his gain from terrorizing me. Further, why was he unarmed and dressed in peasant homespun and why were all items of possible identification, rings, purse, sword, removed from his body?" she continued. "In addition, why was his head torn away from his body at the time of the accident? Wouldn't it seem more likely that he would have been unhorsed by the blow; his whole body left hanging, hands struggling to release his neck from the crotch of the limb whilst his mount galloped on?" she persisted.

Giles looked at his Lady somewhat sheepishly and said quietly, "Excellent questions, my Lady, to which I have no answers, I fear."

Apollonia smiled at her steward and said encouragingly, "Nor do I, Giles, but I should like to find some." Thus declaring her intentions, she continued, "One additional fact which must be added as number three or four on your excellent accounting is that I noticed Sir Wilfrid had been bound, hand and foot, before he died. The marks from the bindings, still visible on his wrists and ankles when I saw the body, made me suspicious that he was being held against his will and possibly had been lashed to his saddle. If his head was torn from its torso by the forward gallop of his horse, the body must have been firmly affixed to its saddle at the horn and the stirrups, don't you think?"

"Indeed, my Lady, it would surely have been so," Giles agreed wholeheartedly. Without saying another word, the steward grasped in an instant his mistress' mental agitation over the death of an old, loathsome acquaintance.

"But who would have been in a position to take Wilfrid prisoner and why?" she wondered out loud. Then she stood and with the determined upward lifting of her shoulders announced in her posture that she had made a decision. "We shall pay a call upon Lady de Guelf in Cliffbarton. I should like to know more of the activities of Sir Wilfrid during recently past years," she said. "Several days travel must be arranged, Giles." With that to occupy him, Giles stood to leave the chamber but the Lady added one more direction. "See that Nan is told of our needs and is prepared to accompany us."

Giles excused himself at once and strode from Lady Apollonia's solar with purpose; he knew he must work quickly. Her Ladyship would wish to make her call upon Sir Wilfrid's widow as soon as possible and the journey from Aust was a significant one. Cliffbarton was a remote manor, including the village of the same name on the coast of Somerset overlooking Porlock Bay. He and Nan would be sufficient company for Lady Apollonia and they were all good travelers. But they must begin with a well-planned route, fresh horses for the journey, and provisions to sustain their travel through the better part of four days' ride each direction.

Chapter Ten

Father and Son

Lady Apollonia loved to travel and was always exhilarated by the prospect of a journey. She relished being in the English countryside, especially riding through the beautifully wooded hills and valleys of the southwestern shires. But this trip was brimming with exciting possibilities, the interview with the widow of Sir Wilfrid being uppermost in her mind. Happily, Apollonia also knew that the road they must travel would take them first to Axbridge where they would lodge with her middle son, Thomas. She was grateful for any excuse to visit with Thomas and share briefly in his constant state of enthusiasm for whatever projects were consuming him at the moment.

Father Thomas was, among all her grown sons, the most scholarly and erudite. Yet his call to the priesthood suited him perfectly, especially the living at Axbridge. The town was a favored royal possession richly benefiting from the presence of a royal hunting lodge. Serving as the resting place for aristocratic hunting parties after long days' chase on the high plateau of the Mendips, Axbridge flourished through royal presence and patronage. Its borough status confirmed by charter, the success of the town and its market celebrated with a great market cross, Axbridge was crowned by its noble church. An especially beautiful cruciform building, topped at the crossing with a great square Norman tower, the church seemed to grow from the grey rock of the surrounding hills. Father Thomas, as its priest, was devoted to the care of the souls of his parish. He officiated at each of the daily round of church services finding great spiritual comfort in the celebration of masses which defined the calendar as well as the daily life of the town. His mother had seen to it that his personal income was more than adequate to support his ambition devoted to study and pastoral care. Father Thomas was totally unmoved by those who urged him to leave his parish flock in the care of a vicar and flee to London where churchmen could achieve power and wealth to rival any courtier in the land.

He had collected a good library and was always a ready purchaser of new manuscripts, as every merchant in the county knew. He loved to translate works otherwise limited to readers of Latin, into the common English of his shire. And Father Thomas loved to teach.

His school for boys received students from the surrounding countryside who had displayed ability and desire to learn. The very basic curriculum in which he drilled his young disciples also included his own requirement that they acquire an ability to express themselves literately in their mother tongue. Lady Apollonia knew that Thomas' rectory would be in its usual state of masculine chaos but he would warmly welcome his mother's party.

After spending the night in Axbridge, her party would continue on to Stogursey Priory. The Benedictines there were an alien cell of the Abbey of Lonlay but Lady Apollonia was well-known to be a great friend of these French monks. Natives of Normandy, they had been living for years under a cloud of suspicion as the King of England continued at war with the King of France. A reputed epicure, Stogursey's Prior always welcomed the Lady Apollonia's visits. He had recommended Guise to the Lady's service years before as a cook whose talents surpassed any in England. The Lady was a generous guest who would bring news to their isolated cell and an evening's opportunity to converse in the Prior's native tongue while they savored a glass of the Priory's excellent Bordeaux.

Finally, the party would lodge at Dunster Priory for two days allowing Lady Apollonia with Nan's company to make a call at Cliffbarton House. Dunster Priory and its community of Benedictine monks was a small dependent cell of the splendid Abbey at Bath. It maintained half of the imposing Norman church of Saint George in Dunster, comfortable living quarters, and an impressive collection of barns and stables in its ecclesiastical establishment. The monks of Dunster, though frequently at issue with the townsfolk, enjoyed the patronage of the great family of Luttrell, new masters of the castle which loomed high above the town. Lady Apollonia's patronage had also been invited by the Dunster monks to gain her support in the building of a glorious new tower for Saint George's, soon to be constructed at the crossing between nave and quire. Her visit would be welcomed by the monastic community in Dunster as well.

While his Lady and Nan would be making their sympathy call in Cliffbarton just outside Dunster, Giles would be sent to pursue a separate line of inquiry in Dunster, gathering local gossip from its wool market and the favored drinking establishments of the town. He would also pay a call upon an old friend, active in Dunster's vital wool trade, who had lodgings on Church Street in the heart of Dunster town. Messages were sent ahead to the places of lodging along their route; provisions were packed for the journey and instructions given for work to continue at Aust during their absence. Before departing, however, Lady Apollonia personally gave instructions to Friar Francis and Brother William to look more closely into the reports of the horsemen of the Apocalypse and sightings of the devil dancing on human graves. They were to put it about that the Lady was gravely concerned by these signs and portents. They were also allowed to suggest that those bringing information would be rewarded. Apollonia made it quite clear that her clerics were to try to locate reliable witnesses ready and able to describe that which they had truly seen.

Nan entered the Lady's solar as Friar Francis and Brother William were leaving. She brought her list of preparations for the journey for Lady Apollonia's approval. Waiting patiently until the door was closed tightly behind the departing clerics, Nan asked to speak privately with her mistress. Apollonia bade her continue as she could see Nan's eyes burned with information eager to be shared.

"I have examined everyone in the servant's hall, as we devised at Kingswood, my Lady," Nan whispered excitedly. "There is only one member of your household whom everyone agrees has been acting strangely for the past month." Pausing to add emphasis to her words, Nan's pale face and small chest drew in a huge breath as might an angel in a judgement painting prepare to issue a call to repentance. "It is Gareth!" she said.

Displaying unemotional but sincere interest in Nan's findings, Apollonia recognized at once that Nan was accusing her master of the stables as the culprit guilty of hanging butchered ravens from the lintels of the kitchen doors. There was little time to pursue Nan's complaint against Gareth now as they were preparing an early departure, but she encouraged the maid to share all that she had learned from her inquiries.

"All the servants complain that Gareth has become moody and sullen of late, my Lady. He refuses to speak, he is irritable and suspicious of all the lads and he has been keeping very much to himself sometimes he has disappeared for days!" Nan said excitedly. "Oh, my Lady, don't you see, if Sir Wilfrid was plotting evil against you, Gareth is the only man of your household who would have been known to the Lord of Cliffbarton." Her face flushed with worry and concern, Nan obviously wished that Lady Apollonia would take action against the stable master at once.

Apollonia paused and remained very quietly staring into the hearth fire which crackled brightly, sending little celebratory showers of sparks above the glowing logs. Thinking carefully through everything Nan had told her she lifted her face at last and smiled at the dear maid, as small and feisty as a fighting cock who stood ready to protect her against any threat.

"You have done very well, Nan and you are quite correct that only Gareth, of all our household, could have known Sir Wilfrid. I shall speak with Gareth when we return from Somerset." Apollonia could see that Nan was prepared to react in protest.

"Think clearly, dear Nan, if the threat to us were from Sir Wilfrid, then it would likely have been eliminated with his death." Rising to place her hands upon Nan's shoulders, Apollonia lifted one hand to smooth the wrinkled lines of worry which puckered Nan's forehead. The maid's head, at her full adult height, barely reached the level of her Lady's shoulder. "What you have discovered is very important to all of us. Some serious trouble has possibly afflicted Gareth and I will surely investigate the cause of the change in his behaviour when we return. Thank you for bringing this worrisome news to my attention."

Nan curtseyed obedience blushing and encouraged as always by her Lady's gracious appreciation but unable to conceal her anxiety that they might be leaving a serpent behind within the precious walls of Aust manor. Apollonia could see Nan's continuing worry but preferred to say nothing more about it. Instead, she asked Nan to describe their state of readiness for the journey to Somerset. When that was complete, Nan was sent to fetch Giles.

Giles reported to his Lady that he had left good men in charge of the harvest and shearing. He would be ready to join her and Nan early the next morning so as to take best advantage of the daylight. Satisfied with her servants' excellent preparations, Apollonia dismissed Giles and encouraged him to take a good night's rest. As he was about to leave her, Giles paused to ask for one additional clarification, "What are your wishes concerning the head of Sir

Wilfrid, my Lady?   Shall I have it carried to Abbot Harold at Kingswood?"

Lady Apollonia did not hesitate before answering, "No, Giles, let it remain here for the moment.   Shan't matter if we keep it yet awhile."

Chapter Eleven

Chaucer's Overture

"Mother, you won't believe the wondrous good fortune that has been mine." Young Father Thomas was hugging a manuscript to his breast as he hurried to assist his mother from her horse. "Master Chaucer's great _Canterbury Tales_ has been brought to me from London. Wait till you hear "*The Prologue*", Mother; Chaucer's language is the people's English at its best!" Thomas was so distracted with the joy of his newest literary acquisition he was unaware he had kept his mother standing in the lane by the rectory, his thoughts racing with his words pouring out in their profusion. "I shan't have to force the boys to read this Mamam, they will delight in it! I shall ask each of them to write a prologue as final exercise from their study. I have it! They can each pretend to be squire to the knight and write of their admiration for their master. Oh, but what a fool I am!" He swept his mother into his free arm and planted a welcoming kiss upon her cheek. "I am so glad to see you, dearest Mamam. Come in, come in, all of you and rest from your journey. My house is yours! Greetings Giles. Blessings on you Nan. Do come in and refresh yourselves."

Apollonia's party gratefully welcomed the opportunity to wash away the dust of their journey, share a simple supper provided with Fr. Thomas's blessing and further graced by his manifest pleasure in their coming. After the meal, they gathered in the priest's parlor and settled into a small circle drawn near the massive fireplace. It was a sparsely furnished chamber but contained two large chairs next to the hearth with several small high backed stools easily pulled close to the fire's warmth. That which it lacked in seating, it compensated in shelves, built deep enough to hold and order a growing collection of manuscript folios, volumes that were Father Thomas' pride and joy. Lady Apollonia, always pleased by her son's fascination with literature, had begged Thomas when they arrived to fill their few hours before retiring by reading for them from his ecstatically welcomed newest addition to his collection.

"I have always loved the richness in your voice, dear Thomas. Please let us listen to the words from your new copy of the writings of Master Chaucer," she said earnestly.

Warming their toes next to the crackling fire, the Lady, her steward and Nan were as eager as children to hear any new tale but Geoffrey Chaucer was already acknowledged by the growing literate population of England to be one of the kingdom's best writers. In expectant silence, they watched Father Thomas put on his spectacles, draw the candle nearer to light his page and then turn to the opening paragraphs of _The Canterbury Tales._ Nan and Giles were not only good listeners their powers of concentration enabled them to enter into the flow of the story effortlessly and both of them were smiling as Father Thomas' rich expressive voice began to read.

"Whan that Aprill with his shoures soote
the drogt of March had perced to the roote,
And bathed every veine in swich licour
Of which vertu engendred is the flour;..."

Apollonia enjoyed a good reading as much as anyone in her household but tended to listen as something of a literary critic as well as an eager member of the audience. She leant back in her chair, loving to absorb the marvelous chords of her son's rich deep voice as they magically transformed the words of the **Prologue** into living images complete in her mind's eye. "Master Chaucer is more than a truly engaging poet," she thought as she felt herself captivated by his verse. "His witty selection of word, color and familiar story all crisply dance to his poet's magical rhyme."

She looked fondly upon Giles and Nan as each sat on the edges of their stools; so intent that their fire-lit faces seemed transported through Thomas' vivid recreation of each of the **Tale's** characters: the noble but humble Knight, the contrary tendencies in the Prioress as well as the aggressive vitality of the shrewish Wife of Bath. Apollonia could sense they were enabled to see these characters, as real as flesh and blood, while never leaving the realm of their imaginations. But she was forced to smile at herself, too. This was the first of Geoffrey Chaucer's works she had heard and could not help but think him brilliant. His verbal brush applied sharp twinges of irony, deep shadings of sarcasm with hilarious japes at the pretense of _noblesse oblige,_ the insufferable self-righteousness of some of the regular clergy as well as the arrogant ignorance of the commons. These were all people they knew. "Chaucer's skill with English expression enthralls the listener but requires one to think as well. I like that."

Apollonia declared to herself. "Why not have a copy of this work for my own leisure? I must speak to Thomas. He is certain to know a good scrivener."

As entertaining as Thomas' reading was, Apollonia found it impossible to free her mind from constantly returning to the plaguing questions still surrounding the death of Wilfrid de Guelf. Her thoughts could not resist straying to her search for clues or connections which she may be overlooking. Suddenly, as Thomas stopped speaking and removed his spectacles she realized his reading was ended.

"Father Thomas, it is a grand beginning," Giles said warmly. "I long to hear more. Will Master Chaucer truly include two tales from every one of the Pilgrims he describes?"

"In faith, Giles, Master Chaucer left the work unfinished at his death thus I must wait to complete reading my copy of the _Tales_ before I can answer your question. But I shall introduce the 'Knights Tale' to my pupils and I can barely wait to hear the boys' reaction to its grand use of mythology and chivalry all written in their own familiar English. What a pleasure it will be for them!"

Thomas' excitement and glowing enthusiasm brought happy tears to his mother's eyes. She looked at the fire in silence so enjoying the present moments as Giles and Nan moved to retire offering their "good nights" and continuing to thank him for his reading. Apollonia's mother's heart was truly moved as she fondly noted how Thomas still unselfconsciously addressed her as "Mamam" echoing days of his early childhood years when he was unable to pronounce "Madame" as his older brothers had been taught to do. "And you have become the best of priests, my son," Apollonia thought proudly to herself, "devout, honest, hard-working, and generous in your service to your people." As if he were at her side, Edward's warm-hearted chuckle suddenly sounded in her mind. "Ah, Edward, my love," she smiled to herself welcoming the memory of her gentle husband, "It is you, isn't it?" She asked to herself. "It is your blessed courtesy, loving respect and concern for others freely granted not only indulgence but true goodness. Thank God you truly do live in our sons."

Later in the evening, as Apollonia and her son were seated alone chatting quietly, the logs in the fireplace glowed red and broke into final fiery embers. Thomas spoke pointedly to his mother, "Mamam, I do welcome your visits but I could not help noticing your preoccupation this evening and I also suspect that you must have other purposes in coming this long way. May I ask why you are traveling so far into Somerset?" His earnest eyes querying her, frankly expressed a great concern for her safety.

She bent to take his hands in hers and returning his steady gaze said quietly, "Of course, you may always ask anything of me, my son. But I must begin at the beginning of a rather long tale which has, as yet, no ending."

Summarizing briefly for her son the events that had occurred since the discovery of Sir Wilfrid's body and the circumstances of its bizarre accidental decapitation, Apollonia explained that she felt compelled to visit the widow of Wilfrid de Guelf because she needed to know more of Wilfrid's life, with whom his service had been given and what has he been doing within the past decades. "I readily confess, Thomas, this journey is more devious than a heartfelt sympathy call upon a grieving young widow. I simply cannot sort out any solutions until I have more information. Chiefly I must know what has Sir Wilfrid been doing during the interim years since our last meeting decades ago? Why was he in Gloucestershire and why was he being pursued?" Apollonia stopped short of sharing with her son her personal conviction that the strange death may touch lives far beyond the de Guelf family in Somerset but he seemed to grasp her larger concerns.

"Father always said it was useless to attempt to discourage you from something you had determined upon, but Mamam," his eyes and his voice pleaded gently, "remember these are dangerous times and people of consequence have been undone by asking impertinent questions."

Apollonia smiled at her son's concern. "One's best defense, at this or any time, is in being an unimportant person," she said. "I am an old woman on a journey of compassion, Thomas, without position or power to threaten anyone. Should some truth emerge which may be dangerous in other hands, it will remain neutral and unexposed in mine. But I have faith that there is value in truth for its own sake. 'Know the truth and the truth shall set you free.'" she spoke into his ear. Before Thomas could express any further objections, the Lady rose and kissed her son gently. "To bed, Thomas, kindly give me your blessing. I am a weary crone who needs her rest and the morrow comes early."

At first light the following day, Lady Apollonia and her little company left the rectory to mount up and continue on the road towards Stogursey Priory. Embracing her son warmly as he stood to hold her foot and assist her mount, the Lady whispered into Thomas' ear, "Do you think it might be possible to have the Chaucer copied?" His brows suddenly knit together as they did when he pondered any new assignment. Apollonia always thought she could see his mind at work on such occasions. She knew that he would be mentally searching for the best scribe in his school. "We shall return within a week," she continued, "and if it is not too great a burden perhaps you will have arranged a copyist by then?"

Apollonia's party began by riding south, through Wedmore, then west to reach a parallel route with the winding estuary of the River Parrett. Turning south again to Bridgewater to pause for a midday meal and find a safe crossing of the river they continued following along the twisting, winding lanes which meandered into the Southwest. Stogursey Priory, not far from the Somerset coast of the Bristol Channel, had its priory lands in the gentle rolling west county given it early in the 12th century by a pious Norman magnate of the Conquest Period. As Lady Apollonia's group approached the Priory gates late in the afternoon, a great bank of fog was rolling inland from the cold waters of the channel beyond. Fortunately, they were safely installed in the Prior's guest parlor by the time the fog outside swallowed the entire region in its swirling grey anonymity.

Their third traveling day was begun after the liturgical office of prime had been sung by the monks in the brilliantly painted Romanesque priory church. Stogursey's Prior Phillippe accompanied Lady Apollonia into the courtyard already welcoming her back on the return journey. With profuse thanks for her gift of a statue of her name Saint Apollonia now standing in a delicate ogee niche of the eastern apse of the Priory's new Lady Chapel still incomplete and requiring additional pious gifts, the Prior wished the Lady and her party Godspeed as they traveled on towards Dunster.

The fog of the evening before had dissipated only to be replaced by a heavily misting rain that accompanied them through the final portion of their journey. Thoroughly soaked, the traveling party experienced a great sense of relief when coming over a hill; they could see at last the town of Dunster lying in the mist-shrouded valley below. As if aware of the end of the journey, even the horses picked up their down-hill pace and gratefully halted after they entered the

Priory gates allowing themselves to be led to the dismounting blocks. Leaving their mounts in the care of stable hands in the courtyard Lady Apollonia, Nan, and Giles gratefully entered the guest lodgings of the Priory. Warm fires had been prepared for their arrival so the women wished Giles a hasty good night as he walked on to his accommodation. Soon as possible they were stripping away their wet garments, changed and grateful at last to thoroughly dry out. After a light supper they slipped into the church for vespers. But by service end they were pleased to escape the damp chill of the evening, hurry to the roaring fire in their chamber and retreat into their beds.

After breaking their fast the following morning, Lady Apollonia donned a fresh black riding habit with a crisp white wimple and was adjusting her black veil over the bodice and sleeves of her costume. Nan entered her room to announce that Giles had started off to the Dunster wool market as he had been instructed. The Lady nodded and then asked Nan if she were ready for the final short leg of their journey to Cliffbarton House. "I'm more than ready, my Lady, especially since the beastly rain has ceased and we shall have a bit of sunshine to cheer us." Nan said honestly.

Their ride up to the cliffs overlooking Porlock Bay needed sunshine to encourage visitors to continue on to Cliffbarton House. It was a desperately lonely and forsaken trail they followed. No trace of habitation appeared along the way; all warmth of human company seemed far behind in Dunster. When at last they approached the walled manor which had been home to Wilfrid de Guelf and his ancestors even the sun had chosen to withdraw behind austere grey clouds. A constant pounding of waves against rocks far below the cliffs upon which the manor house stood, from which it took its name and seemed to emerge, played a sustained base of groaning, throbbing, crashing warning.

Upon their arrival Nan pulled the bell rope at the gate and they entered the courtyard after its massive gates were drawn reluctantly open to receive them. A young groom emerged as if questioning any arrivals at this place but soon aware that they were but an old woman and her maid led their horses to a nearby dismounting block. Nan asked that the steward of the household be summoned to announce them to their mistress. When the steward came he too appeared unprepared to be receiving guests. Nan told him to announce the arrival of the Lady Mary Apollonia of Aust, who, while visiting nearby Dunster, had come to share her widow's sympathy with the recently bereaved Widow de Guelf. Still hesitant the steward seemed to be weighing his options but finally led Lady Apollonia, followed by Nan, through the main entry portal into the great hall to wait in its slovenly maintained interior while he left to announce their arrival to his mistress.

When he returned at last, Apollonia could see he was not in the least prepared to receive casual visitors yet he drew himself into his position and led the ladies up a tower stairway to the private apartments of the manor. There in a small tidy chamber hung with rich tapestries, a young mother sat on a large thick carpet playing with her toddling son in front of a cheery hearthfire snapping and crackling in vain against persistent drafts.

Rising to greet her elderly guest, Lady de Guelf called for a chair to be placed near the fire. "Even summer's warmth does not penetrate these walls, Lady Apollonia," the sweet young face was friendly but serious. "Winds from the channel seem to guarantee that chill prevails in the stone of this house no matter how we strive against it." Once her guest was seated with Nan at her side, refreshment was brought by a single maid servant who was then dismissed. Lady de Guelf obviously wished to speak with her visitor alone.

"My Lady of Aust speaks only when need compels her since the tragic death of her third husband," Nan said to their hostess, "but as your husband's assault occurred upon her lands she feels it her duty to call upon you and express her deepest sympathy, Lady de Guelf."

The young mother returned to the carpet where her son played happily with two new puppies. Although her attention seemed riveted upon her child, she was wary and anxious to learn the true nature of Apollonia's unexpected visit. "My Lady of Aust is indeed gracious, making a very long journey to express her sympathy. As I can no longer know the love of my own mother but with my sweet child do supremely value the gift of motherly compassion, I truly thank you kindly," she said.

"An additional occurrence contributed to my Lady's desire to call upon you," Nan continued. "Many years ago, your lord Sir Wilfrid served as liege man to my Lady's first husband, Sir Geoffrey Montecute. They were companions in all things." Lady Apollonia's lowered eyes searched for any reaction from the young mother as she played with her son. Lady Anne seemed distracted by the child but clearly listened with great care to Nan's speech. "If the knight's destrier should be found wandering in the woods of the Severn River and Lady Apollonia believes it to be the mount of your husband, she would prefer to know your preferences for ..."

"Sell it!" Lady Anne cried out immediately, "and...and send the monies to Kingswood Abbey," Lady de Guelf exclaimed without thinking. "My dead husband's body will lie there and my wishes are that any profit from that which was his knighthood shall go to support prayers for his soul." Suddenly the young mother lifted her head and looked directly up into Apollonia's eyes. The Lady of Aust returned her gaze and could sense in her violet eyes a depth of terror and pain sufficient to cause young eyes to glaze old, young hearts to wither and die. "If you knew Sir Wilfrid, my Lady," she said, "then I need not tell you what an evil creature he was. Being the last of a dreadful issue I do not wish that my little Wilfy will ever know the truth of his father's memory."

The rush of words poured suddenly out from the Lady Anne as if long pent up anguish and emotion found at last an avenue of release. "I wish to know nothing of the circumstances of his death, nothing! Buried far away in Kingswood Abbey, Wilfrid has anonymity there and the evil legends inspired by his life here will, in time, die with him." Pausing only to take in deep agitated breaths as she spoke, Lady Anne seemed to need to hear these decisions declared into the ears of others.

"The village of Cliffbarton is already deserted and stands derelict after the ravages of plague. I shall see to it that the church is pulled down and that horrible effigy smashed. Soon there will be new, clean pages in the history of the family de Guelf upon which my son shall be allowed to begin afresh his own honorable accounting of his life's story."

Apollonia could sense months of desperation haunting Lady de Guelf's words and her heart filled with compassion for the young girl. Remembering the Christian name which Abbot Harold had mentioned, she smiled gently and spoke directly to her with quiet reassurance in her voice, "Anne, my child, you need never fear that I or my household would abuse your wishes or destroy your hopes for your beautiful son."

At the sound of her Christian name, spoken as if by her own mother, Anne's eyes swam in a sudden rush of tears. She put her head down and wept silently.

"I have not come to expose Sir Wilfrid," Apollonia continued, "only to protect my own against any chance of retaliation. Will you help me?" Lady Apollonia bent to place her hand on the quaking shoulders of the sobbing girl.

At her touch, Lady Anne lifted her tear stained face and gasped between her wrenching sobs, "But what can I possibly do? I have been kept here since the birth of Wilfy. No one comes to this place for none have been allowed. I know nothing because I am told nothing and I am served by a collection of malcontents who have been unsupervised for years." The Lady's plight was one of designed helplessness but she knew she was at last in a position to begin to make a difference.

"You can greatly assist me with information if you have it, my child," Lady Apollonia said as she took a kerchief from her sleeve and gently wiped the tears away. "I think that your plans for your son are very well conceived and I believe that you will, with God's help, be able to direct little Wilfy away from a dark and wicked heritage towards a more hope-filled future. I will do all I can to see that any rumor or remembrance of evil associated with the Lord of Cliffbarton is suppressed." Seeing the girl's body begin to relax, Apollonia continued, "In the interests of my cause, however, can you tell me anything about the activities of your deceased husband within the past two years?"

"I have only been married for the past two years, your Ladyship," Lady Anne said, now more calm and composed. "I am not at home here in Somerset, I come from Adwick le Street, south Yorkshire," she said as if the memory gave her pleasure. "My earnest desire was to enter the convent at Nun Monckton and I believed my father ready to provide the dowry necessary for the nuns to accept me. At their urging, I was waiting till I had entered my twelfth year as they preferred to receive girls who were mature and convinced of their vocation." She put her head down again, "It was shortly after I had turned twelve that I first saw Sir Wilfrid."

Apollonia could see that speaking of her married life caused the Lady Anne to delve into unpleasant memory still painful and resented. "Unknown to me," she said with lowered eyes, "Sir Wilfrid approached my father with an offer of marriage requiring no dowry. I was married to a man older than my father because it was seen to be an excellent connection for my family." Now her voice grew flat and empty, "I was told nothing of the carnal demands of marriage." Lady Anne shuddered. "My father said that my husband would instruct me."

Lifting her head and looking at Apollonia after some moments of silence, she began again, "I am sorry but I can tell you very little about my husband's activities. He preferred that I remain ignorant, you see." Anne paused again to force herself to re-gather memories which she had dispersed and suppressed. "Wilfrid was in the service of the Earl of Hereford, commanding a group of men at arms guarding Pontefract Castle when we met. But I know that he had also been with the royal court at Shene in the days of King Richard's good Queen Anne. Wilfrid delighted in pouring contempt upon the Queen's sober German household and their respect for the learned Master Wycliffe. I only know that he traveled several times to Shene from Pontefract after we were married as he said he had business there."

Frowning, Anne spoke as if she were thinking aloud, "It always seemed odious to me that Wilfrid could acknowledge his change of allegiance so casually. Although he served his court for several years he felt no loyalty to King Richard after his fall. Wilfrid called him a silly ass and an ignorant boy. After the Earl of Hereford had returned to England from exile, he sided with the lords' appellant against King Richard. Wilfrid was among the first of Richard's henchmen to support the Lancastrian seizure of the throne." Looking up at Apollonia, Anne's face became defiant, "but I was not supposed to have intelligence of his activities. I was not even told that we would leave Yorkshire. We had remained there for less than a year but when I was found to be with child my husband announced that we would return to his family's estate here at Cliffbarton."

Lady Apollonia had only one further question, "Do you have any idea what the purpose of Sir Wilfrid's most recent journey may have been?"

Anne grew thoughtful and began to speak hesitantly, "Wilfrid told me nothing of his destination . . . most secretive about his purpose but I suspected that he was returning to Pontefract or possibly Shene from the orders which I heard him give to Manfred, his odious squire. He left Cliffbarton, oh, surely it was a month and a half ago, accompanied only by the loathsome Manfred." Lady Anne made no effort to hide her feelings towards her husband's servant. "Manfred was a weasel of a man, capable of any evil. I thank God daily that he, too, has failed to return to Cliffbarton for I shall never allow him to return to my service."

Suddenly recalling a curious aspect of Wilfrid's behaviour, Anne continued, "It may be of no interest to you, my Lady, but Wilfrid was quite excited about some prospect of riches to be gained from his last journey and he became nearly giddy when he thought of it. He would only tell me, 'It has kept us comfortably but now I shall make you a queen, little rabbit,' and then he would laugh horribly."

Nan suddenly shuddered noticeably. Lady Apollonia could see that she was personally disturbed by the conversation; her usual composure was deteriorating into silent agitation. Certain that sharing more old memories of Sir Wilfrid could not be welcome to Nan or to his widow; Apollonia decided it was time to end the interview. Rising, she extended her hand to the young mistress of Cliffbarton. "Thank you for your hospitality, Lady Anne, your candor and willingness to share your memories have been very helpful to me. I congratulate you on your fine healthy son and I shall pray for you both and for his future happiness." Lady Anne preceded her to summon her servant as Apollonia moved to walk towards the chamber door.

Pausing to exchange goodbyes, Apollonia expressed her desire that they might meet again and extended her invitation to the Lady de Guelf. "When you next return to Kingswood Abbey may I have your promise that you will lodge with me in Aust?" The young woman rose to her tiptoes to embrace and kiss the taller Apollonia with a warmth and gratitude promising a future meeting. "I feel I must return home to Yorkshire, my Lady, but I should be grateful to accept your hospitality as we travel north," Lady Anne assured her. Following the servant, Nan and Apollonia descended from the solar and were taken back to the courtyard where their horses were waiting.

Chapter Twelve

Effigy's Legacy

As they mounted and prepared to leave Cliffbarton House, Lady Apollonia said quietly, "I am truly sorry, dear Nan. This visit has forced black memories of childhood upon you once again. Would you prefer to wait for me here whilst I ride into the village? It is my morbid curiosity I grant you, but I must visit the church before we leave this place."

Nan's normally pale face reddened with indignation at the suggestion and her bright blue eyes flashed with spirited denial. "No my Lady, what are you saying?" Suddenly realizing that Apollonia must have noticed her discomfort in Lady de Guelf's solar, Nan hurried to explain. "I did not wish to interrupt. Please forgive me, my Lady. It happened when Lady Anne spoke of Sir Wilfrid's laughter. By all the Holy Martyrs, I swear I could hear it! The sound of his bestial cackle returned to my ears as if a fiendish spirit haunts that chamber. I-i-it was merely a horrible echo from long ago, my Lady. Truly, my pain is exorcised and long forgotten not keenly felt daily like the suffering forced upon his poor Lady wife." Nan's simple honesty matched the earnest pleading in her plain face. She did not wish to be left behind.

"Your spirit has always been a generous one, Nan," Apollonia said as she reached to touch her hand. "You and I shall pray for the young widow and try to find a way to follow events in her life. I promise you we shall find ways to silence Wilfrid's evil laughter." Apollonia looked up at the descending autumn sun. "But we must hurry. Before we have lost the light, let us away to the village church." Urging her horse forward with Nan mounted and determined to follow every step, Apollonia continued down the path towards the deserted village of Cliffbarton. The sun was weak and pallid as it slowly began to sink towards the horizon. Clouds mottled the grey blue sky, lashed into angry reddish-grey welts by the unrelenting winds blowing against the riders' faces as if to resist their progress and push them back.

The women rode into the main crossings of lanes through the village green now grown high with grasses and nettles. For the first time in many years, Apollonia felt raw fear seize her heart. Was this extension of her investigation truly necessary? She and Nan were totally alone in this God-forsaken isolated empty place. No one would ever know if danger befell them here. Apollonia had not even told the Lady Anne that she intended visiting Cliffbarton village. She had not been able to think of a reasonable excuse for such impertinence. It was, she had to admit, her unquenched curiosity piqued by Anne's hysterical reference to the derelict church with its horrible effigy. "We shall not tarry here, Nan," the Lady said to reassure them both. "My questions about this place will be quickly answered within the church and then we shall turn our horses back towards Dunster town."

"Whatever you wish, my Lady," Nan answered calmly.

Wildly shifting winds created eerie movement of shadows among the ruined hovels gathered haphazardly about the deserted village green. Somewhere a door banged in taunting rhythmic throbs; an unhinged shutter rattled garishly against a cob wall. The Lady's palfrey grew skittish, anxious and resistant. Apollonia dismounted and led the beast with gentle murmurs of assurance; Nan followed her Lady's example as they continued to look for the church on foot. There would be only one.

From the green, a hill rose overlooking Porlock Bay. Standing upon its summit, an ancient church clutched the high ground like a looming sepulcher. It was small and primitive Saxon construction, a tall rough-hewn rectangle with long narrow slits in its walls for windows and a clumsy Romanesque arch framing its entry beneath a rudely constructed wooden porch. After a short climb, they entered the churchyard where the horses could be tethered and allowed to graze upon the overgrown grasses. Apollonia looped the reins securely over a small branch and walked straight towards the coffin shaped chapel. Nan slipped around her mount with the grace of a sparrow, tethered him quickly and hurried to remain close to her Lady. Effluvia of rot and decay crept into their nostrils at the entry porch that stank from heaps of detritus and thick piles of bird droppings. Filthy nest materials hung like ancient hair strung in chaos along its inner walls. The iron-strapped oak door hung arrogantly ajar beckoning visitors into its dripping black bowel. Stepping carefully to avoid some of the animal filth and loose snares of broken flagstone, Apollonia walked into the nave and paused for a moment to allow her eyes to adjust to the darkness.

As the shadowed void slowly focused into dark shapes hovering about them, Apollonia and Nan were stunned by the sounds of movement amidst the bone-chilling damp of the place. A frenzy of creeping life scurried at their intrusion and then settled into sullen apprehension somewhere in the blackness. Wind rushing through unseen crevices sustained an undulating urgent cry over their heads. Water dripped pointedly and one wall shone with slimy iridescence. The empty church was alive with silent watchful eyes waiting within its dead stone darkness.

Apollonia squinted to hurry her eyes in concentration on the collection of family monuments which lined the walls of the dank interior. The largest was a freestanding tomb placed directly in the center of the main aisle near the eastern apsidal end. A regal table and canopy of vaulted stone, it contained an exquisitely carved life-sized alabaster figure of a knight. Its intricate canopy forming a delicate arch over the full length of the effigy rose to a crown of towering pinnacles. Such grandeur in this primitive place seemed grossly incongruous. Apollonia walked towards it her quiet steps shattering the empty silence.

Pushing aside a great curtain of cobweb draped from the vaulting of the canopy to the effigy's heart, Apollonia bent her upper body to lean into its marble canopy for a closer look. Feeble light streaks struggled to pierce the interior gloom from the narrow lancet windows above the altar. Invisible stray threads of web brushed her cheeks and attached to her eyelashes. Chill crept up through her feet from the damp stones below and she shuddered involuntarily from the cold, the damp and the decay of spirit in these walls.

The sculpted knight appeared to be the kind of effigy so often seen in multitudes of churches throughout England, impossible repose in full body armor and helmet. The knight's stance with crossed legs and bent arms seemed quite familiar. But the effigy's gloved hands were not held in prayerful silence. The left armored arm lifted a clenched fist bent threateningly at its elbow and the face which peered through the opening of the bascinet with visor removed portrayed no gentle paladin. Closely spaced, narrow open eyes leered above its grim smirking mouth fully framed in drooping mustache. Apollonia thought the face repulsive and yet defiantly proud. Its slant eyes, their pupils deeply chiseled, were smoldering and resentful, looking straight into the future as if hurling a silent curse from beyond the grave.

The effigy torso was twisted, its vivid posture threatening to spring to life at any moment. The right arm crossed the body so that its hand firmly grasped the hilt of its broadsword. Its right leg, bent at the knee, appeared to be crossed over the left. "Oh precious Lord Jesu!" The words escaped from her lips. Apollonia could not believe what she was seeing and leaned further into the canopied space.

Beginning normally at the hip, the human right leg transformed from sculpted armor at the effigy's thigh to a muscular shaggy animal leg. The lower half of the knight's crossed leg was that of a goat furred, bent and terminated in a cloven hoof. Without realizing it, Apollonia had stopped breathing momentarily. She starred at the leg and its cleft hoof, her mind stunned into recognition. There could be no doubt of its intent. The knightly effigy blatantly celebrated its role as minion to the ruler of the underworld. To underscore family allegiance, the heraldic achievement of the de Guelfs was emblazoned upon the interior wall of the canopy above the knight's head with a banner arcing over all to proclaim: "Malefic Triumphant." After moments of utter stillness, Apollonia sucked in a great gasp of startled breath.

"Blessed Mother of God," Nan whispered, leaning cautiously around her Lady for a better look. "Who was this, then?"

"It says, 'Rainauld de Guelf, 1109'. No doubt, this is an early ancestor of Sir Wilfrid, Nan. Whomsoever he was, he wished to terrorize folk even from the far banks of Hades." Apollonia could not take her eyes from the macabre effigy. "No wonder the Lady Anne wishes to smash this abomination!"

Nan could feel her flesh creep as she peered around Apollonia's bent figure to look more closely at the effigy. Her sudden scream shattered the icy stillness and continued its piercing stabs into the darkness as she hysterically pulled her Lady away. A loud flutter of black wings shook the vault overhead and squeaking fur bodies clamored over their feet. With her head tucked into the tomb canopy, Apollonia had not seen the monstrous black spider furiously descending its disturbed web curtain. Now erect and fully aware of the spider's charging legions, Apollonia backed carefully away, taking Nan into her arms to soothe her terrified screams as the eight-legged behemoth lurched aggressively towards the women with an army of arachnids crawling from every crevice of the tomb's alabaster sculpture. Slowly retreating from the area around the tomb and crossing herself in earnest thanksgiving, Apollonia released Nan from

104

her arms but kept her hand and led her urgently towards the door. Both women hurried their careful steps through the portal filled with a welcome sense of release as they finally crossed the threshold and left behind its collection of primordial corruption. Outside, they found themselves breathing in deeply the sharp wind howling through the trembling trees more than ever anxious to fill their lungs with its freshness from the open sea.

Mounted again and looking back from their waiting horses, Lady Apollonia and Nan were suddenly aware that the sun had disappeared behind low-lying grey clouds. An aura of gloom spewed from the church and hovered above the darkening ghostly ruins of Cliffbarton. With an audible sigh, Apollonia wearily turned in her saddle for one final view of the desolation around them. "Oh Nan, There is truly nothing to salvage here. It will be a blessing indeed that this village disappears from the face of the earth. Such a legacy bears no revival."

"Aye, my Lady," Nan said failing to hide her anxiety. "But days' light will not linger. Shall we return to Dunster, now?"

"Yes, oh yes, Nan, let us be on our way."

Apollonia and Nan pushed their mounts out of Cliffbarton, trotting down from the cliffs, grateful to be back on the trail towards Dunster. As they drew nearer to the town their hearts thrilled to its human sounds, to its welcome cooking odors and the living presence of people in community.

Looking forward to the refuge of the Priory and riding steadily through the town, neither woman had exchanged a word on the return journey but both watched eagerly for first sight of the great cross on the Priory gatehouse. Autumnal evening light accompanied them through the town slowly beginning to fade into the darkness. Riding past St. George's wall, they entered the courtyard of the living accommodations of the Priory. Nan hailed a monk who scurried to find stable hands. Dismounting from the warm bodies of their horses, both women realized how cool the evening had become. Fussing that her Lady must lift her woolen shawl to fight the chill, Nan then tied a thickly knitted triangle of wool round her own shoulders. They hurried on to the Church as vespers were already begun. Lustrous voices were offering the opening intonations of the call to worship.

Finally after supping, Apollonia and Nan seated themselves closely to the fire in the Priory guest apartment; speaking quietly as if still trying to overcome the chilling shock of their adventure when Giles knocked upon their door. Having refreshed himself, he had come straightaway to make his account to the Lady Apollonia as he felt he had gathered important information but wasn't quite certain of its meaning. Nan rose to answer his arrival at the lodging door and seeing it to be Giles, urged him to enter quickly.

"Greetings, Nan," he said quite pleased with himself, "Did you have successful hunting?"

"We have seen an amazing sight this day," she whispered pointedly as he walked past her and into the room.

"My Lady," Giles said as he approached her, "I am truly relieved to find you safely returned to the Priory." Giles took his responsibilities for Lady Apollonia's safety very seriously. "It did not please me to be separated from your company today but I do believe I have gathered some news which may be helpful to us." Having closed the door Nan returned to her chair by the fire. Giles drew up a seat for himself while noticing the flush of adventure still glowing upon Nan's pale cheeks.

"We are anxious for your news, Giles, please tell all, sparing no detail," Apollonia encouraged her excited steward.

"As you know, my Lady," Giles began. "I rose early to be at the market whilst it was bustling. Indeed, Dunster's market day demonstrates English commerce at its best," he said proudly. "There were traders and merchants doing a fine bit of trade, with goods from all parts of the kingdom, I vow." Giles described how he jostled among the locals in the market crowds making discreet inquiries after the lord of the manor, Wilfrid de Guelf. "Most frequently, folk would look fearful and walk away at the mention of de Guelf, my Lady."

Knowing that all roads in any market town lead to the inn, Giles moved on to visit the low, dark interior of Dunster's Red Lion. He took an inconspicuous place in a corner, tankard in hand, to listen a bit as the locals spoke among themselves. At first he could hear nothing unusual but then he noticed several rustics laughing over the very strange habits of some foreigners whom they had seen recently. To a Somerset man, a visitor from Cornwall is foreign; therefore, Giles felt he must move closer in order to determine the true nature of these aliens. It didn't take long for him to realize that the yokels were referring to three knights from some unknown country across the sea. The object of their laughter was the language which the gentlemen spoke. No one could guess what it was but to one of the rustics, its guttural, grunting reminded him of swine snorting. "His comic imitation of the sound caused them all to howl." Giles added with amusement.

Giles then decided to make a discreet inquiry of the landlord and jostled through the regulars towards the great huge barrels from which his host was drawing ale. Wishing him God's blessing and good custom, Giles waited until a lull in his exertions would allow a quiet chat with the gregarious, rotund, publican. "At first," he said, "I simply asked about the hilarious visit of the foreign knights which the lads across the room were loudly discussing. The landlord smiled happily and said, 'Aye, they was a queer lot, a'right.'"

"Then," Giles continued, "attempting to draw him out, I asked from whence they had come. He scratched his bald pate and said he didn't rightly know but somewhere over the water surely. 'They paid right well for their bed and board,' he assured me with pleasure."

Then, Giles said, he decided to try another tack and asked the landlord what was the nature of their business in Dunster. "This question drew a puzzled response, my Lady. The landlord seemed a bit embarrassed but finally said, 'Oi don't rightly know, Master, it were turrble hard to fix ther meanin' but Oi reck'ned they was owed som' braass outn my lord o'Cliffbarton.' Adding weight to his speculation that they were seeking repayment of debt, the landlord said that the foreign knights kept asking after Sir Wilfrid only until they finally realized that he had left the county. Then, they too, called for their horses to be ready and galloped away early the next morning."

"I asked the landlord if he could remember when the foreigners' visit had occurred," Giles continued. "He began by saying that it must have been a fortnight ago, but, no, he decided it must have been the better part of four weeks past, 't'were before the great storm struck, Master,' he assured me," Giles said. "I didn't know quite what to make of it, my Lady, but it seems likely that these knights were in pursuit of Sir Wilfrid to collect a debt. Perhaps it was they who captured him."

Having filed this information away in his mind, Giles said he continued on to visit with his old friend, Martin Wickham, a merchant of Dunster whose substantial house stood not far away on Church Street. "Martin has done very well for himself since our boyhood days in Corsham, my Lady," Giles continued. He failed to add that Martin had heartily congratulated him on his own success in raising himself to the position of steward in Lady Apollonia's household.

"After a fine meal, we sat comfortably enjoying the leisure of remembering old times," Giles continued, "laughing at our boyhood escapades and asking after news of old friends. Aware as I am that Martin prides himself on knowing everything happening in Dunster, I broached the subject of Sir Wilfrid's recent death with him. 'The world is well rid of him!' my old friend said forcefully and I asked him to explain himself."

"Martin told me that Sir Wilfrid had been away from Cliffbarton a great deal in recent decades and most folk were grateful for his absence. Little more than two years ago, Sir Wilfrid had returned to his manor with a new young wife who was about to deliver their child." Giles could see Nan nodding knowingly at the mention of the Lady of Cliffbarton. Continuing with his story, however, he kept his Lady's maid upon the edge of her chair. "Martin said that Sir Wilfrid kept to himself upon their return, stayed away from the town and allowed no visitors to Cliffbarton House. To ensure his isolation, his reeve put it about that anyone, pilgrim, musician, juggler, peddlers, any innocent traveler, would be whipped if they dared to set foot upon his lands." Nan gasped audibly but urged Giles to continue.

Saying that he had only one additional point of interest, Giles referred again to his friend's conversation. "Martin also mentioned that it was rumored Sir Wilfrid had connections with the House of Lancaster, that at one time, he served the great John of Gaunt himself. Martin said he didn't believe the old superstitious nonsense about the de Guelf's serving Satan but it was a great wonder to him that a man so totally corrupt and wicked could flaunt justice and the church and remain in the good graces of the king. He always seemed to find his way to the winning side, My Lady," Giles said. "Somehow he managed to maneuver himself into the court party during young King Richard's reign and yet he also emerged with those who held the favor of the new Lancastrian King Henry. But most annoying of all, Martin told me," Giles concluded, "Sir Wilfrid, who neglected every estate and honor which he owned seemed to grow richer in his middle age, though no one could tell the source of his wealth."

Giles sat back in his chair allowing Lady Apollonia to ponder over the value and relevance of his news. The fire crackled and popped merrily but the three continued in thoughtful silence. At length, the Lady turned to him. "Thank you Giles," she told him earnestly, "for this is excellent information." Then addressing her maid, she mentioned casually that they, too, had experienced a very interesting day. "Nan, dear, why don't you share with Giles our adventures in visiting Cliffbarton House and the village church?" Nan was quite pleased to be allowed to tell her tale, while Apollonia starred into the fire meticulously piecing together all the day's gleanings.

Her imagination aflame, Nan became quite animated in her description of the deserted village of Cliffbarton, the horror which they found in its derelict church, and their fervent thanks to God in leaving the foul place. Her description of the tomb effigy of Sir Wilfrid's ancestor proved the de Guelf's served the Devil, Nan insisted. But she totally captivated Giles with her description of the innocent, valiant and beautiful young Lady of the manor, now liberated by widowhood and determined to stamp out the evil de Guelf story in behalf of her son.

Lady Anne seemed to Giles, a character out of one of his favorite French romances. He had not seen her but in his imagination he was certain that she was as worthy of courtly love as any of the ladies of Arthurian legend, a shining example of womanly virtue emerging victorious with one delicate foot resting upon the head of a vanquished demon.

Chapter Thirteen

Stewardship Renewed

Lady Apollonia never allowed herself to question the chosen vocations of any of her handsome sons. The three eldest were establishing themselves in the world through the profession of arms: Hugh would soon be appointed deputy to the sheriff of Wiltshire; Chad and Alban chose to serve with the Marcher Lords in defense of the realm against the Welsh uprising. Thomas had gone to Cambridge to study and seek his call through ordination for the priesthood. But the youngest, gentle and uncomplicated David had no vocation for war or scholarship. Renouncing the world at the age of twenty he had entered the Cistercian Abbey at Tintern, whole-heartedly embracing the purity of its rule built upon a rigorous discipline of manual labor and prayer.

Apollonia had buried their father, Edward Aust, in the village churchyard in 1391. Her third husband, Robert Windemere, a wool merchant of Corsham and dear friend to Apollonia and Edward, died shortly after a year of their marriage in 1394. Thus, David's decision a year and a half later, to renounce the world and enter Tintern Abbey, capped a series of losses which lacerated her already grieving heart. Apollonia knew in her soul that David's decision was made with fervent conviction and faith in his calling to the religious life. Willingly and liberally she gave him her blessing and a substantial gift to the Abbey at the beginning of his novitiate. But she sorely missed her youngest son with his terrible puns, his smiling freckled face and generous sweet nature. It was as if a portion of her very being had been taken from her.

She felt the loneliness and the heavy burden of responsibility keenly. It seemed that late in her life she had become totally in charge but the solitary nature of that position was intimidating. At the same time, she told herself, she was not too old to learn or to contribute. She could not envision her life within conventual walls as she still wished to order her last years according to her own desires. Thus it was in the same year of 1395 when David entered the monastery, that Apollonia announced to her brother, Ferdinand, her intention to live celibate. She had, with the counsel of her chaplain and the Abbess of Lacock, decided to follow the rule of the *devotio moderna*, giving the rest of her life to a discipline of work, charity, and contemplation. "I can't renounce the world, Ferdinand," she had quietly confessed to him, "but I feel alienated by it." The colors of mourning would continue to be her habit of dress. Though not cloistered, she chose to spend her remaining years as a bride of Christ.

Ferdinand agreed with Apollonia's decision which had already received the approval of the Bishop of Worcester. His sister had always been a bit of the mystic he thought, religious and quiet as a mouse. She had fulfilled her obligations to marry and bear children. Now, he thought, it was proper that she concern herself with matters of the spirit as he surely would do some day also. But in his silent thoughts Ferdinand was sincerely grateful that she had decided not to enter a convent. Apollonia had a good mind for figures and ran her estates well. Till her sons returned from war and service, she would be needed to keep things in order. "Well, Polly," he told her, "you're old enough to know your own mind and spirit. Do what you must do. I shall offer no objections."

In the mysterious rhythm of life closing one door while opening another, shortly after David left his mother's world to enter the monastic community, Giles Digby joined the household of the Lady of Aust. Giles was the same age as David and though he knew nothing of Apollonia's pining for her youngest son, Giles sensed a special place opening for him the moment he had agreed to serve her. Their very first meeting took place after a humiliating incident happened to him in the market of Corsham, a town on the road between Bath and Chippenham. The Lady had traveled there from Aust to discuss storage of the season's fleeces with the master of her warehouse and chief wool buyers.

The warehouse and several stone quarries had been left to Apollonia in the will of her adoring third husband. An elderly widower, Robert Windemere had been for years, a friend of hers and Edward's. In respect for her excruciating grief at Edward's death, Robert waited months before revealing his feelings to Apollonia. Having been for many years her secret admirer, Robert was overjoyed when she consented to be the companion of his latter years. They were given little more than a year's collection of happy months together after their wedding. A serious outbreak of sweating sickness struck Corsham late in the winter of 1393, most severely afflicting the very young and the elderly. Although Robert had lived a vigorous, wholesome life, at sixty he seemed to have no strength of resistance to the ravages of fever which carried him away in a matter of days. In early January of 1394, Apollonia stood in the wind and snow, looking down into a husband's open grave for the third time. After the graveside service and the final blessing of the priest, other friends and family had gone. The pitmakers hurried to fill the grave as they wished to escape the frigid cemetery and return to the warm hearth of the local inn to heal numb fingers and revive their own spirits. Apollonia had remained at Robert's final resting place as if reluctant to leave this dear loving friend. As she watched the frenzied shoveling, she was suddenly seized by a strong sense of her own mortality. She didn't fear death but life, she recognized clearly, had distilled into a limited collection of priorities for her. With her mourning had come an even greater sense of personal isolation.

It was a busy market day in Corsham in February of 1395 and Lady Apollonia was walking across the stone pavement of the marketplace with one of her trusted Wiltshire wool buyers when she saw a group of tradesmen gathered round a young man, threatening him with angry gestures. What-ever he had done, she wondered, he was at a distinct disadvantage trying to defend himself against such a crowd of accusers. Quietly she asked her companion if he knew any of the details of the furious exchange they were witnessing. "Aye my Lady," her buyer said knowingly, "the young lad was left a mountain of debt when his father died a fortnight ago. Then two days past a fire in the family ironmonger's shop destroyed all of his property. Young Master Giles has indeed found himself in desperate straits. He has lost his home, the shop and any hope of ever repaying his creditors."

"What do you know of the character of the lad?" Apollonia asked.

"He is a good lad, is Giles Digby," said the buyer, "and well educated too. His father saw to that. But I fear there is little left for him now short of gaol for debt he shall never be able to repay, my Lady."

Lady Apollonia asked that the buyer speak to the gathered tradesmen, take a listing of the debts owed each of them, and send the young man round to meet with her that afternoon in Windemere House on Fish street. The wool buyer knew that this Lady was famous for her good works but he felt he must caution her. "My Lady, these debts are large ones indeed. I must tell you that Giles' father had lived well above his station far too long."

The Lady thanked him graciously for his concern and asked him once again to kindly do her bidding. With bowing acknowledgement of her wishes he agreed to see her request fulfilled. Later that afternoon, the frightened and distressed young man presented himself at the door of Windemere House. Very well dressed, he might have been mistaken for one of the dandies of the town but his adolescent face was a mask of confusion and distress. Nan showed him into the room where Lady Apollonia waited to receive him. Giles' fear only increased as he was presented to the intimidating silent woman, garbed in black who seemed to refuse to look at him. With a gesture, to the chair that was brought for him, he sat. Then to his surprise Nan, the servant who had answered the door and brought him through to this chamber also took a chair seating herself in their midst.

Nan spoke first presenting the Lady of Aust to Giles and indicating that his present difficulties had come to her attention in the market that morning. "My Lady wishes to know what your education has been, Master Giles," Nan asked.

Giles addressed Nan as he responded, "My father sent me to the boy's school run by the priests of Corsham when I was very young. Later I went to the cathedral school in Salisbury only returning to Corsham after a disastrous fire ruined my family's hope of gain."

His face pale and drawn, Giles was having difficulty seeing where this conversation might lead him but he was too desperate to refuse this interview. "I can read and write and do sums. I was a chorister in Salisbury and have some skill in Latin but have no wish to take holy orders." He put his head down and added somewhat sheepishly, "It was never my father's intention that I be 'prenticed out, because, I believe, he hoped I could become a gentleman some day." Such a possibility seemed so preposterous Giles felt foolish having said it.

Now Lady Apollonia spoke to him directly, "Are you willing to work hard, Master Digby?"

Somewhat startled by this question from the silent woman in black, he responded quickly, "I will do anything, anything, to find some way to overcome the chasm of debt which faces me, my Lady."

Suddenly he realized that he was pleading directly to her. Apollonia's grey eyes held his in their penetrating gaze.

"I am in need of a young assistant steward of my household at Aust," she said. "A fine old reeve from my husband's affinity, bailiff to me these twenty years past, now needs to have younger arms and legs to assist him. But he is demanding and exacting and would expect long days of hard work from you as you learn your duties."

As Lady Apollonia spoke and Giles began to realize the position she was offering him, his face glowed with hope soon dashed by the crushing reminder of his situation. "My Lady, I would be tireless in your service and would gladly give myself body and soul to learning the requirements of your household but I am not in a position to leave Corsham at this time." Giles then went on to explain that the tradesmen of Corsham who had accosted him in the market that morning were demanding immediate payment of debts owed them or they would order his arrest and imprisonment. "My life is pawned for debt," Giles said disconsolately, "and I cannot redeem it."

Lady Apollonia pulled from her sleeve the list of debtors and amounts owed which had been prepared for her. She handed it to Giles and said, "Is that the total amount of your debt?" Looking at the list, Giles seemed thunderstruck; even now he had difficulty comprehending how much his father had borrowed. Shaking his head hopelessly as he read through the lengthy notation he nodded and said sadly, "Yes, my Lady, it is; it is. . .quite correct."

Apollonia was impressed by Giles' frank admission of his situation unadorned by excuses or desperate fabrications. This young man possessed qualities of honesty, fidelity, and candor she admired most. Laying the list on the table next to her Apollonia responded to his bowed head in her quiet voice. "I will arrange to lend you the entire amount of the debt if you will agree to two conditions. First, that you will join my household and work diligently to learn the duties of steward. Secondly, that you will transfer to me, as security for my loan, the burned out property that was your father's house and shop that I may use it as I wish. Are you willing to agree to those conditions, Master Giles?"

Lifting his head with inquiring hope, Giles looked again directly into the Lady's grey eyes. "Oh yes, my Lady," he said fervently, "I will accept all your conditions and promise to serve you with the best of my abilities. I shall gladly sign to you the use of my property but what can you possibly do with the ruins?"

Lady Apollonia smiled, "Your land is in a valuable location of the town not far from my wool warehouse. It is not often that such properties become available there and I have need to build a house in that district for my warehouse master and his growing family. When you have worked off the full value of the loan in service to me, the property will return to you as a residence or rental investment. We can, I believe, be of good service to each other in this matter, Master Giles," she said gratified to see his boyish face and blue eyes brighten at last.

Giles shook his head and agreed numbly, speechless and still wondering at such good fortune. He hardly dared to believe that he had become free from the threat of imprisonment. If this Lady wished to take advantage of his property she certainly could have procured it more cheaply. Miraculously she included a position for him in the bargain. Giles couldn't guess why she had chosen him but neither could he refuse the lifeline she was extending to him. Throwing care to the winds, he fell to his knees. "With all my heart, I shall serve you unconditionally, my Lady!" he exclaimed. "At this moment I have no better return for your great kindness than my thanks. But I pledge by all that is holy, you will never regret this gracious act in my behalf."

Although the period of trial at Aust manor kept Giles in an anxious state of readiness, he soon discovered that he had talents for managing and organization which were encouraged and developed within his Lady's directives. The years of his assistantship seemed hectic and arduous but full of energy and enthusiasm for his new tasks, he found he enjoyed dealing with the day-to-day and the season to season requirements of his position in the household. Soon, Lady Apollonia found that she could use Giles as delegate for nearly any matter concerning her farms and other businesses. Four years passed quickly in learning, study, and adequate scolding as well. When the old reeve died, young Giles moved effortlessly into his position as chief steward of the extensive household of the Lady Apollonia of Aust.

Chapter Fourteen

On the Wings of the Doves

Honest in most things, Lady Apollonia did not like having to acknowledge that she was growing old. But by the time their traveling party approached Axbridge on the journey home from Somerset, the Lady whispered to Nan that she needed to rest. Six days of riding along rough country lanes had taken their toll. Her aching bones and muscles cried for respite and an extra day or two with Thomas would provide the perfect restoration, she thought.

It was decided that Nan would remain with her in Axbridge while Giles continued on to Aust. Certainly Giles was needed there; harvest and shearing times were the most demanding of his year and required the chief steward's personal supervision. Beyond that, however, Giles was certain that his Lady was anxious for him to discover if any other news had arrived at Aust to shed light upon their recent inquiries. Either way he was anxious to return as he always felt somewhat irresponsible leaving her affairs in the hands of his assistants.

Their party had barely dismounted after arrival at Father Thomas' rectory when Nan went into action. While her Ladyship chatted with her son, the faithful maid was busy in the kitchen arranging for a huge tub to be carried to the Lady's bedchamber. The cook was given no choice but to work around Nan in his preparations for the evening meal as she saw to the filling and heating of great cauldrons of water.

Immediately after they had supped, Nan urged Apollonia to bid her son an early good night. Willingly and gratefully, Apollonia followed Nan upstairs where the tub was filled and steaming in the midst of the bedchamber. Helping her Lady to strip off her traveling clothes, Nan held Apollonia's arm as she climbed into the tub. The Lady sank gratefully up to her neck in the warm soothing bath piquant with refreshing herbs. She soaked until every muscle in her body felt softened and relaxed. When Apollonia emerged from the tub, Nan, armed with a rough towel, rubbed her Lady's skin until it glowed red. After wrapping the Lady's body in a warmed gown, she tucked her under the furs of an already warmed bed. Lady Apollonia slept the sleep of infants that night so assuaged and restored that she did not wake till the sun was high in the sky.

Breaking her fast much later than usual, Apollonia felt truly refreshed and renewed. Nan, however, proceeded to hover over her Lady throughout the morning, always ready with a warm posset or some new caution against the possibility of overtiring herself. By mid-afternoon, Apollonia had been ministered to sufficiently and announced to Nan that she and Thomas were going for a long walk. Needing to move and fill her lungs with fresh air, she took her son's arm and they strolled off, out of the town and into the hills. Climbing to a quiet spot that Thomas knew offered a breathtaking view of the valley below, Apollonia was overwhelmed by the beauty of simple pleasures in life. The varying panorama of beautiful countryside flowing out from beneath her feet to the farthest horizons seemed to re-establish her equilibrium. Yet, though her sense of well-being had returned confidently, her mind could not remain at peace.

With rest and restoration, her nagging curiosity had also returned with a vengeance, still full of unanswered questions concerning the death of her first husband's henchman and especially his possible involvement in the usurpation of the English Throne by Henry Bolingbroke. She was silent at first as she and Thomas sat together breathing in the scents and fragrant color of the scene stretched below them then suddenly Apollonia asked her son, "Thomas, have you heard any particulars of the attempted Earls' rebellion last January?"

Thomas was startled by the nature of her question but he answered her without second thought. "No, Mamam, but I truly believe any rebellion to restore King Richard only hastened his death," he said sadly. "So much is unknown and speculation abounds but there is little doubt of one fact, as long as Richard lived to provide the focus for disaffected rebels, King Henry could never be secure on his throne."

Thomas looked troubled and admitted that he was sorely perplexed by the events of the past two years. "I cannot believe that the dethronement of Richard was necessary, Mamam. No matter how many of the great Lords despised him, felt injured by him, he was our anointed king." This was an admission which amounted to treason at worst or sympathy with the rebels at best. Had he been with anyone

117

other than his mother, Father Thomas would never have uttered such a sentiment.

"Once the king had been removed and Henry IV crowned and anointed," he continued, "as his subject I have no choice but to give him my unquestioning allegiance." Then he added with a frustrated sigh, "But I cannot condone murder even in the best interests of king and country. In short, precious Mamam, neither the cause of rebellion nor that of loyalty to a monarch with blood on his hands gives me any peace of mind during these troublesome times."

Apollonia took her son's hands, clasped them in her own, and looked into his eyes. "Forgive me for asking such a question, Thomas. Yours is the cause of Christ and I know that you need no reminder of your life's true vocation." She settled back against a tree and looked out at the green hills surrounding them. "Peace is never found in the courts of kings, my love, only within our souls. Keep your heart and mind in Him."

Thomas smiled, always grateful for her sincere support of his vocation but finding in her well-known curiosity an interesting contradiction to her own counsel. "I thank you my Lady Mother," Thomas said with feigned formality. "You are correct as always. But why is it then that you, so desirous of peace and tranquility, continue to concern yourself with the activities of kings and courtiers?"

Apollonia blushed like a child caught with its hand in a honey pot. "*Mea culpa*, Thomas," she laughed at herself, "My curiosity truly does confound my own peace of mind. I confess to you 'reverend father,' I am afflicted by a personal quest to seek the truth and my un-feminine need to know the why of things."

Feeling as if she must offer some explanation for her original question, Apollonia spoke candidly, "My mind cannot relinquish puzzling over the strange events which surrounded the death of King Richard and the possibility that my ancient adversary, Wilfrid de Guelf, was in some way involved in it. I know that Sir Wilfrid was favored by service with Richard's Queen Anne. He was an active member of the court party to King Richard's Queen and yet was welcomed to serve the Lancastrian Henry but I have not been able to discover what Wilfrid might have done to enable him to change allegiance so freely and without censure. I also know that he was being pursued just before his death but I have not been able to discover a clue as to the identity of the pursuers or their motives, only that they were foreigners."

Thomas could see that his mother was obviously absorbed in her personal methods of investigation through meticulous collection of facts. He knew that once she had applied herself to a great puzzle she would persist unto its solution. Her body reclined with luxurious relaxation against the tree trunk but he could see that her face was tense with speculation. Suddenly aware of his gaze upon her, Apollonia sat up and took his hand again. "Forgive your mother's inconstancy? I am so grateful to be here with you in this lovely place but still my mind wanders!" she said, "I confess it readily to you, my son and father in the eyes of the church."

"Peace my child," Thomas chided her, "I, too, have been curious about your journey into Somerset and wondered what you may have learned from it." He had been hoping for some comment from his mother of her visit with the widow de Guelf but hadn't wanted to inquire without her inviting the subject. Lady Apollonia was delighted to tell him of the sweet young creature she had discovered grafted upon an evil family tree yet determined to erase the wrongs of the past. "I found myself exceedingly sympathetic with Anne de Guelf," Apollonia admitted.

She also described Giles' interesting stories from the inn and from his old school friend, Martin, still living in Dunster. Conversation flowed freely between them through the hours of the afternoon. Thomas was amazed at his mother's ability to gather the tiniest bits of information, sort them into categories, and place them according to their value as important pieces of her self-assigned puzzle. The sun was near the western horizon by the time they walked back to the rectory where Nan awaited them anxiously.

Greeting Nan, Lady Apollonia told her and Thomas that she felt they must begin preparations to return to Aust in the morning. "But Mamam," Thomas objected, "Giles won't be expecting you for several more days. I could not possibly allow you and Nan to travel unescorted from Axbridge and I truly cannot leave the parish just now."

He insisted that they must wait till Giles returned but Lady Apollonia was feeling far too restive to linger and suggested a compromise. "We shall use the services of your sturdy Badgeworthy, Thomas," Apollonia announced and she walked on towards the dovecote to put her plan into action while Thomas continued to object to such an abrupt departure. "With no desire to invite your resentment, Mamam, you must remember your years! A lady of your age tempts serious repercussions should she fall ill in a weakened state. Truly, Mamam, you must not be tempted to continue your travels so soon. I implore you to reconsider." Lady Apollonia said nothing. She smiled at her son and nodded, truly pleased by his earnest concern.

When Thomas had first arrived in Axbridge, he was delighted to learn that the rectory had a dovecote. The idea of using birds to carry messages to his mother in Aust was especially appealing to him. At his suggestion Lady Apollonia installed a rack of rectangles, each large enough for a nesting dove, in one of the high eves of each of her houses. In every dovecote, she and Thomas kept several birds trained to fly between their respective roosts, carrying messages between mother and son, Apollonia and her favorite monasteries as well as between her and important business contacts. This gave them the tremendous advantage of being able to transmit to Giles in Aust a tiny note attached to a pigeon's leg in the relatively short period of time it would take a dove to complete the journey.

Lady Apollonia's plan was a simple one allowing her and Nan to meet Giles halfway on their journey home. By morning Giles would receive her message telling him to meet them at Bishopsworth in order to escort them home. There would be time for him to acknowledge the message, flown by a return carrier sent from Aust and arrive in Axbridge that evening.

On the morning after the exchange of messages when Apollonia and Nan departed Axbridge, Thomas' crusty old servant, Badgeworthy, keeper of his birds and general dogsbody, was told he would accompany the ladies. When the two parties reached Bishopsworth, they would part. Giles would accompany Lady Apollonia and Nan the remainder of the way to Aust while Badgeworthy happily returned to Axbridge. They would also exchange the messenger birds, returning each to its nest of origin, ready for another flight should the need arise.

Lady Apollonia and Nan were prepared to depart early on the designated morning. Giles' answer had been received and Apollonia could no longer be detained. Thomas was aware that his mother was accustomed to have things proceed according to her will. He knew her

120

to be quite competent but he always felt a nagging responsibility to protect his widowed, aged parent whether she wished it or not.

"Promise me, Mamam," Thomas said as he assisted her to her horse, "that you will promptly send a message announcing your safe return."

Apollonia assured her son it would be done, kissed him tenderly, and thanked him for the lovely days of rest and renewal which he had provided her. Then the Lady and Nan rode out through the rectory gate followed by Badgeworthy's stolid and grudging company. The world welcomed them with shades of yellow, rust, and green, translucent in the early morning sunshine. Having not yet turned onto the road towards Bishopsworth they could still hear Father Thomas calling out to them from the rectory gate, "Forgot to tell you, Mother, I have found an excellent scrivener. Master Chaucer's *Canterbury Tales* should be ready for you by Martinmass!"

There were no further words exchanged by the little party as it journeyed on. Lady Apollonia was deep in thought. Nan, too, seemed engrossed in her own concerns and Badgeworthy didn't think women worth conversation. He was a man dedicated to celibacy with absolutely no call to Christian service. Having grown up in a small cottage the youngest child among ten sisters, he could think of no greater hell than being confined in their company. There was always an elder sibling, teasing him, pinching him, betraying him or telling him what to do and it was always a SHE! Badgeworthy spent his childhood turning more and more into himself, refusing to allow that any company in life was necessary if it had to be female. But having been trapped into marriage as a teenager by sweet talk and the encouragement of his physical desires, he spent much of the rest of his adult life running from every occupation that required contact with women. When he arrived in Axbridge, a widower in his fifties, he decided he would seek employment by the local vicar. At least employed by the church he could manage his living with little need of female contact. Father Thomas was a gentle superior who appreciated the services Badgeworthy offered him. The boys of the school loved to follow him about as he saw to the priest's horse, two cows in the parish barn and the doves. Their schoolboy banter suited him and they never seemed to mind if his only response might be a grunt.

As the weather was fine and the road to Bishopsworth a fairly easy one the hours passed quickly. They soon passed a milestone indicating the village lay just ahead. Riding into the center of Bishopsworth they could see Giles already waiting for them on the village green near the church. He was standing beside his horse loosening the straps which bound the pigeon cage to his saddle.

Approaching, Nan greeted him cheerfully and Badgeworthy almost smiled and seemed to offer a grunt of satisfaction that his odious task had been completed. He and Giles exchanged the cages in which each had carried his dove. Then Badgeworthy made a silent obeisance to her Ladyship and started off towards the inn. He would, no doubt, bend the landlord's ear for an hour expounding his opinions as to the untrustworthy ill-tempered nature of females. Having been released from the trials of marriage to a scolding, vengeful, harridan when her death intervened twenty years earlier, he felt himself an expert on the subject. He would boast of his good fortune to be part of a manly priest's household where women were normally forbidden to enter past the visitor's parlour. Eventually, having slaked his thirst and his ire, Badgworthy would begin his return journey in misogynistic solitude.

Lady Apollonia had no desire to make a prolonged stop in Bishopsworth though normally she would have enjoyed a few quiet moments in its lovely parish church. They were all in need of nourishment and the local inn could provide that adequately. But she was anxious to return to Aust, especially as Giles told her of Brother William's request to speak with her as soon as she had returned. Apollonia knew William would request an interview only if he had discovered something meaningful to her concerns. As soon as they had refreshed themselves and their horses, Lady Apollonia and her party were in the saddle again. This time they rode more purposefully, the journey passed quickly and they arrived at Aust Manor late in the day.

Chapter Fifteen

William and the Apocalypse

Brother William was the perfect almoner. Entrusted with dispensing charity to the poor and the sick in his Lady's name, he also saw his role as that of brother to any and all who were in need. Originally from Lincolnshire, he had been a young canon regular, attached to a Gilbertine monastery which contained communities of both sexes. Practicing a rigid segregation of men from women, the canons of the rule served mass and heard confessions of the Gilbertine nuns. It was Brother William's kind and gentle goodness which had terminated his association with the monastery but he would never learn such a truth.

Always sensitive to any accusation of alleged lapses between the sexes, the Gilbertine Abbot had expelled Brother William from the community without telling him the nature of his crime. A nun of the order, jealous and resentful of his kindness to a younger sister, had charged William with expressing carnal desires and attempts to touch her while in the confessional. Such accusations were regarded as adequate to declare William, not only guilty, but also impure and unfaithful to his vows of chastity.

Expelled from his community in shame and disgrace William was forced to follow the path of pilgrims and beggars. All attempts to offer his clerical services were rebuffed as even the common folk despised and mocked a dishonored priest. It was as a beggar that he had come to the household of Lady Apollonia but Friar Francis recognized his speech as that of an educated man and reported William's presence among those seeking alms. The Lady asked her chaplain to send the wandering cleric to her as she wished to speak with him. During their interview, Apollonia was appalled by William's ragged and malnourished appearance but impressed with his warmth and concern for his fellow wanderers. She asked Brother William if he would be willing to serve as her almoner and assist her good Friar in the growing demands for care of the poor and dispossessed that regularly appeared at her gates. William was overcome by her willingness to grant him a position of trust and confidence. There was no doubt in his mind, a miracle had been granted to him. God had brought him to the household of this Lady as a beggar so that he might truly know how beggars were forced to live. More than a sense of divine grace, Brother William believed he had been granted a purpose in mission stronger than he had ever known before. His life would still be dedicated to serve God's poor but Lady Apollonia would provide him the means as well as the access to community among whom he would minister.

Too grateful to merely dispense alms from his Lady's largesse, Brother William also made a regular circuit of visits to cottages and villages around Aust. As the Almoner of the Lady of Aust, he was personally known and welcomed in nearly every peasant hovel and village inn. He loved poor people and they found in him a cleric whom they could trust. When Lady Apollonia had asked her household clergy to "put it about" that she was interested in reported sightings of the horsemen of the Apocalypse, she knew local folk would share their fears and secrets with Brother William as he was always the more likely to be accessible to them. It appeared from Giles message that her confidence in Brother William was to be rewarded once again.

Made aware that the Lady was due to return, Brother William waited in the hall reading from his breviary. He rose to greet her as she entered with words of warm welcome and sincere thanksgiving for her safe return. William knew that Lady Apollonia would be anxious for his news but he remained standing respectfully until she had been seated. Asking Giles and Nan to remain with them Apollonia indicated the nearest chair for William to occupy. Then she looked inquiringly into his eyes and William replied at once, "Yes, my Lady, I have found several interesting narratives which I believe may interest you. Although most of the folk I visited had simply heard the tales which flourished in the market place since the great storm, I spoke with two who claimed they could tell me where such things had been seen."

Nan and Giles were so anticipating the tale that William brought that their minds were creating questions even before they had heard it. Brother William, realizing that his Lady wished him to continue, went on. "It was during a visit to Pucklechurch that I first believed I had truly discovered an eye witness, my Lady. From a

124

bench in a back corner of the village inn, the fellow came to ask if he could speak with me after I had announced your interest in the strange occurrences during the storm." William described him as being of slight build and dark complexion. "I believe the lad is a poacher as he preferred to remain in the shadows whilst we spoke. He said he knew the woods and hills well and was frequently out late into the night. He would say nothing of the reports of the devil's horsemen, only that he had seen the devil himself, dancing on a tomb slab at Colerne Leat." Lady Apollonia's eyes grew bright with intense recognition. "He swore by the blessed Virgin, though it were a dark night and mist spread throughout the graveyard, he could see the creature jumping and howling in demonic glee as if he had stolen souls from the grave below."

"I truly thought, my Lady," Brother William went on, "that this would be the sum of my information to be brought to your attention. But traveling back to Aust, I stopped in Almondsbury to visit my good friend, Jarvis the publican, and enjoy a sip of his fine ale. On the odd chance that he might have some news, I mentioned your interest in the Four Horsemen and so on, and Jarvis told me that indeed there were two in the village with relatives who had seen them on the last night of the horrible gales."

"Four mysterious horsemen were observed riding on the Bristol road towards Aust singing in some fiendish language. Three of them were knights in foreign dress and the fourth was a huge hooded creature that seemed to flop about in his saddle as if skeletal Death himself were riding a great pale horse." William paused and then added, "I questioned the publican very closely, my Lady, and I trust everything he said to be an accurate reporting. It was of course hearsay but he swore he is cousin to the witnesses and would stake his life on their word."

Lady Apollonia remained silent but Nan and Giles were both murmuring aloud to each other at these mysterious happenings. Giles was the first to speak, "Brother William, did your friend give any other detail of the knights: their armor, their insignia, or any identifying badge?"

Shaking his head William could only add, "These were illiterate common village folk and it was at the height of the storm, Master Digby. The night was too black and wild for them to notice such fine details. But the family who saw the riders lives in a small cot close to the Bristol road. They heard the strange singing voices and hurried to their door only able to see the four horsemen in flashes of lightening as they galloped past, I'm afraid."

Nan was thinking of her childhood home and couldn't restrain herself from asking, "But what of the devil in Colerne Leat? Are you certain that the man with whom you spoke was trustworthy? He could have been telling a good story to achieve alms from you, nothing more."

"Your suggestion would have merit, Mistress Nan, but the man was unwilling to take anything from me," Brother William answered. "I believe he was truly frightened by his vision in the night and it was my clerical garb which reassured him. He made no attempt to cadge. When I tried to give the poor lad a penny, he begged me to give it to the church and pray for him. This did not seem the behaviour of a charlatan or churl," Brother William concluded.

They all agreed that a poor man who refused a coin would indeed be more likely concerned for his soul than his gain. Still Brother William's tales had the ring of fantasy about them. "I, for one, have difficulty accepting the commons' resort to superstition and magic as explanation of events, my Lady," Giles volunteered at last. "Shouldn't we be looking for some reasonable account for these sightings?"

"I believe that Satanas lurks in many forms to entrap unwary souls," Nan murmured quietly, "but what can these sightings mean to us?"

"There is no need for good folk to fear," Brother William said reassuringly to the little maid. "But Master Digby has put a fine point upon it. More likely these were men abroad in the storm that night rather than demons. The great unanswered questions remain: who were they and what their purpose was?"

Evening was descending and Lady Apollonia felt a need to retire to her chamber for a brief rest before supper. Standing to give her hand to her loyal cleric, she offered her sincere appreciation. "Brother William, I cannot thank you enough for your excellent account. You have brought me far more good grain of fact than I ever expected we should be able to sift from the chaff of gossip and rumor abroad in the county."

Truly pleased by her words, William turned a bit pink about his cheeks and lowered his head. "I await your command to continue to pursue any further line of inquiry you may wish, my Lady," he added with a shy smile.

Apollonia smiled and placed her hand on his shoulder. "At this moment, my will is to rest and I urge all of you to advantage yourselves of a good night's repose. I shall take supper in my chamber and resort to private devotions before retiring. Kindly convey my apologies for being absent from household vespers to Friar Francis."

As Brother William bent to kiss her hand and take his leave, the Lady made one more request of him. "I have so much to be thankful for this day. Would you offer a prayer of thanks and ask God's blessing upon us all before we part for the evening?"

"Gladly my Lady," the canon responded, and as they all kneeled about him, he signed and prayed over their bowed heads with the simple words of a man of great faith. Listening again to the prayer of her good and faithful almoner, Lady Apollonia felt genuinely grateful to be home, able to retire to her own chamber, but most especially to her own bed.

Chapter Sixteen

Pursuit of Night Riders

Giles was gone before sunup the following morning, riding to check and guarantee proper storage of the grain harvest in one of his Lady's farms northeast of Aust. Immediately after Prime, the sunrise service sung in chapel, Nan happily retreated to her sewing room. Travel was not the stimulating tonic to her it seemed to provide her Lady. Nan preferred to remain at home, comfortable within familiar surroundings, especially in this, her domain of fresh, herb scented fustians and linens. As the Lady had no need of her this day, Nan had drawn a table full of her mending and sorting tasks close to the window. Singing to herself, she couldn't have been happier than to be spending this day far from any horse, cart or wagon. She would celebrate this lovely day at home!

Lady Apollonia, however, urgently wished to locate some physical evidence of the route of the horsemen described by Brother William's witnesses. She had summoned Owen to accompany her immediately after breaking the morning fast so that they might ride out together and find Alwan. Though early, the morning did appear to be brightening from its dull, grey beginnings. Lady Apollonia carried her rain cloak in the contrary wish that its presence might discourage possible showers. She feared that rain would greatly complicate her hopes of discovery as the passage of time had already obscured important evidence. It would be difficult enough to find tracks more than three weeks old but a hopeless task in pouring rain. Arriving at Alwan's hut, she and Owen were delighted to find the forester sitting by his door mending traps. The clearing around his dwelling's entrance was arrayed with snares, nets and traps many created from his imagination and born out of his years' experience with animal habits and specific needs of terrain.

Seeing Owen and his Lady approach, Alwan dropped the work of his hands while his face erupted into a massive smile. He stood at once and doffed his broad brimmed hat to greet Apollonia. Owen shouted the familiar Welsh greeting between them and leaped from his horse to clamber about the collection of gear lying, as if for inspection, about the clearing. Alwan, sensing a special honor, was immensely pleased by his Lady's visit. He cherished a love and respect for her which had grown through years of being part of her household and proudly wearing the badge of her affinity. Moreover, Lady Apollonia had become for him a living example of goodness that grants esteem to others, to men and women of all stations. A young man of medium height with lean powerful limbs, long striding legs and silent graceful movements, Alwan assisted her dismount and immediately brought a stool upon which she could rest. Apollonia was always made aware of Alwan's worshipful attitude towards her. The young man never attempted to conceal it; had neither the guile nor pretense to wish to hide his feelings. This unspoken understanding guarded their friendship as Apollonia acknowledged her responsibility to be worthy of his worship while still searching for occasions when she could express her limits and look to him for guidance. "Gramercy, Alwan, grace and peace be with you. Shall we have rain this day, what say you?" she asked in full confidence of his ability to settle her annoyance at the grey clouds overhead.

"Nay, m'Lady, ne' rain, be they 'igh cloud, racin' wi' th' wind, Oi reken."

"Praise to God for his mercy. I am in need of your tracking skill, Alwan, and the trail which we seek will not be an easy one." Alwan responded with a nod and directly sat himself upon the ground at her feet attentive to her will.

Lady Apollonia returned his ready smile and placed into his hands a small parcel of currant pastries which she knew he especially enjoyed. "These will keep well in your larder until we return," she said. "I gathered the currants myself and know them to be fat and sweet." He received the gift with a shy smile and put it inside his dwelling immediately. To avoid any distraction from the task which she had come to ask of him, he returned promptly to resume his place.

"You are a valued servant, Alwan," she said, looking into his uplifted face. "I believe that you are the most skilled forester in the shire and your ability to locate the whereabouts of the head of Sir Wilfrid was an amazing display of that special skill." Alwan's heart soared in the warmth of her praise and the weathered brown skin of his cheeks glowed russet.

"Now I must ask if you would be willing to assist me again but this time we shall be searching for a vague and very cold trail."

"Aye, m' Lady. What'eer ye may wish." Alwan shook his head enthusiastically urging her to continue.

"I would like you to accompany Owen and me to Almondsbury this morning, as I hope, my excellent forester, you shall be able to discover the hoof prints of that one particular horse which you said were so distinct under the tree where Sir Wilfrid died." Listening as if anticipating her every word, Alwan continued to nod in agreement.

"In faith, I am hoping that we may discover the tracks of three unknown riders, whom I believe were accompanying Sir Wilfrid on the night of his death. But it will be his mount with its distinctive shoe you described for me which, I pray, will lead us to them. A strange group of riders were seen near Almondsbury on the Bristol Road towards Aust and if this group included Sir Wilfrid's horse I am hopeful that we might be able to determine where it was they intended to go on the night of the great storm." Apollonia could see a marked change in Alwan's expression. He was thinking of the length of time elapsed since his earlier discovery and the heavy commerce upon the Bristol road. Normally optimistic and willing to succeed in any task given him by his mistress, Alwan could summon but meager hopes of success in this effort.

"Bes' we be off straightawaiy so's not to miss bes' light, m'Lady," he said firmly.

Apollonia always enjoyed being with Owen and Alwan as music was guaranteed to accompany all that they did. Seldom found without their instruments near to hand, Owen usually had his small harp slung across his back while Alwan's flute hung from his belt. They were both blessed with buoyant voices and each seemed to have an endless store of songs in Welsh and in English. Sometimes Alwan would begin a song and Owen would join in. Others were begun with Owen's clear voice and Alwan adding his mellow baritone an octave lower. Many of their songs were of heroes, of lady loves, and of ancient kings. Some of the comic ones were about common folk; the most humorous told of the foibles of weak priests and renegade monks. "Singing hearts make light work," Lady Apollonia remembered a joyous friar once told her. Listening to these pure and unselfconscious young men's voices fill the air with song made their journey along the road from Aust towards Almondsbury pass very quickly. Eventually bright sunshine illuminated the canopy of trees overhead and birds' song seemed encouraged by the human melodies. Alwan had been correct, Apollonia smiled to herself, as the day had brightened considerably by the time they saw the first milestones to Almondsbury appear in the distance.

There were not many occupied cottages along the road but one, especially, they noticed nearly opened its door upon the way. It was within two miles of Almondsbury village and remote enough to have no other neighbors. At that place Lady Apollonia asked Alwan to begin his search. Any other man would have given up with endless excuses at the Promethean impossibility of it. Alwan said nothing but his worst fears were realized as he contemplated the condition of the highway. The muddy roadway bore deep criss-crossing scars of many carts, heavy-laden with harvested goods traveling towards Bristol markets. Undaunted Alwan painstakingly examined the slough of wheel ruts, washouts, animal droppings, amidst a multitude of hoof prints left by draft and pack animals and driven herds, stamped in mad array one atop the other. He asked Lady Apollonia and Owen to remain in a nearby shady grove where they could sit comfortably and keep the horses tethered. Then he walked slowly along the sides of the road, first the right and then the opposite.

Again Alwan walked nearly to Almondsbury on one side of the road. Then he crossed and began walking slowly back along the other side. He approached the cottage then continued walking back towards Aust, going some distance before crossing to the other side and duplicating his efforts by walking slowly back to the spot where Apollonia and Owen awaited him. Pausing to ponder a moment, he called out to his waiting companions and asked them to bring the horses and walk along behind him. He said that he thought he had found one hopeful imprint farther out from the village but he could not be certain. It was pointed towards Aust, however, so he felt they must walk further along the road in the hope of finding a surer marking.

Near the intersection of the Awkley to Tockington lanes which branched off from the Bristol road, Alwan found the sure print he had been seeking in the left berme, wandering a bit as if the horse were being led rather than controlled by its rider.

"Wier go'n the roight waiy tiz certain m'Lady," he shouted encouragingly. "Oi've not made out t'other t'ree riders in th' mire o' th' road, but Oi know Oi 'ave found 'orse Sir Wilfrid were rid'n."

Lady Apollonia smiled confidently at him. "Carry on, Alwan, we shall remain close behind you." He returned to his search walking at a snail's pace and looking as if he were sniffing every square inch of their path. He had one hopeful mark to follow and that encouraged him. The strangely shaped shoe of Sir Wilfrid's horse reappeared regularly enough out of the left berme of the muddy road to keep Alwan on the track like a relentless bloodhound.

Finally, a section of the lane intersecting the Bristol way leading towards Oveston and Elberton captured his entire attention. Thick forests lined both sides of the lane but Alwan kept his eyes on the road pushing on as if driven. With a sudden hoot and howl he shouted back to the Lady and Owen. "Oi've fou'n 'em awl, M'lady!" and he dashed into the woods.

Apollonia and Owen had all they could do to keep up, especially as Owen had three horses to lead along. Alwan was well ahead of them but suddenly stopped. On the relatively undisturbed floor of the woods the four horsemen's tracks had become more distinct and easier to follow. Alwan began to run about excitedly in a rough circle beneath a great canopy of large oak trees. Apollonia approached the area with Owen following more slowly. "The four horsemen must have turned off the road in the worsening storm, possibly seeking shelter in the woods," she thought to herself.

Alwan called her to look at a collection of hoof prints surrounding one particularly massive oak. "Thay woaited 'eer," he said excitedly. There was no mistaking it. The riders must have had difficulty calming their beasts, jittery and terrified by the raging gale. Among their stamping hoof prints were marks made by the feet of at least three dismounted men, huddled together, anchoring themselves against the wind by clinging to the trunk of a sturdy tree.

"Alwan, " Lady Apollonia called softly to her forester, "See if Sir Wilfrid's horse prints leave this place." The sharp well-trained eyes of the tracker began to search from the center of the group of hoofprints to the perimeter of the area. Walking in an ever increasing circle he called out from an area of broken branches. "'EE's tak'n awf 'ere, M'Lady, "'an 'ees 'eaded fore Pilnin'"

To be certain of the direction which Sir Wilfrid's mount had taken during the storm, Alwan, forgetting his "by your leave," took the reins from Owen's hand and remounted his horse continued to follow the tracks out of the clearing. Lady Apollonia and Owen, too, quickly returned to their saddles and pressed on in his wake riding slowly through the dimmer light and treacherous terrain of the thick woods. They passed near to Awkley but Alwan did not stop and as he continued, so too his followers in cautious pursuit. Finally the Lady and Owen saw Alwan pull up in a thicket of brush and gorse beneath a huge oak tree. One low-slung, sinister forked branch reached out beckoning towards the forewarned and wary party gazing at it now with circumspect wonder.

"Is 'ead were jammed t'ere, when I foun' im," Alwan pointed out a flat, shelf-like projection in the thick limb crotch. V-shaped like the forearm, elbow, and upper arm of a powerfully muscled assassin, this mighty limb had become the pincers by which Sir Wilfrid's head had been snared and relentlessly torn from his body.

"Invaluable Alwan," Apollonia exulted, "I knew you could do it! You have brought us full circle. By locating the tracks of his mounted captors, you have determined the place of their refuge against the storm, the moment of Sir Wilfrid's breakaway, and his thundering path towards death. Well done, my faithful forester, well done, indeed!"

Excitedly Lady Apollonia dismounted and walked around the tree examining the limb very carefully. Then, completely startling her young companions, she dropped to her hands and knees for a closer look at the earth beneath the tree. The horseshoe tracks were well-preserved in this untroubled area of the forest and they spoke of a great beast's stamping, lunging and pressing to flee in terror.

Rising at last, the Lady regained her composure quickly righting her headdress somewhat askew from her excited leap from her horse to the ground. Brushing off her skirt and attempting to resume her normal self-possession, her flushed face betrayed the true state of her aroused enthusiasm. "Excellent work, Alwan," Apollonia said repeating herself enthusiastically. "You have found all that I hoped and more."

Savoring her lavish compliments, Alwan's face glowed contentedly. Then his Lady added, "I think we can return home now but I shall need you to come to the manor first thing in the morning prepared to travel for several days?"

Alwan said that he would be ready as she wished. "And you Owen, will you be willing to travel with Alwan? I should like you both to make a journey for me into Wales beginning tomorrow morning. Is that agreeable?"

Owen could hardly agree quickly enough. "Oh yes, my Lady. Whatever your errand, I am ready now!" After spending one whole day doing nothing more important than leading horses in Alwan's wake, Owen was thrilled to think that he was to be sent with Alwan on an important mission. Looking at his older friend, Owen could see

Alwan's eyes shining with equal anticipation; both of the young Welshmen could sense adventure in the offing. But they must wait till the morrow to learn its particulars and so they all turned towards Aust with songs not only to cheer their journey but also to celebrate all that lay ahead. Alwan rode near his Lady until the party reached his clearing. He then waved a hearty Godspeed to Apollonia and Owen as they continued on the path towards Aust. With an unusual burst of speed, the forester set about gathering in all of his gear still spread about the hut. Once all parts and pieces were collected and stowed carefully, he could turn his attention to supper and his currant cakes.

Chapter Seventeen

Alwan and Owen Lay a Snare

As the Lady emerged from her chapel the following morning, Alwan and Owen were eagerly awaiting her with their horses saddled and ready in the courtyard. Signaling them to come to her, the lads followed into the hall where she drew aside to a quiet corner and bade them be seated. "Your assignment is somewhat fluid. I fear I am unable to be very specific. But to begin, I wish for you both to take the ferry from Aust to Wales. Speak freely with the ferryman during your crossing and encourage him to tell you about those whom he ferried across after the great gales."

She paused for a moment to see that they understood her intent. "I want you to learn anything that you can about three foreign knights, quite likely they are German knights," she said and as if to offer explanation she added, "Owen, you will remember the lands of the German Emperor that you have studied with Friar Francis. It is possible these knights are his subjects."

"Yes my Lady, many German principalities comprise the Holy Roman Empire," Owen said quoting the words of his teacher.

"Indeed, Lad, that is so. You have learned your lessons well." She continued her instructions. "If the ferryman tells you that he carried such knights across to Wales, ask him if he noticed which way they turned, towards Caldicot or to Chepstow."

Owen and Alwan were earnestly silent taking careful note of her words. "If the ferryman says no such persons crossed with him, return and report to me immediately. Should that be the case, our quest is ended. But should he remember them and I believe he will, you must take the road towards the nearest town in the same direction. Once these knights entered Wales someone will surely have noticed their foreign ways and be able to tell you where they have gone."

Now Apollonia's face grew very serious. "Above all else, I trust you both to be concerned for each other's safety and to do nothing which will bring suspicion upon yourselves. But if you can find the foreign knights, you are to take up anonymous positions where you may quietly watch them. I wish to know as soon as they move to return to England. Should that happen within a matter of days you are to return also and report their movements to me. If they seem prepared to remain indefinitely come home and we shall make other plans. Here are two purses adequate to keep you well on your journey."

Lady Apollonia asked each of her young men if they had any questions or reservations concerning the task she had given them. Neither offered any and both seemed anxious to move on towards the ferry. Alwan was quiet in his acceptance of responsibility while Owen seemed to tremble in excited anticipation. Lady Apollonia placed a hand on each of their shoulders calling the Father's blessing upon them and wishing them Godspeed. "I shall pray daily for your early safe return. But I require your pledge that you will employ great care and take no foolhardy risks." With that injunction, her hand especially squeezed Owen's shoulder.

Alwan and Owen swore they would respect her every wish but such was their excitement that Apollonia could tell they were thinking of their quest, glad to be going to Wales and even happier to be making the journey together. They seemed so young and eager yet so like elder and younger brothers, she knew they would closely guard each other's safety. She couldn't have selected better agents, she told herself, to achieve the information which she guessed would be found across the Severn but neither could she suppress her concern for the unknown they may encounter.

For centuries the village of Aust had been an important staging post on any journey to south Wales. Beginning as a place to ford the treacherous Severn River in very ancient times, Aust was mentioned by Roman chroniclers when an entire legion was lost there. A flash tide caught the invaders off guard and destroyed them as surely as the closing of the Red Sea had drowned Pharaoh's chariots.

The local residents, on both sides of the river, were well acquainted with its perilous currents and tidal phenomenon, granting it a wary respect. Strangers were fortunate to find themselves in the hands of a native boatman when needing to be ferried to the opposite bank. Any attempt to cross without such experience at the helm was foolhardy indeed.

Alwan and Owen knew the boatman of Aust ferry well enough to realize that he was dour and uncommunicative with all his passengers. They also knew he was Welsh. Lady Apollonia, by instructing them to ferry across with him, assumed they would be able with their songs and their knowledge of his language to succeed in

136

opening doors to his information which would remain solidly closed to any other interrogator. Thus it was they began their fair weather crossing full of songs of the heroes celebrated by the Welsh bards.

A short dark Celt of unknown years, the boatman pushed off from the dock, skillfully guiding the ferry into the swirling currents. Alwan and Owen's songs flowing from the bow of the boat obviously pleased him. Nothing could touch his Welsh soul as sweetly as poetic lines sung from the bards' heroic epics or songs of the grand days when Wales was an independent kingdom. Fully occupied by the steering of his boat through eddies and currents which could capsize the unwary, the boatman did not converse with his passengers. He had no time for speech during the crossing and waited until he had safely docked the craft on the Welsh bank to heartily thank Alwan and Owen for their songs. He shyly inquired if they could stay their journey long enough to favor him with one verse of a favorite tune.

Glad to oblige and as it was well known to them, Owen recited a poetic prologue to the song which Alwan began in his full rich baritone. Adding a bright descant, Owen joined Alwan and they finished the ballad in flowing harmony. The boatman was so truly pleased that his morose countenance disappeared altogether. Gaelic appreciation and thanks flowed from his lips like the rushing river they had just crossed.

Modestly ignoring the praise yet acknowledging the thanks, Owen asked the boatman, with the open-hearted simplicity of a boy, if he had seen many foreigners making their way to Cymru. His tone steeped in disgust, the ferryman responded that far too many English were going to suit him. But Owen persisted, "Do ye ever see any foreigners from over the water?" At this the boatman smiled and said three very stupid ones did cross with him not long ago, just after the gales. They couldn't speak any intelligible language and they were so ignorant as to overpay him for the crossing.

Alwan casually wondered aloud what in the world such folk would be doing in Wales? Which way would they go? The boatman muttered that he cared not at all if they went straight to Hell but, as he remembered, they turned to take Chepstow road. How curious, Alwan remarked to their new friend, that it should be the very same direction he and Owen were traveling. But, he added with a smile, they would be returning within a week or two and would be glad of his services once again. Being careful not to overpay the ferryman, they thanked him for the safe crossing and mounted up to follow the road towards Chepstow.

Riding up from the Severn till they came to the estuary of the River Wye, Alwan and Owen continued in high spirited and exuberant enjoyment of the easily successful beginnings of their Lady's mission. Following the east bank of the Wye, they could see from a distance why Chepstow had always been regarded as a major key to the conquest and occupation of Wales. It was a flourishing small river port which received ships from Bristol, Gloucester and European vessels as well. But looming like a gigantic shadow over the town below, the long curtain walls of Chepstow Castle announced an aggressive English presence at the main point of entry to the Welsh side of the Wye Valley. Riding across the bridge over the Wye, Owen and Alwan were stunned into silence. They had never seen anything so impressive or so intimidating.

With the decline of its military role during the past century, the castle had been converted to use as a nobleman's residence, presently held by Thomas Mowbray, Duke of Norfolk. Knights traveling into Wales would have undoubtedly been welcomed at the castle, especially since the uprising of Owain Glyndwr had been proclaimed within the past month. To make their first inquiries, however, Owen and Alwan decided to seek out the company of other Welshmen taking their ale in the inn nearest the castle gate. Giving their horses over to a stable hand for feeding and care, the two travelers from Aust entered the dark, low beamed public room of the inn now filled with local tradesmen and townsfolk.

Silence seized every tongue in the room as Alwan and Owen entered. In Welsh Alwan hailed the landlord and shouted out a need of tankards enough to clear the dust of the road from their throats. Magically, Alwan's Welsh tongue secured the lads' acceptability and brought a return of the normal hum of conversation as their drinks appeared quickly in the hands of a Celtic wench with mischievous dark eyes. Welshmen in the best of times maintained a silent, some said sullen, distance from any Englishmen whom they considered foreign occupiers of their homeland since the days of the first King Edward. Now with the claim of Owain Glyndwr, descendant of Welsh princes, to be the true Prince of Wales, hope of throwing back the English had rekindled in the hearts of many; others of more cautious nature preferred to express no opinion. Silence by representatives of both views seemed prudent, at least until the full identity of strangers could be established.

Alwan and Owen were adopted by the regulars when a series of songs was begun from one corner of the crowded room and the verses of the lyric were continued round the room. Their voices blended easily into the songs which had probably begun as simple folk tales put to music. Soon, however, someone tried to raise a song of Welsh victory and the assembled group seemed reluctant to risk joining in. Owen, lifting his harp to his chest, began to sing a tale of Arthur, legendary king in England but heroic Briton to Welsh thinking. The room quieted again as imaginations took flight through the ballad's celebration of days of glory long gone, long remembered. It was a safer subject and the men of Chepstow were content to listen to Owen's beautiful voice as it filled the rooms and touched their hearts.

Owen blushed at the generous praise accorded him by all in the room as he finished and soon Owen, the minstrel's son, and his elder companion were being urged to join smaller groups, share their conversation, ale and song. The evening passed joyfully, lavishly spent in music and poetry. At each interlude, Owen or Alwan would ask his companions about the possible presence of strange foreign knights in the town but no one remembered seeing any such newcomers. At the closing hour, Owen and Alwan bade their new friends a hearty good night and followed the landlord to the lodging chambers overhead. Casually inquiring of him how business had been and were many foreigners coming to Chepstow during these days, the landlord scowled saying scornfully, "If there were, they weren't lodging 'ere." Instead, he continued to complain, English knights were coming in great numbers but riding on to the Marches where the lords were in need of troops to put down Glyndwr. If foreigners were coming to Chepstow, he added, they were staying at the castle during these troubled days probably unwilling to lodge with the locals.

"But we've heard that even some German knights have come to take part in the fighting," Owen said, his eyes wide with innocent wonder.

"If that be the case, lad, they've not mixed with the likes o' us," their host said with emphasis.

Lying together alone in the dark room, Alwan and Owen fell to whispering between themselves. They were disappointed in having found no clues to the whereabouts of the three German knights whom their Lady had asked them to trace. Asking casual questions among the locals throughout the evening had achieved no more encouraging news than that received from their landlord. Their first day, begun with such a sense of excitement, had ended in dismal failure.

"Surely," Owen whispered, "if the knights had come to Chepstow town someone would have noticed their foreign ways and strangers' accents. Perhaps we have come to the wrong place, Alwan, perhaps the ferryman led us astray."

"We cawn't gi'e up s' soon, Owen," Alwan told his young friend. He knew from long experience that if one trap did not catch the prey often a new design in a new place might succeed. "In th' morn we mus' try th' cawstle. Landlor' be roight a'roain. Knights ne'er stay wi' th' common folk if t'ere be welcome by th' cawstle gentles." Thus it was decided that they must go to the castle and gain entrance by seeking employment there. Once inside its walls they might discover the whereabouts of the knights or at the very least learn if their journey to Chepstow had truly been in vain. Owen was excited by the romantic prospect of actually entering the massive stone walls of a real castle. Throughout his youth, he had read tales and sung songs of the great castles of myth and legend with their halls filled by companies of brave knights and lovely ladies. Alwan's more practical thoughts, however, concentrated within his favorite province enlarging the idea that such an impertinence would be a most unusual test of his forester's skill. Chuckling at himself he whispered to Owen, "Oi've ne'er laid a snare big as this'n."

After breaking their fast the following morning, Owen and Alwan left their horses in the care of the inn's stable and walked together up the road towards the castle's ramparts carrying only those belongings which they could carry or normally wear on their backs. As it neared the river, the road turned and began a long incline upward. The castle's outer gatehouse could be seen straddling the road ahead, halting all travelers upon the way. From the angle of approach taken by Alwan and Owen, the castle appeared to be tall and massive but narrow. What they could not realize was the tremendous length of it beyond the visible wall of the eastern lower bailey.

Stretching on behind the great gatehouse guarding the main entry lay another large middle bailey concealed by its east curtain wall. A huge rectangular keep stood between the middle and a succeeding upper bailey which was crowned at its uppermost end by a towered courtyard leading to the higher gatehouse and barbican. If they could have seen the castle from the river, the travelers would have craned their necks to take in the prodigious wall of stone projected skyward from a sheer rock face, defending a portion of the Wye nearly an eighth of a mile long.

Alwan and Owen were speechless. The castle seemed to grow ever larger and more intimidating as it glowered upon them directly ahead in their path. Neither would have had the courage to proceed with their plan had they not accompanied each other. Their larking about had ended abruptly as they left the town behind and each lad slowly began to realize the brazen effrontery of their scheme. Armed men were posted about the great gatehouse and the drawbridge was down but these things added little to the young travelers' sense of security. Twin towers, guarded by sets of cruciform arrow-slits in each of three levels seemed the horns and eyes of a monstrous evilly squinting head; its gaping maw dripped with metal capped teeth from the suspended portcullis; its drawbridge tongue lay beckoning to lap them up.

The Duke of Norfolk's pennon was waving brilliantly from the main tower and had the travelers from Aust been aware of its significance, they might have guessed their presence would be more warmly received than their imaginations now conspired to assure them of the contrary. To deal with the threat to south Wales from the Welsh uprising, the Duke of Norfolk was in residence examining the state of readiness of Chepstow should he be ordered to garrison the castle against Owain Glyndwr. The Duke's army of retainers and household affinity filled the castle walls which on the inside appeared to be crawling with feverish activity needed to support such a large retinue. Every man wore the Mowbray livery and each member of the household was marked by the ducal badge.

Approaching the gatehouse, Alwan and Owen were roughly halted by one of the guards. "What's this then? State your business or be off, vagabonds!" The brute made a barrier of his halberd and with it shoved the two lads back from the gate. But Alwan's permanent grin presented his first line of defense. Doffing his hat he said quickly, "'Tis service we wish to offer, master. Be t'ere no need in kitchen f'r ready 'ands or ears in 'all needin' songs?" The guard kept his halberd levelly aimed at Alwan's midsection but sent a comrade to seek the opinion of a superior. Soon Alwan and Owen were allowed to pass.

The gatehouse ceiling above them was pierced with murder holes and drumming sounds of swiftly moving feet surrounded them as they timidly walked through the inner passage between its towers. Strange and frightening to two nervous souls below unaware of its source the noise emanated from a suite of rooms on the floor overhead. These were the lodgings of the constable of the castle through which a herd of harried retainers were running simply to keep up with the demands of the recently arrived Duke of Norfolk.

Directed to proceed across the lower bailey towards the kitchen, Alwan felt Owen take hold of the hem of his tunic. This shy grasp for reassurance pierced the woodsman's gentle heart as he faced, for the first time, his role as elder protector and leader of their expedition. Alwan knew Owen to be courageous and intelligent for his years and a trustworthy companion at all times but at that singular moment in their lives, the boy was afraid. Alwan turned his face to one side and whispered behind the back of a hand in mock triumph, "We did 'er, Owen, we'r in." Owen smiled weakly but lifted his shoulders and sucked in a huge breath. Grinning confidently, Alwan pushed his hat rakishly to one side and exaggerated the nonchalance of his loping gait. Beneath a grinning bravado, however, the self-appointed leader wondered silently how to convince himself of the nature of their victory. Indeed, they had won entry but now inside the castle each of the Welsh lads wondered to himself what could they possibly learn of the plans of the gentles? What lay ahead only God would foretell.

Chapter Eighteen

In the Courts of the Great

They were indeed welcome as they soon learned. Armand, the castle steward was a startlingly thin man with a gourd-shaped head and twitching face, nearly collided with Alwan and Owen as he rushed to meet them in the middle of the bailey. Even standing in stationary position, Armand seemed a study in perpetual movement. His foot beat a steady tattoo upon the ground, his hands opened and closed in rhythmic accompaniment, his torso leaned from one side to the other all the while he impatiently demanded a description of their skills. "But be brief, my lads, be brief!" he hastened to add. Upon learning that Alwan was accomplished at skinning and dressing game for cooking and that the lads together performed as traveling minstrels, Armand heaved a sigh of relief which appeared to drain his entire body. "Praise be to God," he mumbled crossing himself. "We haven't a moment to lose. Follow me!" he commanded and he ran off with the lads scurrying along to keep up with him. "Cook will put you both to work straightaway," he called over his shoulder. Owen and Alwan looked at each other in sincere alarm for this desperate man. They had never heard anyone speak so rapidly.

Rushing his charges to the ground level door of the kitchen, the steward placed them under the direction of the master cook. Before he left, however, he rattled off a list of instructions. They must find their way to the minstrel's gallery early and be ready to play in the hall the moment his grace entered. "My Lord of Norfolk likes to have music throughout his meal and, thus far, we have found no truly pleasing musicians in this God-forsaken country," he gasped for breath. "Do not be tardy, have your instruments with you and do your best to please or we shall all suffer the consequences!" As he spoke, the steward's bony limbs continued to bend and press forward as if winding up towards a new explosion of activity. When Armand abruptly left them to rush out of the kitchen, Alwan looked at Owen and they both inhaled a great breath. Smiling to each other, each felt himself gasping from the vocal exertions recently poured upon them.

Chepstow Castle's huge kitchen was a hub of noise and activity on all sides of the two massive fireplaces ablaze behind a web of spits already turning to roast the hundreds of carcasses needed to serve the ducal household which would gather in the great hall for the evening meal. Alwan, so skillful with a knife that he could do the work of two, attacked the mountain of meat still needing dressing. Owen stayed with him going through the motions but dependent upon his friend's skill to actually complete the task. At Alwan's suggestion Owen began to pluck feathers from a great pile of birds and soon had overcome his fear finding the novelty of their situation quite exciting.

The trestle which served as their work table was in a quiet corner of the busy kitchen prompting Alwan and Owen to sing to lighten their spirits and add rhythm to their work. Servants, pages and kitchen maids crashing through their appointed tasks soon began to pause and search for the source of the songs emanating from a far corner and reflecting down throughout the noisy kitchen from its vaulted ceiling above their heads. Drawn to the worktable where the lads sang unaware of the notice they caused, Owen and Alwan looked up to see themselves surrounded by a small audience full of encouragement to the musicians. Alwan's lined brown face grinned broadly welcoming the praise but even more this chance to begin to meet a few of the denizens of the castle kitchen: Crispin, Nel, Babs, Gerard, Antony, an entire corps of serving hands whose work kept them running between ground floor and the upper halls, many stopped long enough to drop a cheery, "Well done, lads!" or at least whistle and hum along behind a cheeky wink of appreciation. Alwan noticed that Owen, too, more relaxed now with his position seemed to warm to their new acquaintances quickly. A congenial pair, Alwan and Owen soon found themselves being asked if they might sing a favorite request or a jollier tune and, of course, many repeats of a few folk tunes of questionable morality to lighten the daily grind.

Throughout the morning and into the afternoon Alwan and Owen were pleased to learn that the kitchen was the heart of the castle where the entire service staff came at one time or another during the day or into the evening. It was the perfect place for inquiring ears to overhear gossip and chatter as the servants freely expressed their opinions of the castle's lordly inhabitants safely out of earshot. By mid-afternoon songs and teasing banter had established an especially friendly exchange between Alwan and several of the serving wenches. He and Owen were delighted when a few casual questions helped them to learn that the German knights had come to seek the hospitality of the duke several weeks earlier. But two of the knights, the good-looking younger ones, they were told, had already taken ship from Chepstow to return to their homeland across the water and were not expected to return. Only one remained and he was the most frightening of the lot, a saucy redhead named Freda told them. She served to clean the German knight's chamber and serve him when necessary as he had no squire nor body servant accompanying him. She surely did not like it. He was so difficult to understand and his long melancholy face never smiled. He kept very much to himself, Freda told them, brooding about as if waiting for Judgement. She truly wished that he, too, would have returned home with his companions and freed her from his suspicious and ill-tempered scolding.

Freda was full of gossip and delighted in sharing her tales with the new kitchen boys. She told Alwan and Owen that a great quarrel had erupted among the German knights shortly after their arrival at Chepstow. Hiding in the corridor near their chambers, she had listened as the Germans argued vehemently amongst themselves. Shouting and cursing, she knew no word of their tongue but was sure the knights were swearing, they had nearly come to blows before the older warrior refused to speak further with his fellow knights and ordered them from his presence. In disgust, she said, the younger men departed the following day without ever looking back at their dour former companion standing upon the castle wall.

Owen asked if Freda could point out the old knight to him in the great hall. "Oh sweeting, ye shan't miss 'im. 'Ee sits at table lookin' like 'oly Jerome in the wilderness," she told him, " 'an ee cuddles wi' no'on. Cold as th' bishop's bum, ee is."

Unnoticed by Freda, Owen and Alwan exchanged a fleeting nod of triumph. Once they had definitely identified the knight they were well placed to be able to watch him and his movements from a proper distance. Although their Lady of Aust had assigned them to follow three, as only one knight was left, they would attach to him like a thistle.

Excited anticipation seemed to drag out the hours still required of them in the kitchen. Scarcely concealing their impatience, the young men were finally released by cook who sent them to the well to wash and then upstairs to prepare for their first experience of entertaining at the evening meal in the great hall of the castle. "You had best be worthy," the dubious cook told the rustic looking lads with emphatic warning. "All the greats will be in the hall this night!"

To serve Chepstow Castle's great hall, pages had to carry their huge trays of meat and wine vessels from the kitchen at ground level through a long service passage and up a steep flight of stairs. At the top of the stairway, a central service entrance to the hall passed between the buttery and pantry. All of the important functions of these spaces were hidden from view by an exquisitely carved wooden screen, so massive that it strode across the width of the end of the hall like a free-standing wall topped by a narrow stage.

Having arrayed themselves in the livery tabards emblazoned with Norfolk's crest, Alwan and Owen entered the dark area behind the great hall screen. They were told to ascend a narrow circular wooden stairway, ingenuously carved to integrate with the foliate designs of the screen. Emerging with harp and flute upon its uppermost platform which served as the minstrels' gallery, their mouths dropped in wonder as they overlooked the brilliant vast hall, alive with frantic activity beneath them.

It was a sight they never could have imagined. Regal enough to receive a king, the walls were whitewashed to perfection and had the outline of their stone courses painted in bright red. Overhead stone corbels held aloft huge oak ceiling support beams. Every corbel was carved in fantastic arrays of floral and leaf designs with human and animal figures playing amongst the foliage. The beams, too, were transfigured from their earthly woods through lavish carving into intricate design. Every carved detail they could see, from wooden beam to stone corbel and down through the pilasters which lined the walls was a riot of painted color shimmering with gilt.

In the high intervening spaces, between clerestory and mid-level, life-sized wall paintings portrayed deeds of chivalry. Fine Flemish carpets hung along the lowest portion of the walls reaching to the floor to protect from draught those who would sit at the lines of trestle tables. The hangings' bright wool and silken colors presented iridescent scenes of courtly love with knights and ladies splendidly dressed and gracefully posed. Large torches, projecting from sconces arranged regularly along each wall, sent flickering waves of golden illumination adding magic to the hall's overpowering sense of glorious movement and brilliant color.

Owen was glad that he had brought his own harp to this grand place. It was a plain and homely instrument but he knew he could call forth from its strings beautiful rich sounds which would float down from their lofty minstrel's gallery to please the great ones below should his nervous voice fail him. Alwan, too, made speechless by the grandeur before them, tried manfully to assemble his wits. He knew he had an important errand to complete for his Lady and he needed courage to lend support to young Owen whom he saw was trembling.

As Owen's fingers began to flow across the strings of his harp Alwan began to blow dark sweet sounds from his foresters' hand-carved flute. At times he could slip to an upper register with clear bright notes nearly duplicating the warbling of birdsong. The gathering crowd beneath them entered the hall and exchanged its noisy greeting. Taking their places according to rank at table, the members of the duke's household were delighted by the lovely sounds of the harp and flute. So absorbed in their playing, Alwan and Owen failed to notice as their tense fear melted away and their spirits united within their natural love of music.

Suddenly from the entrance portal, heralds' trumpets announced with fanfare the arrival of Norfolk and his Duchess. The duke and his lady swept majestically into the hall as the household stood to honor them. Lavishly dressed in flowing garments of bright greens, blues, and deep scarlet, they sparkled in silks and jeweled embroideries from their heads to their finely crafted slippers. Alwan and Owen were dumbstruck by the grandeur of the scene below them; their instruments hung loosely at their sides. Alwan's eyes fixed upon the graceful ceremony as his grace and the duchess took their places on the dais at the high table and the signal was given for the assembly to sit.

Without realizing that Armand the steward was madly signaling them to begin to play once more, Alwan searched the faces of the cavaliers seated at the high table. Near to its end, far to the right of the Duke, he could see where the only foreign knight of the company was seated. Without doubt, Alwan thought, they had found at last the German knight whom they had sought since their Lady's commission was first given them. Owen, seeing that Alwan was unaware of the steward's frantic command for music, began a lovely forlorn air of homesick love-longing. His bright voice filled the hall, carried aloft by his harp's strong fluid harmonies. The sweet boy soprano lyric startled Alwan from his mind-wandering inattention and the forester collected himself with a mental note to thank the lad for bailing him out. But until Owen's stanzas were complete, Alwan was free to observe the German knight from their excellent vantage on the gallery. He could see that the foreigner did not mix with the company at table and expressed faint interest in the brilliance surrounding him. Freda was right, Alwan thought, the German knight was not difficult to pick out in a crowd. His narrow, fair face with its shock of graying hair seemed sculpted into a mask of stony gloom. He wore a rich dark tunic as simple and somber as the cassock of a pious priest. Slim, straight, with large square shoulders, Alwan guessed he would be tall when he stood and powerful though the passage of years had conspired to lessen his quickness.

At the end of Owen's song, the duke's steward called for more sprightly music and Alwan returned to join Owen in playing a series of their favorite dancing songs. They played through the evening hours, exhausting their repertoire of every ballad, romantic tune, and jig they could remember. When at last the duke and his lady dismissed the table and the members of the household began to drift off to their respective sleeping chambers, Alwan and Owen wearily removed their ducal livery, leaving it to await their return to the minstrel's gallery and descended to find a place to sleep on the hall floor near to the glowing embers of the huge hearth which warmed the space through the night. Grateful that their long day was ended at last, Lady Apollonia's lads lay near enough to whisper together. Unaware of the extent of their fatigue and finding themselves too numb to speak, each of their weary heads dropped into the cushion of an arm and they collapsed into deep snoring slumber.

Chapter Nineteen

Waiting and Watching

At their jobs in the kitchen with the dawn, Alwan and Owen watched carefully for Freda. She was running at a frantic pace, fetching large pitchers of water needed in the knight's chamber to provide his morning wash. Alwan gave her a friendly pat as she hurried past and urged her to return to them when her duties allowed. She smiled and answered willingly that she would be freer to talk in the hours during chapel. The new kitchen lads worked at their chores patiently waiting for the leisure moment to bring chatty Freda back to their sides. They did not have long to wait. Her tasks complete, Freda ran to the kitchen to spend a few delicious stolen moments with the pleasant young Welshmen.

Freda was not much older than Owen but she had known considerably more hard use and worldly ways in her fourteen years than either of the young men from Lady Apollonia's household could have imagined. Several of her front teeth were missing and, although she carried water to many of the folk of the castle for washing, she used precious little of it upon her own person. Her hair as well as her body exuded an odor more barn like than chamber maid. Having taken a definite liking to Alwan and his permanent grin, she sat upon his lap and pressed her body against his as she continued her magpie chatter.

"Chris' blood, ee were in a 'orible mood th's mornin'," she said as she nuzzled Alwan's cheek.

"Why, Freda," Owen asked, "what can be troubling him? Has he not come to Wales to fight for the king?"

"Lor' no, Lad," she laughed, "ee's only coomb ter awsk questi'ns, I vow." When Owen opened his eyes in wide disbelief she patted his cheek and added, "Ee says ee are on a quest, tho Lor' knows ee's ne'er an 'oly man." Freda went on to describe how he questioned all the knights who entered the castle, inquiring after some special person whom he sought. The young knights preferred to avoid him, she said. They were too randy and ready for tilting in the yard or a roll in the hay. Still, Freda said, he asked the same boring questions of every new face in the duke's affinity.

"Well, Luv, whoos'it 'ees lookin fer, then," Alwan said, putting his bloody hand around her waist. Freda squealed and jumped up from the stool where he was sitting. "Keep yer bloody 'ans away," she giggled playfully. "Oi know not an' keer less. But give us a song, Luv, an Oi'll be back soon. Ee'll be wantin' me t' carry away 'is durty water an lin'n." Alwan began to sing a naughty ditty about a flirty maid and a shepherd as Freda reddened with a cheeky grin ran out of the kitchen.

Several days passed and the lads from Aust continued to ask questions among the kitchen folk during the day while observing the knight in his solitary vigil through evening meals in the hall. None of the Duke's kitchen servants were interested in the German knight or cared a whit for his quest. But they all were happy enough to stand between the roaring hearth fires listening while Owen and Alwan sang and entertained. The kitchen was a happier place with the minstrels working there for everyone except the artists themselves. Alwan hated the confinement and Owen grew restless and anxious as nothing seemed to be happening. They were not sure how long their Lady wished them to remain at Chepstow. The German knight made no move to depart and even if he did they could not be certain of his return to England. Still Alwan urged his young friend to be patient, reminding him that one must never hurry the traps. Quarry didn't move, he told Owen, until assured that it was safe to take the bait whatever that might be.

It was at the end of the first week of their sojourn that Freda came rushing into the kitchen one morning with her grand announcement, "Ee's go'in, b'god, ee's leavin' at lawrst." Alwan knew in his heart of whom she spoke. Her detested German knight was preparing to depart from the castle. Freda said that he would attend chapel with the duke's family then take leave of his grace before the sun reached noon. Freda put her arms around Alwan sitting upon his stool as she had done every morning since he had arrived. He leaned into her neck and whispered into her ear, "So Luv, 'owed you do it, then? 'Owed you git 'im to be mov'n on?"

"Bless me," she said merrily, "Oi did'n do enythin. T'was the ol' knight who coomb 'ome t' th' duke las' even'n." Freda went on to describe an old companion in arms of his grace who had returned to join his lord's contingent of guards. Evidently the German knight had sought him out immediately, "ter awsk 'is questions." The two old soldiers had retired to the German's chamber and talked late into the evening, she said. She knew what was happening, Freda added because when they said goodnight, the German called for her straightaway to supply his bathing water earlier than usual the following morning. When she appeared into his chamber with basins full at first light he made her begin to gather his things and pack them up while he prepared to leave the castle.

Alwan's thoughts were racing beneath his playful spirit shared with Freda. He and Owen must be prepared to follow the German and they had much to do in advance of his leaving to extricate themselves from their highly visible positions within the castle community. As Alwan was mulling these new developments over in his mind, Freda whispered into his ear that the pretty young squire of the duke's old knight had just walked into the kitchen to filch an extra honey bun for tardy breakfast on his way to the stables.

"Ee must 'ave 'ad a long nite. Mark ye 'ow tir'd 'ee be." Freda whispered into Alwan's ear.

With a flash of inspiration, Alwan got up from his stool and walked to Owen's side. Urging him to follow the squire, Alwan told Owen to see if he could engage him in conversation and try to learn the nature of the knights' late-evening conversation. "Take thee' time, lad," Alwan said encouragingly. He would fend off cook's questions and Freda, too, could help cover his absence.

The squire paused to eat his pastry quickly then wiping his mouth on his sleeve, he walked through the kitchen door into the lower bailey. Owen slipped away from Alwan towards the door in pursuit of the squire taking a fresh tankard of ale with him. Allowing a short distance to grow between them, he followed the squire across the bailey to the timber stables that were built between the towers and against the south curtain wall of the castle. Not stopping until he had reached the stall of his master's horses the young squire wasted no time expressing his displeasure at the animals' state. Irritably shouting curses and complaints which sent stable hands scurrying to brush and feed his master's beasts and clean away the accumulation of muck from their stall, the squire promised dire consequences in future should such lapses occur again. Owen, watching quietly from the entrance, noticed that the squire was yawning and stretching from lack of sleep. His temper, too spoke of a late night's service much resented. Walking up to the squire as if sent from the kitchen, young Owen greeted him and offered the tankard. "God save you squire. Cook asks to be remembered kindly to your master and sends this draught to freshen your morning," Owen said cheerfully.

"Gramercy lad," the squire responded. His sleepy eyes were streaked with red and bore dark shadows beneath their lashes. He gratefully accepted the tankard and emptied it in one long series of swallows. With the wide-eyed curiosity of his years, Owen asked the squire where they had come from and what had brought them to Chepstow. The squire continued to yawn amidst his tale of their journey so Owen wondered aloud had the squire not slept well the night before? Swearing in disgust, the squire said he would have slept well enough had his master not assumed he must accompany him to the chambers of an old German knight who plied them with questions into the night. "What ever could have been so important to stay the gentlemen's parley?" Owen pressed his new friend.

"Some old comrade in arms, tis my belief, lad. I must have dozed off several times as they spoke but the German was determined to know where my lord had seen him last, whom did he serve, and on and on," the squire said impatiently. "It was ages ago and I cared not a whit!"

"Was it a famous knight he was seeking, then?" Owen continued expressing boyish wonder.

"No lad," the squire answered, "it was another old timer I'd never heard spoke of called de Guelf, I think. He had served Montecute, a hero of Poitiers. But that was of no interest to 'im, t'was the place of service which excited the crazy old German."

Owen casually patted the horse's neck and asked, "Is the German knight on a pilgrimage, then?"

"If he is, I know of no holy shrine where he wants to go," the young squire said. "It's in the heart of empty Wiltshire, a manor called Colerne Leat. When my lord told him this de Guelf served with the garter knight, Geoffrey Montecute, the German kept pressing for news of him." The squire was getting bored with his subject but he finished his story. "He's long dead, it seems, but his lands lay not far across the Severn from Chepstow. So after a wasted evening, we returned to my lord's chamber as the cocks were nearing to crow; he to his bed and I to see to the horses."

Owen retrieved the empty mug with the squire's thanks and told him that he had heard news in the kitchen of the German knight's preparations to depart. "Likely you shall sleep better this night,"

Owen laughed as the squire snorted in agreement. Crockery in hand, Owen hurried back to the kitchen. When he returned to Alwan's side, Owen was pleased to find that Freda had been called away. He quietly repeated the squire's tale of his miserable sleepless night and happily noted that Alwan was thrilled with its mention of Colerne Leat. Now they could report to Lady Apollonia whom it was the German sought as well as offer her some idea of his destination back in England. But they must lose no time in finding a way to extricate themselves from their services here in Chepstow. Alwan wanted them to precede the German knight's arrival at the ferry crossing to Aust. If Freda was correct, they had only the few hours remaining before mid morning to achieve a head start.

The forester sent Owen to gather up their few belongings and carry them out, as if going to the garbage pit beyond the castle walls. Once outside the gate, Owen was to hurry back to the Inn to retrieve their horses and settle their account. With horses in hand, Alwan told him to wait inside Chepstow's town wall just next to Rivergate. Watching his young friend slip past the scolding cook heaping frustrated abuse upon his corps of scullery maids, Alwan offered a hurried prayer that God might help them accomplish their Lady's tasks. Crossing himself, Alwan knew time was essential but they must take great care lest they arouse suspicion or call attention to their departure. Alwan continued to sing and prattle merrily as he worked. When asked of Owen's whereabouts, Alwan complained that his clumsy fellow had snapped a vital harp string and had to see it mended before their evening's duties on the minstrel's gallery. Finally, he excused himself pleading a call of nature and left the kitchen. Instead of turning towards the servants' garderobe he left from the kitchen door and continued straight through the main entry gatehouse.

Keeping his pace measured and singing a little ditty to calm his spirit, he greeted the guards who now recognized him as one of the entertainers and they waved him through with lighthearted japes. "Out with it minstrel, what's it you're always smiling about. Looking for a tumble in the bushes with Freda, are ye?" They all laughed and Alwan laughed too, tipping his hat and winking slyly as he passed them by. Walking his unhurried loping pace across the drawbridge, he started the long descent towards Chepstow town whistling merrily. Picking up the pace as the castle faded into the distance behind him he began to run as he neared the bend in the river skirting round the town. Soon he was running as fast as he could, grateful to call upon his forester's speed and endurance to carry him free of walls and guards with their jangling intrigues.

Running past the Chepstow well, he could see Owen waiting at the Rivergate with the horses. His heart was pounding but he drove himself to pour on the speed. Shouting to Owen to mount up, Alwan swung into his own saddle and they trotted through the gates of Chepstow town. Galloping across the Chepstow bridge and down the river road following the Wye's east bank, they didn't slow the horses until they reached the entrance of the Wye River joining the Severn. Turning towards the broad Severn's banks, they gave their horses full rein and poured on the speed until the ferry crossing came into view.

The ferryman was just tying up from a crossing when they arrived in a great cloud of yellow dust. Leaping from his horse, Alwan approached the gnomish creature and asked if he would carry Owen and his mount across straightaway. Frowning, the boatman would have refused immediately as it was his custom to rest awhile, hopefully waiting for additional passengers who would make the crossing more profitable. Then, squinting his tiny eyes upward into Alwan's face, the boatman broke into a broad smile of recognition. He could see at once that his countryman was harried and in need. So he turned about, asking no questions but gestured Owen to climb aboard. Owen looked to his friend with questioning eyes. "Why will ye not cross with me, Alwan," he asked.

"Oi mus' watch fer the knight 'ere," he whispered to Owen. "If'n 'ee stays t' this side o' th' river, Oi mus' be 'ere ter track 'im." Alwan pushed Owen onto the ferry and would not allow him to refuse. He told the boy that he must go straight to Lady Apollonia as soon as he landed. "Tell 'er everthin', Owen!" Alwan said. He was to recite every detail of their adventure and tell her of their news. The Lady would know what to do next.

Owen did not wish to leave his friend behind but could think of no further objection. The ferryman made his decision for him. Without a word, he steered his craft into the rising waters and was soon doing battle with the Severn's swirling currents. At last, with Owen and his mount on the ferry, Alwan's heart could cease pounding. He turned his horse around and trotted back towards the gates of Chepstow. When the German knight departed the town, Alwan wished to be ready to follow as near as his shadow.

For the first time since their great adventure had begun, Owen felt hurt as he stood on the ferry's deck so much that he feared that he may begin to weep. He wasn't a bairn he told himself and made a mighty frown, pursing out his lips and wrinkling his forehead. He truly wanted to remain with Alwan until they could make their exciting report to Lady Apollonia together. Worse yet he may miss some exciting thing happening on the far bank as Alwan was tracking the German knight. Ashamed of his pouting, Owen stopped to remember the importance of his task. Alwan was depending on him to bring the Lady Apollonia to the Aust side of the ferry for her next instructions.

The ferryman looked over his shoulder at the lad and normally wouldn't have said a word, but today, seeing his troubled face, thought better of it. "Not a song for the crossin'," he shouted. Owen smiled sheepishly and began a cheeky ditty of an old English lord who played the fool to chase pretty Welsh maids.

Paying the ferryman a good sum for his trouble, Owen requested that he remain on the Aust side till his friend Alwan summoned him from the far bank. "All's depends 'pon t'e custom," the boatman replied. But Owen knew the old Welshman grasped that there were reasons for his request. He would hold his return, if he could, till summoned by Alwan from the far bank. Mounting up, Owen thanked the good boatman heartily and galloped off towards the manor house. "Holy Mother, let my Lady be at home this morning," he prayed urgently as he rode.

Chapter Twenty

Raven's Oracle

The days since Alwan and Owen left for Wales had passed all too slowly for Apollonia. At times she was convinced that she had been unwise to send two unsophisticated young men to spy on and outwit foreign knights. In other moments she would assure herself that no other members of her household had a better chance of pursuing an unnoticed inquiry in Wales. Alwan and Owen had their language and musical gifts, their native intelligence, and their ability to melt into the masses. All would be well she told herself again and again but she prayed urgently that God would protect them and bring word of them soon. When she wasn't on her knees in the chapel Apollonia told herself that she must keep busy in the kitchen, in the garden, even in the barns. Work and activity would calm her spirit best by directing her thoughts elsewhere and, she reminded herself, had yet another troubling mystery to investigate within her own walls.

She had decided to tackle that nagging problem by walking down to the stables on the very morning after Alwan and Owen had left for Wales. She intended to have a quiet chat with Gareth, her stable master. No matter what the outcome, she had no wish to embarrass a good man of many years faithful service to her. Entering the long stone stable with its oak beams and stone tiled roof, Apollonia could hear Gareth's voice shouting harshly at his stable lads. They were all good boys but bound to be troublesome at times. Still she had never heard such irritation in his exchanges with them before. When her dark silent figure appeared unexpectedly in the periphery of his gaze, Gareth stopped in mid-sentence and a guilty blush spread over his face. Swiftly he doffed his large brimmed hat and offered his obeisance to her. Apollonia gestured to him to accompany her and he followed obediently as she walked well away to a quiet spot between the hayricks.

Turning as she waited for him to come closer she could see that Gareth was distressed and very uneasy. He knew that if the Lady required something of him, Giles would normally have transmitted the Lady's request to him. Her unannounced presence in the barn seeking him out indicated that she wished to speak with him alone and he feared she may have reason to be displeased with him. He stopped a few paces from her hat in hand but his head and body defiant. Her face was not angry; she displayed no emotion at all. But her eyes looked directly into his and she said simply: "You know I have lived in debt to you these many years for services only you could grant me, Gareth," she began. "But it has recently come to my attention that you have been spending long periods of time away from my stables."

"Naught 'as been lef' undone," he replied hastily, then remembering himself, he added, "m'Lady."

"I harbor no doubts of your faithful service, Gareth," she said quietly, "you were my only hope of escape once many years ago and I remain grateful for your risks in my behalf to this very day. But it is unlike you to be absent from the manor without requesting permission."

His hands fell to his sides and his proud head dropped. Not sure at first Apollonia realized after a few moments that Gareth was near to tears. "Oi've done a stupid thing, m'Lady. Th' pries' in church alway warn'n 'gains' pride lead'n t' fall'n inter sin," he blurted.

Apollonia said nothing at first she simply stood silently allowing Gareth to regain his masculine composure and then she continued encouragingly, "No matter the sin, Gareth, there is always forgiveness to one who is truly repentant."

"But Oi don' wish t' repent," his handsome face lifted to speak with conviction. "Oi fancy Oi shall stay wed, com' 'ell er 'igh wa'er." Before Apollonia could express her surprise at the strange announcement that this long-time bachelor had married, he began to confess the "'orrible muddle" of his very own making. Not a voluble man, Gareth poured forth his simple story of having fallen in love with a maid in nearby Ingst. She was a pretty sixteen year old, so precious to him that he could not risk bringing her to live at Aust.

"T's Jan'ary wedded t' May, m'Lady. "Cawn't ye see 'ow the lads wull lawf." Apollonia could see that Gareth was thoroughly miserable. Although his tan, weathered face was crowned with a full head of greying hair, Gareth's was still a comely face set upon strong shoulders and a youthful, slim, well-muscled figure. But at sixteen, his wife was young enough to be his daughter. Secretly wed, he had made his pretty bride remain with her father because he feared she would soon tire of him once surrounded by all the good-looking young lads about Aust stables. He stole away to Ingst, every spare moment he could devise just to be with her. But the lass was growing unhappy with the arrangement and pressing him to make a home for them.

Apollonia knew the village of Ingst and she thought she also knew the bright and spirited maid of whom Gareth had become so enamored. "I should not mind if you choose to live in Ingst and come each day to oversee your responsibilities in the stable, Gareth," Apollonia said quietly. "Do you have a man capable of supervising in your absence?" she inquired.

Gareth's face suddenly brightened with the realization that the Lady had solved his dilemma in one sweeping statement of permission. "Aye, m'Lady, Hank be a good lad an' as careful o' the beasts as St. Francis," Gareth said happily. Oi been trustin' 'im whilst Oi were goin' these past months."

"What is this I hear of a great horse being found wandering near Ingst?" the Lady asked casually. "O course I were meanin to tell thee, m'Lady. But Oi been so muddled o' late." Gareth said with a look of real surprise at her unexpected change of subject. "E were wanderin in the woods an' no oon could cap'tur 'im. But Oi co'od tak 'im in 'and. So Oi put 'im in yo'or barn ne'er Ingst. E's worth a poun' o brass ifn no'on claims 'im."

By the time Apollonia walked away from the stables she was convinced that her worries of threat within her affinity could now be laid to rest. Gareth had thanked her profusely; delighted to learn that she had no objection to his living in Ingst though it had never occurred to him to ask. The Lady pledged as her wedding gift to the new couple sufficient material to add on to Gareth's father-in-law's cottage. But she also cautioned her stable master to grant his young wife a fair measure of trust. Her youth and beauty, she assured him, did not necessarily mean that he had married a flirt. Finally offering her sincere congratulations, Apollonia could see that Gareth was restored to peace within himself. Before allowing her to leave him, however, he begged her to hear of one other concern which had been worrying him but which he had not been in a position to confess before this moment. In the past months while he had been making his secret evening trips to Ingst, hurrying back through the forest before dawn Gareth had often seen another member of the Lady's household trapping and collecting live ravens.

From the stables, Apollonia walked on towards the brew house. She, too, felt more lighthearted and grateful. It was quite possible, she told herself, that her household had been terrorized by nothing more

158

threatening than their own superstition. But to be sure, she knew she must speak with Mad Mag alone and very carefully. Mag was known for her outrageous tantrums when she would howl and throw things. But she was such a familiar and well-meaning local character that no one truly feared her. Mad Mag had lived in Aust for unknown years; no one knew just how long but first serving the manor when Apollonia's husband, Edward Aust, was a boy. No one knew how old she was but everyone in the household respected her strength when aroused. No one knew where she had come from but her ale and beer were renowned in the county. Edward had told Apollonia that he suspected some terrible beating had destroyed Mag's wits. Beneath her ragged hair, her misshapen head and scarred face still spoke of a hideous thrashing long years before by an unknown hand. Edward and Apollonia had always required the rest of the manor household to be patient with the woman, to humor her and encourage her to return to the brew house where she held sway entirely on her own. She was a powerful woman, short, squat and stubborn and, for some reason, whenever she was told to do something, her only response was: "Shant!" Mad Mag would put her massive arms crossed upon her equally massive breasts and shout, "Nary O'i shant".

Finding the brewmistress standing upon a ladder stirring a huge vat, Apollonia called to her by name. "Mag," she said, "you must stir the vats harder."

Mag immediately threw down her pestle and shouted, "Shant!" Then she climbed down to the floor where the Lady stood quietly waiting for her. Apollonia held out her hand to Mag and the old woman put her gnarled calloused paw into the Lady's palm. Stroking the hand and speaking very softly Apollonia brought up the subject of her concern. "There were many dead ravens in my house, Mag," the Lady said gently.

"Blood sacrifice! Blood Sacrifice!" whined Mag. "Save thee again' evil, Lady," she whimpered over and over again.

"So you hung the ravens upon the doors to save us, Mag?" the Lady inquired softly.

"Shant!" shouted Mag, "Mus'n kill but on'y blood wull saf' thee!"

Apollonia had long suspected that Mag practiced her own version of magic. Gathering forest herbs and animal parts she would hang them around her neck and about the inside of the brew house as protection. Perhaps, in her clouded mind, the raging of the storm had led her to extend her magical spells to protect the manor house. Of one thing Apollonia was certain, although she might never decipher Mag's tortured reasoning she never needed to fear it either. Mag's battered mind sought equilibrium in its struggle against the evils of the world but intended no harm against those who protected her. "We must not pray together, Mag," Apollonia said, and the woman knelt immediately.

They said together their prayers to God the Father, Christ his Son and the Holy Virgin. Then Apollonia rose and put her hands upon the muddled head, with lips still muttering furiously. "Kill ravens, Mag?" Apollonia asked.

Standing abruptly, Mag turned an irregularly toothed grin and shouted, "Shant" and walked back to her brewing vats. Apollonia smiled too waving goodbye as she walked from the brew house. "I must find Nan," Apollonia said to herself. "She so truly loves happy endings."

Days turned into a week and still there had been no word from Wales. At the back of Apollonia's mind a nagging thought kept repeating that Owen and Alwan must have encountered something important to detain them to this extent. That encouraged her to believe that she had put them on the correct trail to find the German knights. But she grew more agitated and worried that the passage of days might also mean that her two young henchmen had found themselves in serious trouble.

To counter her anxiety on this late October morning, Apollonia had retreated to the barn to assist with the recording of tithes brought in by her tenants. She enjoyed being with her people, smiling upon those with new babes, heartening those who struggled against old age, disability or sickness while encouraging the tally man to praise all for a good harvest year. Surrounded by the press of people greeting her, some pausing for a few moments to express complaint or special need, she hadn't noticed Nan's breathless entry into the tithe barn. Moving slowly through the gathered tenants Nan did not hesitate to interrupt her Lady's conversation.

Whispering into Apollonia's ear that Owen had returned alone, Nan stepped back for a deep breath. The Lady rose with stately grace and nodded to each of her tenants. With upraised hand in the sign of the cross she wished everyone peace and God's blessing then she left the barn walking gracefully with Nan in close pursuit. Together they walked more briskly towards the house with quickening pace as they approached the wicket entrance to the golden yellow stone wall surrounding the garden. Once Nan had closed the gate behind them, Apollonia lifted her black skirts and bolted, her long legs running between the garden beds of herbs and vegetables through the line of fruit trees until she burst into the house through its garden door. Rushing up to her solar where she had been told Owen awaited her she paused at its entrance only to restore her breath and gain a moment of composure.

As she entered, the boy was eating a mighty chunk of fresh bread and about to wash it down with ale. Owen put the tankard down immediately and stood up to receive his Lady. He had never seen her in such a state of agitation. "You must forgive an old woman's weakness, Owen," she said still breathless as she straightened her headdress, "the stairs do trouble me more each year." Offering her hand, she welcomed him home to Aust and begged him to sit down and finish his meal. Owen, filled with the importance of his mission insisted that he must not eat, he must speak with her immediately as Alwan had told him he must do.

Thus, the Lady seated herself, urged Owen to his stool and requested that he repeat for her Alwan's message quickly if time must not be wasted. Owen did even better. He began by telling her that he had gained some time for them by his arrangement of stalling the ferryman on the Aust bank of the Severn. Then he told his Lady the wonderful adventure in Chepstow Castle, their service in its kitchen and hall and, of course, their spying on the one remaining German knight.

"The other knights had already taken ship back to their homeland by the time we arrived, Lady," he told her. "But we knew you would wish for us to discover the plans of the one cavalier who remained."

Then Owen described their chats with Freda, the chamber wench, and his own interview with the squire of Norfolk's old knight. "Wilfred de Guelf was the name of the gentleman whom the German knight sought, my Lady, but the squire said he seemed even more intent on learning locations where de Guelf had served in Wiltshire." Lady Apollonia's eyes disappeared beneath half-lids and she seemed very calm now. She offered no interruption to Owen's tale preferring to hear the whole of it as it poured fresh from his memory. But her mind was assimilating and connecting each new fact gathered by the wit and invention of her two young henchmen.

"The squire told me that the German knight grew most excited at the mention of de Guelf's service with Sir Geoffrey Montecute," Owen continued. "He took especial note of Sir Geoffrey's lands and after learning the whereabouts of Colerne Leat, ended the interview and began making plans to depart from Chepstow." At this, Lady Apollonia's eyes lifted abruptly to Owen's face but still she refrained from interrupting his tale.

"Alwan stayed behind at the ferry point on the Welsh bank telling me to report all to you immediately, my Lady. He said he would follow the German knight to be certain of his next destination." Owen paused a moment and then added, "And I am to await him at Aust ferry." Owen had no desire to end this grand adventure just yet. He earnestly hoped that Lady Apollonia would allow him to watch for his friend till he returned. Surely, he could conjure no concentration for his daily studies if Alwan were still on the Welsh side and the tale of their adventure remained incomplete.

Lady Apollonia could see the pleading in Owen's eyes full of concern for his friend and curiosity for the continuing chase. She thought for a few moments as Owen waited in respectful silence and then said to him, "It is most important that you station yourself out of sight but near the ferry to watch for Alwan and probably the German knight also. Alwan may have feared that you might be recognized as the castle minstrels should you be seen together. Therefore, be sure to remain hidden until the German knight has left the ferry and continued on his journey." Owen nodded enthusiastically.

"It is possible that the gentleman may surprise us by traveling another route into England but I think it not likely. He cannot be aware of our need to understand his quest, whatever that truly is," Apollonia said as she continued planning their next effort. "I shall summon Giles and we will both remain here in the courtyard with our horses ready whilst you perform as my eyes and ears at the ferry point. You will alert us as soon as Alwan and the German knight have landed. Alwan was wise to remain to follow the knight but you were equally clever to stall the boatman upon this bank of the river." Owen's breast swelled with her quiet praise of his quick thinking. "If all goes well, Owen, we may not have long to wait. Hasten back to the ferry point and remain out of sight." Apollonia could see Owen's pleasure in her instructions. Without remembering his manners, he forgot his food, forgot his courtesy to her and rushed from her chamber in teenage explosion through the door.

Chapter Twenty-one

Home to Aust

Alwan had positioned himself outside the Chepstow town walls between its roadside well and the castle in a small copse of trees near to the bend in the river. From this vantage he had a fine view of its east curtain wall from Marten's Tower to the main outer gatehouse. The sun rose higher and warmed sharp edges of the autumn breezes toying with the brim of his slouching hat. Sunlight brought such golden beauty to the day he noticed happily as his anxious mood slowly subsided and he felt the prospects for success in their Lady's mission to be rising with the bright star of the day. Having spent far too long to suit him inside the stone walls of Chepstow Castle, Alwan relished the sweet fragrance of the trees and delighted in the sunbeams flowing through the woodsy canopy overhead in translucent shades of yellow, green and russet. The warm and welcome sun also guaranteed him good visibility having burned away patches of hovering pre-dawn mist. All was well, he thought chuckling to himself at the success of their hasty morning's retreat. Owen would be safely on the far bank carrying their news to the Lady Apollonia while on this side of the river, Alwan was in excellent position to maintain a vigilant watch of the yawning gates well before the German knight could have broken his fast and taken leave of Chepstow's resident lord.

Confident and content Alwan waited patiently, whittling a bit and humming quietly to himself. He was especially happy to be near the Wye as he found a great deal of pleasure being able to watch the river and its early morning creatures. He especially admired the perfect fishing skills of the shining black cormorants whose greedy appetites kept them half submerged as they swam along the water's surface ready for an instant dive in pursuit of their next scaly meal. A family of swans swam proudly by, four grey cygnets furiously paddling to keep up with the effortless cruising of their serene parents. A large fly harassed Alwan's good natured horse's hind quarters. As his mount swished and stamped in annoyance, the forester loosened his wide wool neck scarf to make a lethal swat at it.

Alwan watched the sun to judge the hours slowly passing as its brilliant splendor ascended; slowly too, an irritation as niggling as the bloody fly began to gnaw at his complacency. There was no doubt that the day was approaching its mid hour and still produced no sign of the German knight. Could he have altered his plans in leaving, Alwan began to wonder? Had there been unforeseen particulars which kept him in the castle? Fleeting clouds of anxious questions grew in the forester's mind to a full-blown storm of worry. Surely something had gone amiss, he told himself. Then he remembered with a sinking heart that the castle had an upper gate at its northwestern end. Could the knight have departed through that gate like a wary rabbit emerging from its warren at a distant unguarded exit? Why hadn't they waited to be certain he thought furiously?

A splash in the river distracted him momentarily but realizing it was merely the breaching of a large fish, Alwan's thoughts returned to his dilemma. He could not remain in his excellent blind he told himself. He had to know if the quarry had already escaped him by taking another route. Urging his horse forward, Alwan returned to the edge of the road as a single horseman appeared riding through the castle gate onto the drawbridge and down towards the town. With a deep silent gasp of recognition, Alwan swiftly retreated into the copse once again and remained hidden from view until the knight had passed him by. Allowing the object of his long pursuit to gain a good distance ahead of him, Alwan emerged from the trees once again and began to follow on the blind side of the curving road from his quarry ahead. There was no need for such security measures; the knight rode without ever looking back.

Riding at a moderate pace the knight continued into Chepstow town, riding past the bridge across the Wye below the castle gate, thus encouraging Alwan to believe that he must have business in the town before proceeding to the Severn ferry crossing across from Aust. Intent upon his own affairs however, the knight turned his mount at the sloping lane which passed the parish church and led to the harbor on the river Wye. He rode towards the crowded docks with their forest of sailing masts. Crawling with activity the placid ships bobbed aimlessly, securely bound in their shallow berths as they were being made to disgorge or devour great mounds of cargo and stores lining the quay.

"Damn an' blawrst!" Alwan swore under his breath, "Oi truly wish ye were 'ere, M'lady. What'ere shall Oi do now?" Thinking of no alternative course, Alwan continued to follow the knight as he rode along the docks searching among the bevy of moored sailing ships. The knight paused several times to seek information and after questioning various sailors who directed him down the line, he finally stopped at the berth of a ship with strange markings and outlander crew. Leaving his impatient charger tethered at dockside, the tall stately figure walked across the gangplank and went on board. Alwan's heart felt its walls constrict; the knight was preparing to take ship!

Thinking that he might at least learn the German knight's destination, Alwan walked to the gangplank where a number of burly Welsh laborers were rolling great casks of provisions on board. It was a Hanse vessel belonging to the guild of German mercantile cities called the Hanseatic League, Alwan learned from a young hodsman. After taking on its cargo of Welsh lumber and wool, it would call in at Bristol before sailing on to Hamburg. With this disheartening information, Alwan turned away from the vessel and led his horse to more inconspicuous observation post. As he continued to watch, the German knight emerged from the shipmaster's cabin and walked cross the deck towards the gangplank pushing aside sweating seamen to clear his path. He left the ship, returned to his tethered horse and mounted up. Once in the saddle, he retraced his path back up the river lane, past the parish church, and turned back again to cross the bridge and take the Wye-side road towards Severn's ferry point.

In great relief after this second major feint by his quarry, Alwan never allowed the knight's departing figure out of his sight. Maintaining a discreet distance, he followed cautiously just in case the German may take yet another expected turn. That surprise, he thanked God wholeheartly, did not happen. The knight halted only when he reached the ferry dock and was attempting to call the boatman from the far bank as Alwan rode up to join him. There being no response from the opposite bank, Alwan doffed his hat and offered his service to the knight. "Beg pard'n, Mawrster, could Oi 'elp 'ee call'n th' boatm'n," he said politely. The German looked at him quizzically for a few moments and then seemed to realize that Alwan's shire accents were offering to call the ferryman. He said nothing; his stone face betrayed no change of expression but his head nodded in silent affirmation. Alwan, putting two fingers between his lips, let out a mighty whistle and began to wave his neck scarf like a long brown pennon back and forth high over his head.

Owen was sitting with the ferryman, asking endless questions about managing boats on the river, when they saw the summons from the far bank. "Tis Alwan! That's my friend," he said in Welsh. With that, the gnomish boatman seemed to know that this was the important crossing for which he had been waiting half the day. He pushed the craft away from the dock and was swiftly underway. Owen left the docking area as soon as the ferry departed. He climbed a tall tree with plenty of thick foliage and, midst its tangle of branches, perched himself to observe the crossing and return of the ferry. The return journey, he noted with great pleasure, brought two passengers, Alwan and the German knight.

Reaching the English bank and his passengers disembarked, the boatman turned to each to receive his payment without uttering a word. The German continued to remain silent, paid for the crossing, and remounted his horse. Riding up from the river into the heart of the village of Aust, the knight could be seen stopping at the one and only village inn, The Boar's Head. Lingering with the boatman but keeping his eyes upon the movements of the German knight, Alwan was assuring his countryman of the ferry that his services would be well-remembered when to his happy surprise, Owen dropped down from his hiding place and ran up to embrace his friend. "By all the saints, Alwan, I am pleased ye' have returned. What took ye' so long," he said excitedly.

"No quest'ons yit, Owen, ye' mus' run 'n tell 'er Ladyship, th' gentilm'n be at th' Boars Head. Swif'ly, Lad, Oi shall watch fer 'im 'ere whilst ye' fetch 'er." Putting his arm around his young friend, Alwan gave Owen's shoulders a gentle push in the direction of the manor house and sent him flying up the road.

Owen did not stop until he had entered the manor house courtyard. Three horses were tethered there, already saddled and waiting should a hasty journey become necessary. Shouting for Mistress Nan, Owen bounded into the Hall. Nan sent Owen bounding up to the Lady's solar where he forgot himself completely and burst through the door unannounced. The Lady and Giles were going over harvest accounts together as the door crashed against the stone wall of the chamber. "Alwan is back my Lady," he shouted breathlessly, "and remains watchful of the German knight who lingers in The Boar's Head."

Apollonia and Giles stood at once. "Come Giles and you, Owen, go to collect Mistress Nan. Bring her with you to the horses!" the Lady said. "We shall all ride to join Alwan in his vigil near The Boar's Head."

Chapter Twenty-two

Chivalry's True Constant

The German knight seemed more hurried as he finally left The Boar's Head. Having sought and gained directions from the landlord, he returned to his horse and was preparing to leave the village. Alwan, watching from the shadows of the huge trees of Aust church yard, was mounted and ready to follow when Lady Apollonia, Giles, Nan and Owen came down the lane from the manor. Joining Alwan, they could not see the German knight. He had already disappeared down the lanes leading south-east from Aust. Riding to Alwan's side, Apollonia gave her hand to her hardy woodsman with a warm smile of welcome.

"Greetings Alwan, God be praised for your safe return," she said as he bowed over her hand. "We shall ride slowly so as not to arouse the knight's suspicion that we follow him. Haste is not essential as I believe I know where the good knight will go next." Her proud forester was blushing deep shades of dark rose in his twisted cheeks with pleasure to be in her presence once again but felt he must interrupt his Lady.

"Ee's arranged to take ship from Bristol, m'Lady, Oi sawr 'im dicker wi' the German ship's mawrster." Lady Apollonia nodded smiling again at Alwan for his good judgement under pressure. He had not missed a detail in the knight's unfolding plans.

"You must continue to ride ahead, Alwan," she said, "and we shall follow more slowly grateful for your tracker's skills should he lead us astray. The German knight is riding in the correct direction, however. I think he is trying to reach Colerne Leat before nightfall. Let us away and see if we may assist him in his quest."

After a ride of twenty miles, the sun lay on the horizon as they arrived at the dark grey manor walls surrounding Colerne Leat. The German knight had left his horse tethered to a tree on the green and could be seen exploring the village of Colerne in the pale light of early evening. Seeing him on foot as they entered the village, Lady Apollonia halted her party and requested Giles to assist her dismount. She then told Giles and Alwan to take the horses into the manor stables and return to find her after the horses had been tended. Owen would accompany her she said, while she spoke with the German knight.

The German knight was alert to the arrival of this mixed party into the village. But three of the group rode on to the manor house leaving two of its most unexpected members dismounted and walking towards him. His chiseled features turned quizzical as he looked tentatively upon the tall old woman dressed entirely in black who approached him in the company of a boy. With no word of introduction, she spoke to him directly addressing him in Latin. "God's blessing, sir knight," she continued in a quiet voice, "I am sorry that I do not speak your language but I believe we may communicate in the Latin tongue."

"I spik your langvage, Lady," the knight responded, with a low bow, "How may I serfe you?"

Apollonia smiled and said, "I believe you are searching for something which had been in the hands of Sir Wilfrid de Guelf, one of the henchmen of my first husband, Geoffrey Montecute, Lord of Colerne. And," she added gently, "I believe it is I who may assist you in locating your desired object."

The German knight's eyes blazed though his face remained unmoved. He refrained from making any further comment but stared at Apollonia with an attitude of disbelief which would have withered any lesser human.

Returning his gaze looking straight into his eyes, Apollonia continued. "I know that Sir Wilfrid is dead and I know that you did not murder him. He was a totally evil man whose death is mourned by no person. Whatever it is that you seek, if you will accompany me I believe I can show you where you will find it."

Waiting until she could see in his eyes that he did understand all that she had said even if he remained hesitant to believe her, Apollonia quietly turned away and walked towards the village churchyard. As she left with Owen following her lead, the knight hesitated, scanned the area around them for any sign of additional intruders then slowly began walking in the same direction continuing to watch around them carefully to see if any sort of trap were being laid for him. After some moments of consideration and seeing no others about in the village, he followed Lady Apollonia and Owen into the churchyard of Colerne. Walking down a path which skirted the church entrance porch and wandered behind its apse, the Lady arrived at a large stone tomb covered by an impressive black stone grave slab lying in the burial yard. Even in the day's pale remaining light the knight could see carved upon its surface a full-length image of an

English garter knight in armor, his legs spread arrogantly and his feet resting upon a dog and a boar with his hands raised incongruously in prayer.

Stopping at the head of Geoffrey Montecute's tomb slab, the Lady waited until the German knight approached and then said to him, "I am the Lady Apollonia of Aust. This is the grave of my first husband Geoffrey Montecute, liege lord of Wilfrid de Guelf. Peasants' gossip says that the devil was seen here dancing upon this grave just before the outbreak of the gales earlier in the month. That devil was, I believe, Sir Wilfrid and he was probably howling in fiendish delight because he assumed he had outwitted you." She paused again and could see that the German was desperately trying to reckon why she was telling him all of this. How did she know? What did she want?

"I have a quest for truth," she acknowledged to him. "If you wish to dig around this tomb slab, I shall send two of my men with a light and shovels. Once you have reclaimed your lost object you may keep it and I shall see that no one questions your activities here. Is that agreeable with you?" she asked. He fixed an intense stare upon her face scanning every detail of her expression, her manner, and her calm, unthreatening presence. Then he nodded yes, he would accept her assurances and her offer of men to assist him in digging.

Lady Apollonia sent Owen to tell Giles and Alwan they must fetch lights and shovels and return to dig as the knight commanded them. "This manor belongs to me, although I give its use to the Augustinians of Bristol as a place of summer retreat. I reserve apartments for my own use whenever I am in this county. When you have completed your task, I would be pleased to offer you hospitality for the night." With that, she turned and walked away.

She was seated in front of the fire when Giles showed the knight into her parlor. Asking that meat, bread and wine be brought to them, Lady Apollonia told Giles to see that he, Alwan, and Owen took supper. Then he was to see to it that a room be prepared for their guest. She wished to speak with the knight alone Apollonia told her steward. Giles was not happy with this request but he voiced no objections. Leaving a tray on the table between them, Giles withdrew from the chamber. But he stationed Alwan just outside her door should there be a call for help at any point in the interview.

The knight carried a mud-stained sheepskin bag in his hand somewhat larger than a purse but having a similar shape. Before he would sit, he presented himself to the Lady. "I am Casimir of Prague, nephew by marriage to his imperial highness, the Emperor Wenceslaus. You are the only person in this country to know my true name. I come from Bohemia."

Apollonia realized this sharing of his confidence was a great honor. Casimir was not a man to grant such things frivolously. She responded warmly and with cordial grace. "Welcome to this house, Lord Casimir. I am Lady Mary Apollonia of Aust, mistress of Colerne Leat and Aust manor. I hope you will find your simple accommodations here adequate to your needs. My hospitality is offered to you for as long as you like but I understand that you have already made arrangements to return to your homeland."

At this, the forbidding knight smiled and scratched his head like a child wondering over the mysterious insights of a parent. "I do not know how you haf' acqvuired the power of omniscience, my Lady but I detect that you mean me no harm. I am foreffer in your debt as you haf' made my return to my country von of triumph razzer zan failure."

"My omniscience, as you call it, is based upon a strange series of happenstance, your Grace, for which I can claim little credit." Urging him to take the chair opposite her, help himself to their supper and warm his feet by the fire, Lady Apollonia began as they ate together the long tale of the discovery of Sir Wilfrid's body on her lands after the storm, the location of Sir Wilfrid's head by her excellent forester and finally the search for him, Lord Casimir and his companions, from Somerset to Chepstow. When she had finished, her guest sat with his chin cupped in hand wondering at her ability to collect information and her meticulous powers of deduction. "But," Casimir felt compelled to ask, "vy haf you taken such trouble to follow my moofments if you haf' no interest in revenging zis man's death?"

"At first, I was distracted by a need to protect my own interests," Apollonia said frankly, "but once my concerns were settled I wished to know the truth. I believe there is great value in learning the truth for its own sake," she said simply. "Obviously you had taken Wilfrid prisoner which, from my experience of his evil ways, could well have been justified. You and your companions were seeking to flee with him as your captive into Wales when the gale reached its most dangerous pitch and drove you from the road. I have no quarrel

172

with any of your actions. But Sir Wilfrid's curious dress and the absence of all identifying marks of his person plagued my restless curiosity," she confessed.

"As you haf' zolved my dilemma, gracious Lady," he said with a gentle smile, "I shall now zooth your raging curiosity." His face grew softer and though he smiled at Apollonia as he spoke, Casimir's eyes flashed with the bitter gleam of a world-weary man. "Indeed, I confess de Guelf vas our prisoner. He vas a thief. To conceal his identity ve had taken his garments and purposefully humiliated him in peasant rags." Casimir's voice dropped, "I vas prepared to do anysing to vipe the arrogant smirk from his churlish face!"

Casimir said that he and his companions had been sent to England months earlier at the Emperor's command. They were instructed to travel in the guise of mercenary knights seeking to sell their services to a powerful English lord but never to reveal their true names or the nature of their commission to anyone. Trailing Wilfrid for weeks, they had traveled from London to Somerset, to Pontefract and finally to Gloucestershire where they challenged de Guelf and his squire not far from Marshfield. As Casimir and his knights attempted to take them prisoner, Wilfrid and his wretched squire foolishly drew their weapons and tried to flee. The squire was killed and Wilfrid surrendered quickly but his arrogance continued unabated. The young knights, infuriated by his cheek, demanded that Wilfrid return the Bohemian treasure they knew he had stolen. He laughed in their faces saying that he knew nothing of their imaginary treasure. Ignorant German fools he called them and threatened to set the King's sheriffs upon them. "I have power here; I shall have you all arrested as murderous foreign agents!" He shouted and raged that he had connections in the highest places and would never rest until he had seen them all hang as enemy spies!

To protect themselves against his screaming threats of exposure, Casimir and his companions had forced Wilfrid into rough peasant fustian. They took his rings and tore the tokens of his estate from his horse's harness. Angered by his arrogant shouting, they gagged his mouth with rags and bound him to his saddle in preparation for a long ride into Wales. There, in some deserted spot far from the reach of King Henry's justice, they were certain that they would be able to force him to answer their questions. "Ve knew he vould answer under threat. De Guelf vas a coward!" Casimir said with righteous conviction. Planning to conceal themselves by day and travel only after sunset, the knights had kept Wilfrid secure by enshrouding his massive figure in a hooded robe as they pushed on towards the ferry at Aust.

Casimir conceded that the Lady was precise in discerning that they had been forced to stop and seek shelter in the woods. "Neffer, in all my life haf I seen sach a defil storm," he told the Lady. Managing to tether their own horses, Casimir said his companions had removed Wilfrid's robe and gag and were preparing to pull him from his mount also. Terrorized by a nearby lightening strike and fantastic crash of thunder Wilfrid's horse reared, pulling its reins free allowing Wilfrid to kick it into bolting from their camp. The storm was so violent Casimir and his companions had all they could do to calm and control their own horses. Unable to follow Wilfrid's desperate plunge into the darkness, the knights decided to wait with their mounts until the storm showed some possibility of weakening. Wilfrid had fled but they knew he could not dismount without some one to unbind him.

After a period of time when the roaring winds and crushing rain had calmed somewhat, Casimir and the young knights rode in the direction Wilfrid had fled. They finally found his horse wandering aimlessly in the woods, its blood-soaked decapitated rider lolling against their secure restraints. Fearful that they would be accused of the murder of an English gentleman, the knights panicked and threw Wilfrid's body into the roaring Severn that very night assuming that its tides would carry the hideous carrion out to sea. They released his horse into the woods then turning towards Aust, they waited out the final blasts of the storm and took the first ferry of the following day to safe harbor and sanctuary in Chepstow.

"Ve had no idea that the sea, alzo, vould throw him back to be found upon your lands, for vich I am truly sorry, my Lady," Casimir said apologetically.

Safely escaped to Chepstow, Casimir's young companions refused to consider his plans for returning to England to continue their search for the Bohemian treasure and declared they must acknowledge failure in their mission. Casimir accused them of weakness swearing that he would never accept defeat or retreat like a coward. Their anger mounting, the younger knights refuted his charges of cowardice by saying they had already traversed the heart of England and their quarry was dead. He could tell them nothing! They would no longer submit to the leadership of a compulsive madman. After several hours of violent arguments amongst themselves the two younger men abandoned Casimir, accusing him of blind obstinacy which could achieve nothing more than a hangman's noose. Booking their passage on the first ship leaving Chepstow for the continent, the young knights refused to consider any avenue but escape. "They said ve could not get confessions or directions from a dead man," Casimir said simply.

Unwilling to allow their departure to deter him, Casimir explained to the Lady of Aust that he was honor-bound to continue. More than that, he was convinced that Wilfrid de Guelf had retrieved his loot from its hiding place near Pontefract Castle and was in possession of it when he arrived in Wiltshire. Therefore, Casimir reasoned, since it was not on his person when they captured him, Wilfrid must have hid the treasure somewhere nearby. Whom did Wilfrid know in Wiltshire? Where would he have felt secure to hide so great a treasure? Casimir questioned every knight he met inquiring after de Guelf's connections in the West. He truly did not care if Englishmen thought him mad; such behaviour might cloud their eyes and protect his own imperial purpose, he said. His inquiries had produced results only within the past two days he told Apollonia, when he learned of Sir Wilfrid's service with Geoffrey Montecute of Colerne Leat. "Und here it is that you find me, Lady."

Apollonia's eyes never left the face of the solemn Bohemian as Casimir completed for her the details of his relentless pursuit of de Guelf. She marveled at his candor, recognizing his plain-spoken honesty as intended tribute to her. Grateful for that gift of confidence, Apollonia had no intention of asking any further explanation of the nature of Wilfrid's crime or the object of Casimir's secret imperial commission. To her great surprise, the silent Bohemian lifted the sheepskin bag so recently exhumed from the graveyard to the table before them and drew open the stout cords which bound its mouth. Carefully turning down its soft skin sides, he exposed the bag's contents revealing to her unprepared eyes the marvelous wonder it contained.

Chapter Twenty-three

Majesty Redeemed

Apollonia could not contain her startled gasp. Sitting on her table in front of the fire, radiant in the flickering light was a small exquisite royal crown. A series of golden pinnacles, the finely wrought circlet was a masterpiece of the goldsmith's art set with sparkling diamonds and precious jewels. Fearing to touch it, the Lady could not resist leaning closer to wonder at its perfection. Designed to grace a small feminine head, the crown was encrusted with expertly cut diamonds, rubies, and emeralds, each outlined in a continuous stream of perfectly matched pearls.

"Zis is the crown of her highness, Princess Anne of Bohemia, vich she brought to zis country at ze time of her marriage to your King Richard," Casimir said. "Wilfrid de Guelf stole it from ze Queen's treasury at ze time of her death. All the gold and coins he stole are of no consequence; my Lord, ze Emperor, vishes this crown to be returned to Bohemia."

Along with her jewels, the lovely young Bohemian princess had brought a household of ladies-in-waiting, one of whom had been Casimir's younger sister. Apollonia could see pain in Casimir's eyes as he spoke of his cherished sibling's glowing descriptions of the court of King Richard, the royal love of art, music and pageantry. All of these things he knew only from her letters as he had been in Prussia fighting with the Teutonic order.

Casimir had learned from surviving members of the Bohemian household that Wilfrid de Guelf served one of the queen's English courtiers after her marriage. Wilfrid also managed to worm his way into the confidences of Casimir's innocent sister, making himself familiar with the royal apartments and discovering the place where the royal treasure was kept. When sudden death claimed young Queen Anne at the Palace of Shene, de Guelf saw his opportunity unfold in the midst of tragedy. Secretly stealing into the royal apartments while the household was prostrate with grief in the chapel, Wilfrid found his way unchallenged to the great jewel chests of the secret chamber.

Considering the chaos of the royal household, it must have been ridiculously easy, Casimir told the Lady of Aust. Wilfrid had sufficient time to steal a great chest of Bohemian gold as well as the

Queen's priceless crown. Some of the gold was melted and recast with the cooperation of a devious goldsmith in Pontefract whom Casimir had hunted down and threatened torture for information. But the goldsmith could not help the German knights learn the whereabouts of the Bohemian crown, he told them, piteously. The fawning creature pleaded ignorance as Wilfrid, he said, had felt it prudent to hide the crown somewhere near Pontefract known only to him. Whining and sniveling of his weakened heart, the smith was anxious to tell the German knights that Wilfrid had been recently seen in the town, hoping that they would leave him in peace. He had personally seen Wilfrid enter a nearby inn only a matter of days before Casimir and his companions arrived.

More than a decade had passed since Queen Anne's death and with certainty it was now known that King Richard, too, was dead. Possibly assuming it was safe for him to retrieve the crown long forgotten in the chaos of the monarchy, Sir Wilfrid had traveled north to retrieve his hidden treasure and take it home to Somerset. Casimir suspected that Wilfrid thought he would be able to have the crown, also, melted into anonymity while he sold off the fabulous jewels one at a time.

"My sister's body was found after the death of Queen Anne. Ve vere told she died of grief," Casimir said quietly. "I haf no doubt who vas the man who vished her dead and employed a vitch to poison her."

Lady Apollonia merely nodded in response to the knight's quiet accusation of murder. She was not given to emotional outbursts, did not appreciate the silly ideals of chivalric devotion to lady loves or foolish fashionable notions of courtly love. But her whole heart responded in utmost sympathy with the faithful ageing Casimir and his solitary quest to allay the tormented spirit of his murdered sister. Apollonia was convinced that Casimir was honorable and probably correct in his presumed accusation. She knew Wilfrid de Guelf to be a thief, a torturer and a likely candidate for murderer as well. She bore no judgement against Casimir in her heart and could only be grateful that this loyal and long-suffering paladin had granted her his personal confidence. The memory of his story would always remain a wonder hidden away in her soul. "My Lord Casimir," she said quietly, "your sister's spirit surely rests in peace now, fully restored, as will be this beautiful crown, to the honor of her countrymen." Carefully returning the glowing crown to its homely carrying parcel, Casimir begged to take his leave of the Lady.

"I am an old man," Lord Casimir protested, "and I find I am depleted. Graciously grant me your leafe, my Lady?" Giving him her hand, Apollonia bade him God's blessings and a very good night then called for Giles to show him to his chamber and see that his needs were provided.

With Nan returned to her side, Apollonia retired to her own bedchamber while her maid fussed quietly but persistently over the recklessness of her solitary actions. "You were being guarded by a mere boy, my Lady, surely some men of your company should have remained with you during your interview with that foreign knight!" But Apollonia simply had too much on her mind to object. She found sleep illusive that night, her mind still churning from the evening's revelations and the completion to an unbelievable story which she had been privileged to share. She was not surprised during the earliest morning hours to hear the sounds of a horse being quietly led from the stables. Rising to her window, she watched as Casimir of Prague mounted his courser and walked it through the gate of Colerne Leat. As his evanescent figure disappeared into the darkness, she whispered a prayer for his safe journey and God's peace in his heart. She was certain he had begun his long journey home; he was at last on his way to take ship at Bristol, returning a dead Queen's stolen crown to its kingdom of rightful ownership.

At dawn's light Lady Apollonia gathered her servants round the huge kitchen table. Offering no explanation, Giles announced in her behalf that they would all return to Aust that morning. Crestfallen faces greeted this announcement not due to its subject of their return but because no mention was made of the German knight. Owen especially wanted to say, "He's gone, my Lady, the foreign knight took his horse from the stable and has fled." But he feared to risk impudence and bit his lip to guarantee no slip of tongue. It was Giles who broached the subject upon which they all wished she would offer enlightenment. "My Lady," he began, "have we solved the mystery of the death of Sir Wilfrid?"

"Oh yes," she said, "you have all done it for me. But we must not finish the tale until we have gathered to share our adventures with Guise, Brother William and the Friar."

Returning home to Aust, Lady Apollonia and her company rode through a steady downpour. Undaunted and struggling to endure the dreadful weather, each was preoccupied with his own mental solutions to their great mystery. Alwan was singularly happy and least concerned among his fellows for any additional explanations. His Lady was pleased and that was enough he thought. Taking out his flute he played melodies of his own composition, accompanying the mesmerizing rhythm of the horses' hooves and raindrops which continued to fall unnoticed from his nose.

Nan was aghast at the sodden state of the party which finally rode through the manor gates that afternoon. Scolding and pushing she sent the men off to change into dry clothes before chill could settle into their chests and infect the whole household with sickness. She stood next to her palfrey as Lady Apollonia was helped to dismount and would not cease fussing until the Lady had submitted to a hot bath and restorative herbal drink. At last, warmly enthroned in her favorite chair in front of a roaring fire in Aust manor hall, Apollonia convinced her hovering angel of mercy that she was truly restored and ready to receive her company.

Nan wasted no time in hurrying off to summon Giles. He was to bring Guise from the kitchen, collect the clerics, Alwan and Owen, that all might meet with her Ladyship in the Hall. If truth be told, curiosity had infected Nan far more seriously than the threat of sickness. She felt like celebrating, convinced by the Lady's contented smile and sparkling eyes that all had been answered to her satisfaction. Lady Apollonia had announced she wished to speak with them.

As so frequently happens in the west of England after a gloomy grey day of rain, a late afternoon sun was shining brightly near the horizon. Long horizontal rays of sunlight flashed across shimmering purple shadows and mixed their gilded shafts with the wet shiny hues of autumn's pallet. Spilling through the west window of the great hall, the low sun filled Lady Apollonia's reception chamber with the golden glow of a giant treasure chest. Apollonia's servants each arrived in her hall, hats doffed and pleased to see each other while sharing the growing excitement each felt as the puzzle was surely about to be completed for them. Alwan and Owen, Brother William, Friar Francis, Guise and Giles, each greeted Nan and then walked to the Lady's chair to express his obedience to her. Each one of them as a member of the Lady's inner household circle had helped to gather the tangled scattered threads of their emerging mystery. But like the group of blind men examining an Indian elephant recently sent to the king's menagerie in London, none of them could construct a whole image from the single part of his or her contribution. Surely now their Lady would reveal the unknown strands and weave together an entire tapestry of the adventure.

Chapter Twenty-four

Sharing the Tale

Giles bade them all to find a bench or stool and draw it comfortably close to the roaring fire near to Lady Apollonia's chair. He remained standing next to the Lady as Nan brought beer and ale into the hall to add to the festive pleasure of their gathering. When everyone was settled, Giles pulled himself to full height and began by saying that the Lady Apollonia wished to express her gratitude and heartfelt thanks to each of her faithful servants. They had, he said, all served her admirably in a very special good work well done. "Further, My Lady Apollonia credits us with seeking out important clues to the solution of the mystery of the gentleman found dead in the north drains. The horrible spectacle of ravens bleeding into our lower portals, the tragic drowning of so many of the poor lepers eventually brought us to that discovery but only confused our efforts to understand what was the nature of the threat against us. By the grace of God we have protected the innocent and preserved truth and Lady Apollonia wishes to laud and thank all of us, her faithful affinity, for that which she credits as a job well done."

His speech ended, Giles stepped into the shadow. He could see the assembly of familiar faces appreciated the kindly words he offered. All members of the household shared a wholehearted respect for this very young man who had not only grown into his role as Steward of the household but also continually offered his personal respect for each of their contributions . But they had certainly hoped for more. Then, to everyone's surprise, the Lady began to speak. "My dear and faithful ones, I depend upon you all to serve me but also enable me as my hands, my ears and voice, none more than Giles." Giles smiled and nodded his thanks but every person in the hall leaned forward to listen to the Lady's words as her soft well-modulated voice spoke clearly but quietly and no one wished to miss a word. Hardly daring to breathe loudly, their silence enhanced the only other noise within the room as it emanated from the hearth in an irregular rhythm of snapping and crackling tongues of flame. "Therefore, I would be remiss if my thanks were not directed to him and to each of you from my own heart. You all know the broadest outline of our adventure but I should like to add one or two further aspects which will complete its telling."

"But before I continue, I have not properly thanked my good chaplain and almoner for the extraordinary ministry they organized in behalf of our poor leper brothers in Christ," she said. Francis and his fellow clergyman could not look up from their thoughts as each remembered the human horrors seen during the retrieval of bodies after the great storm. Each of them also treasured memories of kindness, goodness and gratitude expressed by the leper outcasts, God's children possessing nothing but still offering to be His servants. "Gentle Friar, Brother William, you will be pleased to know that I have received word from the Benedictines of Shrewsbury; our leper band has, at last, found sanctuary and care in their hospital. You were the means to that end, for which I am truly grateful and I believe heaven's angels join us in rejoicing over your good works."

Her clerics smiled with warm acknowledgment of her news and graceful compliment. "We serve the glory of God, my Lady, but your kind heart and generous gifts sustain all that we do," Friar Francis said.

"Amen to that," echoed Brother William. "There is neither cottage nor church in the shire which does not praise God for your Ladyship's good grace."

Smiling upon the earnest faces of her clerics, Apollonia again picked up the threads of her story. "Well, as you all know, the storm presented our household with an inexplicably hideous corpse amidst the leper dead," she went on, "but I was especially impressed by your intelligent appraisal of the circumstances, Giles. It was your statement of the unlikelihood of Sir Wilfrid being assaulted by common folk and Alwan's demonstration of his death as accidental which set for me the most important questions needing answers." Pausing to look into the fire, Apollonia spoke somewhat distractedly, "I wondered how could such a death occur and for what reasons would a knight have been stripped of all objects of identification?" she said ticking off her points upon her long white fingers. "Someone of equal position and might must have taken him prisoner but what had he done to incur the indignities which led to his death?"

"Then I foolishly allowed myself to be led astray by the terrifying specter of dead ravens. You were eminently correct, Guise," Apollonia turned to her excellent cook, "ravens can be intended as an evil threat and I assumed needlessly that I was their target." Guise could be seen breathing deeply, his chest expanded nearly to the girth of his belly in justification of his wise judgement. "Madame, I am always at your serveece and faithfully serve to protect you," he said with a great grin of gratitude for her endorsement. Sharing a quiet wink at Nan whose pale features suddenly flashed scarlet, the Lady acknowledged their shared secret and then continued.

"Through our visit to Cliffbarton, dear Nan and I were able to gather meaningful truths of the activities of Sir Wilfred during more recent years when I did not know him. We learned that the dead gentleman had been at Shene serving the royal household during the days of the great confusion after our Lady Queen Anne died. After her death, Sir Wilfrid had remained in the north serving King Richard but later King Henry at Pontefract, switching sides with ease but truly loyal to none. For his treachery, this knight had acquired enemies but we also learned he had accrued surprising amounts of wealth while allowing his own lands and holdings to fall into ruin. But most importantly our visit to Dunster also enabled my sleuth Giles to discover that after his return to his family lands in Somerset, Sir Wilfrid was being pursued by three foreign knights." The eyes of Apollonia's audience moved from Nan to Giles and then back to the Lady as she continued.

"Your thought that the foreign knights were pursuing Wilfrid as if he owed them something was particularly insightful, Giles. It was the first suggestion of a compelling motive in this very strange sequence of events." She broke her narrative just long enough to urge her steward to make a note. "Be sure to thank your friend, Martin, for his excellent hospitality to you with a cask of our good Wiltshire cider."

Giles smiled bowing his head to her in acknowledgement once again. "By my faith, a generous gift, my Lady," he said, "Martin shall truly rejoice of it."

Turning next to her almoner, Apollonia continued, "Dear Brother William, you who know the halt, lame, and dispossessed who traverse the lanes of our troubled country, it was you who provided the clues to the route of the foreign knights and their captive during the raging storm. It was also you who discovered the hiding place of the evil knight's stolen treasure."

In honest amazement, Brother William began to protest. "My Lady, I, I did nothing. . ."

Before he could complete his denial, Apollonia asked Brother William to extend an invitation which she knew would please him. "If you should again encounter the unfortunate man of the Pucklechurch

Inn, offer him a trial place in our service. Alwan could surely use an extra pair of hands come Lent."

"God bless you, Lady," Brother William said happily, "I will find him, surely."

"You see, Brother William, I have come to believe that many of the superstitious murmurings of the people have some kernel of truth at their heart however embellished and misunderstood. The terrifying devil and the doomsday horsemen of the storm were Sir Wilfrid hiding his stolen treasure near my first husband's grave and the three German knights who, pursuing Wilfrid into Wiltshire captured him shortly thereafter and forced him to ride towards Wales with them," she concluded. Brother William's eyes flashed understanding. Of course he had, indeed, discovered the whereabouts of those events.

"Alwan, in locating the missing head of Sir Wilfrid, established once and for all the accidental nature of the gentleman's death. Then my excellent forester kindly confirmed the route of the three German knights and their captive attempting escape into Wales. Bless you, Alwan for demonstrating to me that once Sir Wilfrid had fled from his captors, they would, of necessity, be the persons to observe for the completion of our story. I realized that they may well have fled the county but I could only guess they may have chosen to flee into Wales." Apollonia could see Alwan's beaming face. Owen, on the edge of his stool, could hardly wait for her to continue knowing that she was about to introduce their grand adventure.

"This brings us to our team of minstrels who double as Alwan the forester and Owen my page." All in her gathered affinity turned to look to their younger compatriots. Both of her Welshmen were swelling with pride as their exploits now assumed the center of all attention. "Having assaulted mighty Chepstow Castle, you bravely penetrated her gates and followed the knights' story from Aust to Wales and back again. It was you who provided the framework for the conclusion of our mystery." Alwan and Owen felt themselves burning with self-conscious pleasure.

Apollonia continued, "After your experiences in the grand hall of the Duke of Norfolk," the Lady chided, "I am more than ever grateful that you returned to serve our humbler household." How wonderful that the Lady announced where they had been to everyone present! Now, Alwan and Owen would be allowed to speak of it and add the Chepstow tale to their repertoire of songs and adventures when they entertained the manor hall.

"It was Owen and Alwan who discovered that two of the knights left our country from Chepstow leaving only one refusing to depart England before he had restored the honor of his house. I cannot divulge to you the secret mission of the worthy German knight whom you followed so skillfully and faithfully," Lady Apollonia said to Alwan and Owen, "but I am at liberty to tell you all that it is thanks to your help, the knight errant recovered his stolen treasure and will fulfill his quest. He is probably on board a ship at this very moment sailing to his homeland." There was no heart in the room which did not swell in response to this announcement. Assisting a godly knight in his quest was an honor granted to few in their station.

Allowing a moment's rest for her words to be absorbed, Lady Apollonia continued, "Dear friends, Alwan's evidence proved Sir Wilfrid was not murdered and the German knight confessed to me that he and his fellows had taken him prisoner because he had stolen from them. It was they who forced him to wear peasant's clothes and they who bound him to his horse." Apollonia closely watched the faces of her little group as she spoke; their imaginations inflamed by her unfolding tale. "If his death will be blamed upon any creature, the guilt can only be charged against his horse," Apollonia pronounced with great conviction. "Frightened by the raging storm," she said, "Sir Wilfrid's destrier bolted away from his captors and eventually galloped its helpless rider's head into the pincers of a mighty oak limb."

Finding horrific details repulsive, Apollonia continued in a steady controlled voice. "From the remaining hoof prints beneath that tree, Alwan could assure us that only one horse had been present at the place of Sir Wilfrid's death. Possibly frustrated by the restraints of the entrapped head of its rider restrained in his saddle, Sir Wilfrid's mount twisted powerfully back and forth finally thrusting itself free. Snared by his neck and unable to use his hands to free himself, Sir Wilfrid died a horrible freakish decapitation, assisted and witnessed by no man."

A soft communal groan issued involuntarily from the group. Alwan matter-of-factly nodded in agreement with the Lady's interpretation of the tracks of struggle beneath the tree. Owen's eyes widened to saucers and his mind conjured up horrible sounds of crackling bones like those of the birds whose necks they wrung after releasing them from snares. Brother William crossed himself and began to whisper silent prayers. The Friar unthinkingly put his hand to his neck, while Nan kept her head lowered, deep in her own thoughts of the dreadful demise of her childhood tormentor.

Even more quietly now, Lady Apollonia completed her tale, "The German knight also told me that he and his companions found Sir Wilfrid's horse with its grisly burden the same night of his attempted escape after the storm had quieted. Fearing that they might be blamed for Sir Wilfrid's death, they threw his body into the Severn thinking the river's tides would carry it out to sea." Apollonia saw Alwan's eyes light in immediate realization. He was well aware of the power of tides in the estuary.

"As strangers to our county," the Lady said, "the foreigners couldn't know of the peculiar forces that can accompany storms on the Severn. They would never have imagined a wall of water rushing inland." Apollonia lowered her head, remembering the carnage on the day of the burial. "It was that horrible rage of nature, a tidal bore which drowned so many of the poor lepers camped along the Severn's banks. And it was the same surge of flood tide which hurled Sir Wilfrid's headless body back upstream to be found in the drains of our fields."

Lady Apollonia paused as if her summation of the story was ended. Her familiar minions had grown thoughtful as each of them mentally assembled the brutal tale of accidental death in his or her own imagination. Giles was the first to question the Lady further. "But, my Lady, I still do not understand how you knew where Sir Wilfrid had hidden away his stolen goods?" he asked.

Lady Apollonia pointed towards her Almoner. "When Brother William told me of the man who swore he saw a devil in the church yard of Colerne Leat, I could think of only one man equal to the role. Sir Wilfrid had served my first husband and also was well acquainted with our manor at Colerne Leat. He knew the village well and the place of my first lord's burial. I believed him capable of ghoulish delight in using my husband's grave as hiding place for his plunder."

Young Owen thinking back to the message he had carried from her Ladyship to Alwan, timidly raised his voice. "But my Lady, how could you know that Alwan should begin his search for Sir Wilfrid's head from the place where the lepers had camped?"

"Excellent Owen, you have caught me out in my most fortunate mistake. I had assumed then that Sir Wilfrid's horse may have been startled by accidentally riding into the midst of the wretched creatures' camp and then galloped in terror from it. In truth, the lepers were totally innocent of any involvement in this affair. Sir Wilfrid's horse ran terrorized by the storm from an opposite direction towards the camp and not the other way round."

"My Lady," Nan, said with a sly twinkle in her eye, "perhaps you will now tell the reasons for bleeding ravens hung upon our doors in the midst of the storm?"

"Ah yes, thank you Nan. The grisly birds were put there for our protection, Guise," Apollonia said. "As the people of Israel were told to smear their lintels with blood to protect them against the Angel of Death, so also our own Mad Mag sought to insure your kitchen and our household against evil during that dreadful night." "Mon Dieu, mais oui," Guise, now returned to his fastidious perfection of appearance, nodded with great assurance. Indeed, he had known all along. A general murmur of agreement spread among everyone in the hall as each could imagine Mag doing just such a thing. They all were well acquainted with brewster Mag's dabbling in white magic and bizarre behaviour. And it was Friar Francis' turn to laugh at himself now.

"For the love of God, of course," Francis chuckled. "I proudly thought Mag was moved by the power of my sermons. She listened so intently and questioned me with such serious scrutiny. Perhaps my enthusiasm for the Moses' stories must be tempered in future telling."

"By my faith Friar," Giles said with a grin, "few preachers can claim to have inspired a follower of Moses. But kindly modulate future exhortations or Mad Mag may feel inspired to feed the five thousand or turn her excellent beer into an undrinkable wine!" Everyone laughed at the thought of Mag's literal interpretation of Holy Word but none so heartily as the Friar.

"We have one further cause for rejoicing this night," Lady Apollonia announced. "Gareth, my servant and stable master for many years has recently wed." Surprise and unanimous good wishes erupted throughout the group at this news. "He has chosen to live with his new wife in Ingst village but I hope you will all find a moment to congratulate him upon his marriage and offer prayers for his future happiness." Then raising her hand to hold everyone's thoughts, the Lady continued. "I must also share with you the excellent capture of Sir Wilfrid's destrier. After the German knights had thrown the body of their captive into the Severn, they set the great beast free so that they would not be charged with its possession. Gareth not only found the great horse wandering near Ingst, he was the only man in the county able to take it in hand. He told me he put the beast into one of our barns and we have sold it as we were requested to do by the Lady de Guelf. Thanks to Gareth a significant monetary gift was made to Kingswood Abbey where the body of Sir Wilfred lies."

Suddenly the hall was a hum of voices now free to discuss and exclaim at all the exciting bits of revelation that had been shared among them. Smiling with pride upon her household, Apollonia settled back into her chair to savor the warmth of the moment. But Nan, who had been called from the Hall, suddenly returned to speak with the Lady, her face contorted into a forbidding frown. She leaned close to Apollonia's ear and whispered into it: "That hateful Pardoner Brandon Landow is here and wishes to speak with you, my Lady."

Epilogue

Evil Bones Put to Rest

"Oh yes, Nan, my thanks. I have been expecting him. Please show Landow up to my private solar," Apollonia directed. Nan was aghast. "Oh my Lady, you know he can only have come to steal money or sell some fraudulent relic at unworthy cost. Please allow Giles to remain with you as you converse with him. I truly do not trust anything he may say or do."

"You are kindness itself, dear Nan, but this is an exchange I must pursue with Landow privately." And allowing for no further objection, Apollonia retreated from the hall, up the stairs to her solar.

Sitting alone before the fire, the Lady Apollonia looked up as the heavily caped Landow, a wallet brimful of Papal pardons hanging from his shoulder, entered her private chamber. As she had come to show him in, Nan looked pleadingly towards Apollonia but the Lady shook her head in response, Nan retreated reluctantly closing the door behind her. Sweeping off his hugely feathered hat Landow bowed dramatically before Apollonia. "Greetings my most gracious Lady, it is I, your one absolute failure in life!" Landow said pompously.

Lady Apollonia offered no word of casual conversation nor even a welcoming smile. She looked directly at him and demanded immediately, "Cease your exaggerated claims, Landow. Have you brought it with you?"

Landow hoisted a large rounded parcel for her examination. "It is as you command, my Lady, ready for your inspection." He lifted the bag to the table at her side and began to loosen its laces, revealing a grotesquely shaped object meant to be a holy relic. It was a skull sheathed in silver but opened across the front of what had been its face with two crystals embedded into its sockets as eyes. A circular halo surrounded its crown with shafts of metal shooting from it to suggest a heavenly aura. "My silversmith believes it is his finest reliquary work but also expresses a spirit of long-suffering humility in its broken jagged teeth," he said disdainfully.

Apollonia stood to examine the relic more closely from all possible views. "With the skull," Landow added, "I have brought the forged documents to declare that this is the relic of Saint Creedan, an obscure Celtic saint of Cornwall whose holy well is included on the pilgrimage routes into the far West of England." Apollonia examined the documents and their fraudulent copy of the seal of Bishop Stapledon of Exeter. "Where else may we find such relics of this Saint Creedan," Apollonia asked?

"My Lady of Aust," Landow exclaimed, "what can you think of me? I offer documented legitimacy with every relic. You will find no other heads of St. Creedan in all of Devon, Cornwall or Wiltshire. Exeter Cathedral may boast a finger of the saint but this glorious presentation is one of a kind, I pledge by all the holy saints!"

"Do not dare to heap your blasphemy upon me!" Apollonia said slowly but meaningfully. "I have requested your help in this effort and I thank you Landow. You have done very well and will be well paid for your efforts but I have one further task for you. Surely your travels throughout the southwest can take you to Kingswood Abbey?" she asked.

"Bless me, it is one of my best regions," Landow said. "I can sell endless teeth of Saint Joseph, capsules of the Virgin's milk, and several portions of Christ's foreskin as well as locks of the hair of Mary Magdalene there." Lady Apollonia nodded her acknowledgment. "Enough! I am grateful to learn of it," Apollonia told him. "Your success as Pardoner has made you well-traveled as well as rich."

"Well now, I shant put me self forward beyond me station," Landow crowed as if attempting to seem humble, "but I am compelled to allow that no one can resist me best preacher's pitch. I stir such guilt in the hearts of the commons that they pay double for the chance to hold a bit of holiness in hand whilst they pray God for healing." Landow puffed up his chest and seemed to expect some admiration from the Lady.

"I have no praise to add to your collection of riches, Landow, as I also know you to be capable of thieving," Apollonia went on. "I have required your services in this delicate matter and now ask you to take this reliquary and its endorsements to Abbot Harold of Kingswood Abbey. You are to tell him it is a penitent's gift to his monastic church; that his ministry may include the blessings of a Celtic Saint and holy well just as Shrewsbury Abbey in Shropshire offers the relics of Saint Winefred. He is to know nothing more."

"It shall be done as you direct, my Lady," But pausing, Landow obviously wished to ask further grace from Apollonia. "I have always known you to be a true Christian lady. Can you not offer some gentle words of forgiveness for me?"

"Brandon Landow, you came into my household as a lad of ten. I freely admit to envisioning great hopes of your intelligence and wit early on but I cannot condone your unrepentant need to steal from every person in Aust." She spoke with pointed meaning as she looked directly into his eyes. "I truly have forgiven you but I have proof of your thievery and I shall not forget all you have done. You have found your own place protected within Canon Law of the church Brandon and I wish you well." Apollonia sighed deeply and extended her hand to her former liveryman. "I shall reward you for this service after you have returned with the full account of your call upon the Abbot of Kingswood Abbey."

With a deep audible sigh, Landow bent over her proffered hand and kissed it. "Your will shall be done, my Lady. The Abbot of Kingswood will ne'er be acquainted with his true 'penitent.'" Gathering his aggressive self assurance about him and taking up the re-enclosed reliquary parcel he bowed with smirking conceit and swept from the chamber.

After Brandon's departure Lady Apollonia continued alone seated in her chair staring into the fire as she forced herself to consider her intent once again. She could not feel pride in her decision but she knew that alone among her henchmen only Brandon Landow was in a position to assist her. "Truly," she insisted to herself, "this is the best possible service for your head, Wilfred de Guelf. Every church needs relics!" Brandon had been able to transform for her the moldering skull of a truly evil man into a valuable contribution to the treasury of the Abbey church of Kingswood. She knew Abbot Harold would rejoice to receive it!

As if the memory of his long detested face now hovered before her eyes, Apollonia spoke aloud, "I could do nothing for your wretched person Wilfred but I shall see to it your head will be nearly reunited with your body and by the Grace of God will serve a holy cause."

Glossary

Accidie: laziness or indifference in religious matters

Affinity: medieval concept of loyal household, wearing the livery or heraldic badge of one's lord and granting full allegiance and acceptance of his rule in one's life

Almoner: a person whose function is the distribution of alms in behalf of a noble person

Aureole: any encircling ring of light or color, a radiance surrounding the whole figure

Bacinet: a medieval European open faced military helmet

Bailey: defensive walled courtyard surrounding a castle

Barmclooth: medieval name for a kind of fabric

Breviary: a book containing all daily psalter, hymns prayers, lessons, etc., to enable a cleric to recite the daily Divine Office

Cadge: to obtain by imposing on another's generosity

Caryatid: a sculptured female figure used as a column

Cassock: close-fitting garment usually worn by clergy or laymen during church services

Cavalier: horseman, mounted soldier or knight

Chemise: a woman's loose fitting shirt like undergarment

Chevauchee: method in medieval warfare for weakening the enemy by wreaking havoc, burning, pillaging destroying enemy property

Churl: a peasant or rustic or a rude boorish or surely person

Clerestory: medieval architectural portion of building (church) interior rising above adjacent rooftops and having windows for admitting light

Cloven hoof: the figurative indication of Satan or evil temptation

Columbine: flowering plant leaves used as herbal medicine to prevent skin diseases

Conversus/aConversi: a class of servants within the monastic community who were not monks

Corbel: architectural bracket meant to support beams or ribs

Cot: small house, cottage or hut

Cottar: tenant renting land directly from the landowner

Courtesy: In the understanding of those followers of Julian of Norwich from about 1400, courtesy is not meant to be understood as excellence of manners or polite behaviour. Courtesy means loving respect implying not only indulgence of another but also goodness granted freely regardless of sinful behaviour. Mother Julian describes God as our "Courteous Lord".

Cracows: 15th century names for men's fashionable shoes with exaggeratedly long points at the toe

Crossing: the intersection of nave and transcepts in a cruciform church building

Curtain wall: exterior wall about castle or manor house having defensive but no structural function

Cymru: – Welsh language for Wales

Demesne: an estate or part of an estate occupied and controlled by the owner for his use only

Destrier: medieval name for a war horse or charger

Devotio moderna: religious movement of the late Middle Ages stressing meditation and emphasizing the inner life of the individual

Dogsbody: person of all service and assistance or general helper

Dorter: a dormitory, especially in a monastery

Eclat: brilliance, acclaim

Effigy: image sculpted upon a tomb

Entente: an arrangement or understanding between parties

Epicure: a person who cultivates a refined taste in food, art or music

Franklin: in the 15th century, a wealthy freeholder who was not of noble birth

Fustian: a stout fabric of cotton and flax

Garterobe: medieval privy often built into the walls of a castle or manor house

Gentles: referring to the class of gentlemen, those of birth and higher class

Gramercy: an expression of thanks, "grand merci"

Halberd: a shafted weapon with cutting blade, beak and spike

Henchman: in the middle ages a trusted attendant, supporter or follower

Hodsman: an assistant whose work is to carry hods of materials

Jupon: a man's short close-fitting surcot usually padded

Keep: Stronghold or dungeon

Lazar: a person infected with a loathsome disease, usually a leper

League: unit of distance, in English speaking countries, usually about three miles

Leat: small stream or long basin of water

Liege: a feudal vassal granting service or allegiance to a feudal lord

Livery: a distinctive dress, badge or device formerly provided by someone of rank or title for his retainers.

Mea culpa: my fault

Mendips: range of hills in Somerset

Minion: follower or subordinate of person in power

Murrain: any of various diseases of cattle or sheep

Nave: principal longitudinal area of a church extending from main entrance to the chancel

Noblesse oblige: the moral obligation of the rich or highborn to display honorable or charitable conduct

Novitiate: novice of a religious order

194

Opus dei: literally the "work of God" but referring specifically to the services for the divine offices of the church

Page: a youth in attendance on a person of rank

Paladin: any knightly or heroic champion

Palfrey: a saddle horse particularly suited to a woman

pardoner: an ecclesiastical official charged with the granting of indulgences

Paterfamilias: the male head of a family or household

Pennon: a distinctive flag or pennant

Pilaster: a shallow architectural feature projecting from a wall having the shape of a pillar and capital

Placebo et dirige: the vespers for the ecclesiastical office of the dead

Poacher: a person who trespasses on private property

Portcullis: a strong iron grating let down to prevent passage through a castle portal

Postulant: a candidate in process for admission to a religious order

Prie-dieux: piece of furniture especially designed for kneeling upon during prayer

Publican: a person who owns or manages a tavern or medieval inn

Quire: area in a medieval church for the choir

Reeve: an overseer of workers, tenants or an estate

Sanctification: to make holy, set apart as sacred

Satanas: the great adversary of man, the devil

Sconce: a bracket for candles or torches set on the wall

Scrivener: medieval word for scribe

Slype: covered passage

Solar: a private or upper chamber in a medieval English house or castle

Squire: a country gentleman, especially the chief landed proprietor in a district

Steward: one who serves as manager of financial and business affairs, serving as manager or agent for another

Tidal bore: an abrupt rise of tidal water moving rapidly inland from the mouth of an estuary

Tunic: an outer garment with or without sleeves and sometimes worn belted

Villein: a member of the class of partially free persons in a feudal system who served their lord but had some rights and privileges

Virgator: An unfree tenant of the Lord of a Manor in feudal society who was an agricultural laborer supposed to hold a "virgate" (approximately 15 acres). These tenants possessed few rights.

Worship: a title of honor

LaVergne, TN USA
02 November 2010
203105LV00001B/25/P